Life of John Sterling

Thomas Carlyle

PART I.

CHAPTER I.
INTRODUCTORY.

Near seven years ago, a short while before his death in 1844, John Sterling committed the care of his literary Character and printed Writings to two friends, Archdeacon Hare and myself. His estimate of the bequest was far from overweening; to few men could the small sum-total of his activities in this world seem more inconsiderable than, in those last solemn days, it did to him. He had burnt much; found much unworthy; looking steadfastly into the silent continents of Death and Eternity, a brave man's judgments about his own sorry work in the field of Time are not apt to be too lenient. But, in fine, here was some portion of his work which the world had already got hold of, and which he could not burn. This too, since it was not to be abolished and annihilated, but must still for some time live and act, he wished to be wisely settled, as the rest had been. And so it was left in charge to us, the survivors, to do for it what we judged fittest, if indeed doing nothing did not seem the fittest to us. This message, communicated after his decease, was naturally a sacred one to Mr. Hare and me.

After some consultation on it, and survey of the difficulties and delicate considerations involved in it, Archdeacon Hare and I agreed that the whole task, of selecting what Writings were to be reprinted, and of drawing up a Biography to introduce them, should be left to him alone; and done without interference of mine: —as accordingly it was, [1] in a manner surely far superior to the common, in every good quality of editing; and visibly everywhere bearing testimony to the friendliness, the piety, perspicacity and other gifts and virtues of that eminent and amiable man.

In one respect, however, if in one only, the arrangement had been unfortunate. Archdeacon Hare, both by natural tendency and by his position as a Churchman, had been led, in editing a Work not free from ecclesiastical heresies, and especially in writing a Life very full of such, to dwell with preponderating emphasis on that part of his subject; by no means extenuating the fact, nor yet passing lightly over it (which a layman could have done) as needing no extenuation; but carefully searching into it, with the view of excusing and explaining it; dwelling on it, presenting all the documents of it, and

1

as it were spreading it over the whole field of his delineation; as if religious heterodoxy had been the grand fact of Sterling's life, which even to the Archdeacon's mind it could by no means seem to be. *Hinc illae lachrymae*. For the Religious Newspapers, and Periodical Heresy-hunters, getting very lively in those years, were prompt to seize the cue; and have prosecuted and perhaps still prosecute it, in their sad way, to all lengths and breadths. John Sterling's character and writings, which had little business to be spoken of in any Church-court, have hereby been carried thither as if for an exclusive trial; and the mournfulest set of pleadings, out of which nothing but a misjudgment *can* be formed, prevail there ever since. The noble Sterling, a radiant child of the empyrean, clad in bright auroral hues in the memory of all that knew him, —what is he doing here in inquisitorial *sanbenito*, with nothing but ghastly spectralities prowling round him, and inarticulately screeching and gibbering what they call their judgment on him!

"The sin of Hare's Book, " says one of my Correspondents in those years, "is easily defined, and not very condemnable, but it is nevertheless ruinous to his task as Biographer. He takes up Sterling as a clergyman merely. Sterling, I find, was a curate for exactly eight months; during eight months and no more had he any special relation to the Church. But he was a man, and had relation to the Universe, for eight-and-thirty years: and it is in this latter character, to which all the others were but features and transitory hues, that we wish to know him. His battle with hereditary Church formulas was severe; but it was by no means his one battle with things inherited, nor indeed his chief battle; neither, according to my observation of what it was, is it successfully delineated or summed up in this Book. The truth is, nobody that had known Sterling would recognize a feature of him here; you would never dream that this Book treated of *him* at all. A pale sickly shadow in torn surplice is presented to us here; weltering bewildered amid heaps of what you call 'Hebrew Old-clothes; ' wrestling, with impotent impetuosity, to free itself from the baleful imbroglio, as if that had been its one function in life: who in this miserable figure would recognize the brilliant, beautiful and cheerful John Sterling, with his ever-flowing wealth of ideas, fancies, imaginations; with his frank affections, inexhaustible hopes, audacities, activities, and general radiant vivacity of heart and intelligence, which made the presence of him an illumination and inspiration wherever he went? It is too bad. Let a man be honestly forgotten when his life ends; but let him not be misremembered in this way. To be hung up as an ecclesiastical scarecrow, as a target for heterodox and orthodox to practice archery upon, is no fate that can be due to the memory of Sterling. It was not as a ghastly phantasm, choked in Thirty-nine-article controversies, or miserable Semitic, Anti-Semitic street-riots, —in scepticisms, agonized self-seekings, that this man appeared in life; nor as such, if the world still wishes to look at him should you suffer the world's memory of him now to be. Once for all, it is unjust; emphatically untrue as an image of John Sterling: perhaps to few men that lived along with him could such an interpretation of their existence be more inapplicable. "

Whatever truth there might be in these rather passionate representations, and to myself there wanted not a painful feeling of their truth, it by no means appeared what help or remedy any friend of Sterling's, and especially one so related to the matter as myself, could attempt in the interim. Perhaps endure in patience till the dust laid itself again, as all dust does if you leave it well alone? Much obscuration would thus of its own accord fall away; and, in Mr. Hare's narrative itself, apart from his commentary, many features of Sterling's true character would become decipherable to such as sought them. Censure, blame of this Work of Mr. Hare's was naturally far from my thoughts. A work which distinguishes itself by human piety and candid intelligence; which, in all details, is careful, lucid, exact; and which offers, as we say, to the observant reader that will interpret facts, many traits of Sterling besides his heterodoxy. Censure of it, from me especially, is not the thing due; from me a far other thing is due! —

On the whole, my private thought was: First, How happy it comparatively is, for a man of any earnestness of life, to have no Biography written of him; but to return silently, with his small, sorely foiled bit of work, to the Supreme Silences, who alone can judge of it or him; and not to trouble the reviewers, and greater or lesser public, with attempting to judge it! The idea of "fame, " as they call it, posthumous or other, does not inspire one with much ecstasy in these points of view. —Secondly, That Sterling's performance and real or seeming importance in this world was actually not of a kind to demand an express Biography, even according to the world's usages. His character was not supremely original; neither was his fate in the world wonderful. What he did was inconsiderable enough; and as to what it lay in him to have done, this was but a problem, now beyond possibility of settlement. Why had a Biography been inflicted on this man; why had not No-biography, and the privilege of all the weary, been his lot? —Thirdly,

That such lot, however, could now no longer be my good Sterling's; a tumult having risen around his name, enough to impress some pretended likeness of him (about as like as the Guy-Fauxes are, on Gunpowder-Day) upon the minds of many men: so that he could not be forgotten, and could only be misremembered, as matters now stood.

Whereupon, as practical conclusion to the whole, arose by degrees this final thought, That, at some calmer season, when the theological dust had well fallen, and both the matter itself, and my feelings on it, were in a suitabler condition, I ought to give my testimony about this friend whom I had known so well, and record clearly what my knowledge of him was. This has ever since seemed a kind of duty I had to do in the world before leaving it.

And so, having on my hands some leisure at this time, and being bound to it by evident considerations, one of which ought to be especially sacred to me, I decide to fling down on paper some outline of what my recollections and reflections contain in reference to this most friendly, bright and beautiful human soul; who walked with me for a season in this world, and remains to me very memorable while I continue in it. Gradually, if facts simple enough in themselves can be narrated as they came to pass, it will be seen what kind of man this was; to what extent condemnable for imaginary heresy and other crimes, to what extent laudable and lovable for noble manful *orthodoxy* and other virtues; —and whether the lesson his life had to teach us is not much the reverse of what the Religious Newspapers hitherto educe from it.

Certainly it was not as a "sceptic" that you could define him, whatever his definition might be. Belief, not doubt, attended him at all points of his progress; rather a tendency to too hasty and headlong belief. Of all men he was the least prone to what you could call scepticism: diseased self-listenings, self-questionings, impotently painful dubitations, all this fatal nosology of spiritual maladies, so rife in our day, was eminently foreign to him. Quite on the other side lay Sterling's faults, such as they were. In fact, you could observe, in spite of his sleepless intellectual vivacity, he was not properly a thinker at all; his faculties were of the active, not of the passive or contemplative sort. A brilliant *improvisatore*; rapid in thought, in word and in act; everywhere the promptest and least hesitating of men. I likened him often, in my banterings, to sheet-lightning; and reproachfully prayed that he would concentrate himself into a bolt, and rive the mountain-barriers for us, instead of merely playing on them and irradiating them.

True, he had his "religion" to seek, and painfully shape together for himself, out of the abysses of conflicting disbelief and sham-belief and bedlam delusion, now filling the world, as all men of reflection have; and in this respect too, —more especially as his lot in the battle appointed for us all was, if you can understand it, victory and not defeat, —he is an expressive emblem of his time, and an instruction and possession to his contemporaries. For, I say, it is by no means as a vanquished *doubter* that he figures in the memory of those who knew him; but rather as a victorious *believer*, and under great difficulties a victorious doer. An example to us all, not of lamed misery, helpless spiritual bewilderment and sprawling despair, or any kind of *drownage* in the foul welter of our so-called religious or other controversies and confusions; but of a swift and valiant vanquisher of all these; a noble asserter of himself, as worker and speaker, in spite of all these. Continually, so far as he went, he was a teacher, by act and word, of hope, clearness, activity, veracity, and human courage and nobleness: the preacher of a good gospel to all men, not of a bad to any man. The man, whether in priest's cassock or other costume of men, who is the enemy or hater of John Sterling, may assure himself that he does not yet know him, —that miserable differences of mere costume and dialect still divide him, whatsoever is worthy, catholic and perennial in him, from a brother soul who, more than most in his day, was his brother and not his adversary in regard to all that.

Nor shall the irremediable drawback that Sterling was not current in the Newspapers, that he achieved neither what the world calls greatness nor what intrinsically is such, altogether discourage me. What his natural size, and natural and accidental limits were, will gradually appear, if my sketching be successful. And I have remarked that a true delineation of the smallest man, and his scene of pilgrimage through life, is capable of interesting the greatest man; that all men are to an unspeakable degree brothers, each man's life a strange emblem of every man's; and that Human Portraits, faithfully drawn, are of all pictures the welcomest on human walls. Monitions and moralities enough may lie in this small Work, if honestly written and honestly read; —and, in particular, if any image of John Sterling and his Pilgrimage through our poor Nineteenth Century be one day wanted by the world, and they can find some shadow of a true image here, my swift scribbling (which shall be very swift and immediate) may prove useful by and by.

CHAPTER II.
BIRTH AND PARENTAGE.

John Sterling was born at Kaimes Castle, a kind of dilapidated baronial residence to which a small farm was then attached, rented by his Father, in the Isle of Bute, —on the 20th July, 1806. Both his parents were Irish by birth, Scotch by extraction; and became, as he himself did, essentially English by long residence and habit. Of John himself Scotland has little or nothing to claim except the birth and genealogy, for he left it almost before the years of memory; and in his mature days regarded it, if with a little more recognition and intelligence, yet without more participation in any of its accents outward or inward, than others natives of Middlesex or Surrey, where the scene of his chief education lay.

The climate of Bute is rainy, soft of temperature; with skies of unusual depth and brilliancy, while the weather is fair. In that soft rainy climate, on that wild-wooded rocky coast, with its gnarled mountains and green silent valleys, with its seething rain-storms and many-sounding seas, was young Sterling ushered into his first schooling in this world. I remember one little anecdote his Father told me of those first years: One of the cows had calved; young John, still in petticoats, was permitted to go, holding by his father's hand, and look at the newly arrived calf; a mystery which he surveyed with open intent eyes, and the silent exercise of all the scientific faculties he had; —very strange mystery indeed, this new arrival, and fresh denizen of our Universe: "Wull't eat a-body? " said John in his first practical Scotch, inquiring into the tendencies this mystery might have to fall upon a little fellow and consume him as provision: "Will it eat one, Father? " —Poor little open-eyed John: the family long bantered him with this anecdote; and we, in far other years, laughed heartily on hearing it. —Simple peasant laborers, ploughers, house-servants, occasional fisher-people too; and the sight of ships, and crops, and Nature's doings where Art has little meddled with her: this was the kind of schooling our young friend had, first of all; on this bench of the grand world-school did he sit, for the first four years of his life.

Edward Sterling his Father, a man who subsequently came to considerable notice in the world, was originally of Waterford in Munster; son of the Episcopalian Clergyman there; and chief representative of a family of some standing in those parts. Family founded, it appears, by a Colonel Robert Sterling, called also Sir Robert Sterling; a Scottish Gustavus-Adolphus soldier, whom the breaking out of the Civil War had recalled from his German campaignings, and had before long, though not till after some waverings on his part, attached firmly to the Duke of Ormond and to the King's Party in that quarrel. A little bit of genealogy, since it lies ready to my hand, gathered long ago out of wider studies, and pleasantly connects things individual and present with the dim universal crowd of things past, —may as well be inserted here as thrown away.

This Colonel Robert designates himself Sterling "of Glorat; " I believe, a younger branch of the well-known Stirlings of Keir in Stirlingshire. It appears he prospered in his soldiering and other business, in those bad Ormond times; being a man of energy, ardor and intelligence, —probably prompt enough both with his word and with his stroke. There survives yet, in the Commons Journals, [2] dim notice of his controversies and adventures; especially of one controversy he had got into with certain victorious Parliamentary official parties, while his own party lay vanquished, during what was called the Ormond Cessation, or Temporary Peace made by Ormond with the Parliament in 1646: —in which controversy Colonel Robert, after repeated applications, journeyings to London, attendances upon committees, and such like, finds himself worsted, declared to be in the wrong; and so vanishes from the Commons Journals.

What became of him when Cromwell got to Ireland, and to Munster, I have not heard: his knighthood, dating from the very year of Cromwell's Invasion (1649), indicates a man expected to do his best on the occasion: —as in all probability he did; had not Tredah Storm proved ruinous, and the neck of this Irish War been broken at once. Doubtless the Colonel Sir Robert followed or attended his Duke of Ormond into foreign parts, and gave up his management of Munster, while it was yet time: for after the Restoration we find him again, safe, and as was natural, flourishing with new splendor; gifted, recompensed with lands; —settled, in short, on fair revenues in those Munster regions. He appears to have had no children; but to have left his property to William, a younger brother who had followed him into Ireland. From this William descends the family which, in the years we treat of, had Edward Sterling, Father of our John, for its representative. And now enough of genealogy.

Of Edward Sterling, Captain Edward Sterling as his title was, who in the latter period of his life became well known in London political society, whom indeed all England, with a curious mixture of mockery and respect and even fear, knew well as "the Thunderer of the Times Newspaper, " there were much to be said, did the present task and its limits permit. As perhaps it might, on certain terms? What is indispensable let us not omit to say. The history of a man's childhood is the description of his parents and environment: this is his inarticulate but highly important history, in those first times, while of articulate he has yet none.

Edward Sterling had now just entered on his thirty-fourth year; and was already a man experienced in fortunes and changes. A native of Waterford in Munster, as already mentioned; born in the "Deanery House of Waterford, 27th February, 1773, " say the registers. For his Father, as we learn, resided in the Deanery House, though he was not himself Dean, but only "Curate of the Cathedral" (whatever that may mean); he was withal rector of two other livings, and the Dean's friend, —friend indeed of the Dean's kinsmen the Beresfords generally; whose grand house of Curraghmore, near by Waterford, was a familiar haunt of his and his children's. This reverend gentleman, along with his three livings and high acquaintanceships, had inherited political connections; —inherited especially a Government Pension, with survivorship for still one life beyond his own; his father having been Clerk of the Irish House of Commons at the time of the Union, of which office the lost salary was compensated in this way. The Pension was of two hundred pounds; and only expired with the life of Edward, John's Father, in 1847. There were, and still are, daughters of the family; but Edward was the only son; —descended, too, from the Scottish hero Wallace, as the old gentleman would sometimes admonish him; his own wife, Edward's mother, being of that name, and boasting herself, as most Scotch Wallaces do, to have that blood in her veins.

This Edward had picked up, at Waterford, and among the young Beresfords of Curraghmore and elsewhere, a thoroughly Irish form of character: fire and fervor, vitality of all kinds, in genial abundance; but in a much more loquacious, ostentatious, much *louder* style than is freely patronized on this side of the Channel. Of Irish accent in speech he had entirely divested himself, so as not to be traced by any vestige in that respect; but his Irish accent of character, in all manner of other more important respects, was very recognizable. An impetuous man, full of real energy, and immensely conscious of the same; who transacted everything not with the minimum of fuss and noise, but with the maximum: a very Captain Whirlwind, as one was tempted to call him.

In youth, he had studied at Trinity College, Dublin; visited the Inns of Court here, and trained himself for the Irish Bar. To the Bar he had been duly called, and was waiting for the results, —when, in his twenty-fifth year, the Irish Rebellion broke out; whereupon the Irish Barristers decided to raise a corps of loyal Volunteers, and a complete change introduced itself into Edward Sterling's way of life. For, naturally, he had joined the array of Volunteers; —fought, I have heard, "in three actions with the rebels" (Vinegar Hill, for one); and doubtless fought well: but in the mess-rooms, among the young military and civil officials, with all of whom he was a favorite, he had acquired a taste for soldier life, and perhaps high hopes of succeeding in it: at all events, having a commission in the Lancashire Militia offered him, he accepted that; altogether quitted the Bar, and became Captain Sterling thenceforth. From the Militia, it appears, he had volunteered with his Company into the Line; and, under some disappointments, and official delays of expected promotion, was continuing to serve as Captain there, "Captain of the Eighth Battalion of Reserve, " say the Military Almanacs of 1803, —in which year the quarters happened to be Derry, where new events awaited him. At a ball in Derry he met with Miss Hester Coningham, the queen of the scene, and of the fair world in Derry at that time. The acquaintance, in spite of some Opposition, grew with vigor, and rapidly ripened: and "at Fehan Church, Diocese of Derry, " where the Bride's father had a country-house, "on Thursday 5th April, 1804, Hester Coningham, only daughter of John Coningham, Esquire, Merchant in Derry, and of Elizabeth Campbell his wife, " was wedded to Captain Sterling; she happiest to him happiest, —as by Nature's kind law it is arranged.

Mrs. Sterling, even in her later days, had still traces of the old beauty: then and always she was a woman of delicate, pious, affectionate character; exemplary as a wife, a mother and a friend. A refined female nature; something tremulous in it, timid, and with a certain rural freshness still unweakened by long converse with the world. The tall slim figure, always of a kind of quaker neatness; the innocent anxious face, anxious bright hazel eyes; the timid, yet gracefully cordial ways, the natural intelligence, instinctive sense and worth, were very characteristic. Her voice too; with its something of soft querulousness, easily adapting itself to a light thin-flowing style of mirth on occasion, was characteristic: she had retained her Ulster intonations, and was withal somewhat copious in speech. A fine tremulously sensitive nature, strong chiefly on the side of the affections, and the graceful insights and activities that depend on these: —truly a beautiful, much-suffering, much-loving house-mother. From her chiefly, as one could discern, John Sterling had derived the delicate *aroma* of his nature, its piety, clearness, sincerity; as from his Father, the ready practical gifts, the impetuosities and the audacities, were also (though in strange new form) visibly inherited. A man was lucky to have such a Mother; to have such Parents as both his were.

Meanwhile the new Wife appears to have had, for the present, no marriage-portion; neither was Edward Sterling rich, —according to his own ideas and aims, far from it. Of course he soon found that the fluctuating barrack-life, especially with no outlooks of speedy promotion, was little suited to his new circumstances: but how change it? His father was now dead; from whom he had inherited the Speaker Pension of two hundred pounds; but of available probably little or nothing more. The rents of the small family estate, I suppose, and other property, had gone to portion sisters. Two hundred pounds, and the pay of a marching captain: within the limits of that revenue all plans of his had to restrict themselves at present.

He continued for some time longer in the Army; his wife undivided from him by the hardships, of that way of life. Their first son Anthony (Captain Anthony Sterling, the only child who now survives) was born to them in this position, while lying at Dundalk, in January, 1805. Two months later, some eleven months after their marriage, the regiment was broken; and Captain Sterling, declining to serve elsewhere on the terms offered, and willingly accepting such decision of his doubts, was reduced to half-pay. This was the end of his soldiering: some five or six years in all; from which he had derived for life, among other things, a decided military bearing, whereof he was rather proud; an incapacity for practicing law; —and considerable uncertainty as to what his next course of life was now to be.

For the present, his views lay towards farming: to establish himself, if not as country gentleman, which was an unattainable ambition, then at least as some kind of gentleman-farmer which had a flattering resemblance to that. Kaimes Castle with a reasonable extent of land, which, in his inquiries after farms, had turned up, was his first place of settlement in this new capacity; and here, for some few months, he had established himself when John his second child was born. This was Captain Sterling's first attempt towards a fixed course of life; not a very wise one, I have understood: —yet on the whole, who, then and there, could have pointed out to him a wiser?

A fixed course of life and activity he could never attain, or not till very late; and this doubtless was among the important points of his destiny, and acted both on his own character and that of those who had to attend him on his wayfarings.

CHAPTER III.
SCHOOLS: LLANBLETHIAN; PARIS; LONDON.

Edward Sterling never shone in farming; indeed I believe he never took heartily to it, or tried it except in fits. His Bute farm was, at best, a kind of apology for some far different ideal of a country establishment which could not be realized; practically a temporary landing-place from which he could make sallies and excursions in search of some more generous field of enterprise. Stormy brief efforts at energetic husbandry, at agricultural improvement and rapid field-labor, alternated with sudden flights to Dublin, to London, whithersoever any flush of bright outlook which he could denominate practical, or any gleam of hope which his impatient ennui could represent as such, allured him. This latter was often enough the case. In wet hay-times and harvest-times, the dripping outdoor world, and lounging indoor one, in the absence of the master, offered far from a satisfactory appearance! Here was, in fact, a man much imprisoned; haunted, I doubt not, by demons enough; though ever brisk and brave withal, —iracund, but cheerfully vigorous, opulent in wise or unwise hope. A fiery energetic soul consciously and unconsciously storming for deliverance into better arenas; and this in a restless, rapid, impetuous, rather than in a strong, silent and deliberate way.

In rainy Bute and the dilapidated Kaimes Castle, it was evident, there lay no Goshen for such a man. The lease, originally but for some three years and a half, drawing now to a close, he resolved to quit Bute; had heard, I know not where, of an eligible cottage without farm attached, in the pleasant little village of Llanblethian close by Cowbridge in Glamorganshire; of this he took a lease, and thither with his family he moved in search of new fortunes. Glamorganshire was at least a better climate than Bute; no groups of idle or of busy reapers could here stand waiting on the guidance of a master, for there was no farm here; —and among its other and probably its chief though secret advantages, Llanblethian was much more convenient both for Dublin and London than Kaimes Castle had been.

The removal thither took place in the autumn of 1809. Chief part of the journey (perhaps from Greenock to Swansea or Bristol) was by sea: John, just turned of three years, could in after-times remember nothing of this voyage; Anthony, some eighteen months older, has still a vivid recollection of the gray splashing tumult, and dim sorrow, uncertainty, regret and distress he underwent: to him a "dissolving-view" which not only left its effect on the *plate* (as all views and dissolving-views doubtless do on that kind of "plate"), but remained consciously present there. John, in the close of his twenty-first year, professes not to remember anything whatever of Bute; his whole existence, in that earliest scene of it, had faded away from him: Bute also, with its shaggy mountains, moaning woods, and summer and winter seas, had been wholly a dissolving-view for him, and had left no conscious impression, but only, like this voyage, an effect.

Llanblethian hangs pleasantly, with its white cottages, and orchard and other trees, on the western slope of a green hill looking far and wide over green meadows and little or bigger hills, in the pleasant plain of Glamorgan; a short mile to the south of Cowbridge, to which smart little town it is properly a kind of suburb. Plain of Glamorgan, some ten miles wide and thirty or forty long, which they call the Vale of Glamorgan; —though properly it is not quite a Vale, there being only one range of mountains to it, if even one: certainly the central Mountains of Wales do gradually rise, in a miscellaneous manner, on the north side of it; but on the south are no mountains, not even land, only the Bristol Channel, and far off, the Hills of Devonshire, for boundary, —the "English Hills, " as the natives call them, visible from every eminence in those parts. On such wide terms is it called Vale of Glamorgan. But called by whatever name, it is a most pleasant fruitful region: kind to the native, interesting to the visitor. A waving grassy region; cut with innumerable ragged lanes; dotted with sleepy unswept human hamlets, old ruinous castles with their ivy and their daws, gray sleepy churches with their ditto ditto: for ivy everywhere abounds; and generally a rank fragrant vegetation clothes all things; hanging, in rude many-colored festoons and fringed odoriferous tapestries, on your right and on your left, in every lane. A country kinder to the sluggard husbandman than any I have ever seen. For it lies all on limestone, needs no draining; the soil, everywhere of handsome depth and finest quality, will grow good crops for you with the most imperfect tilling. At a safe distance of a day's riding lie the tartarean copper-forges of Swansea, the tartarean iron-forges of Merthyr; their sooty battle far away, and not, at such safe distance, a defilement to the face of the earth and sky, but rather an encouragement to the earth at least; encouraging the husbandman to plough better, if he only would.

The peasantry seem indolent and stagnant, but peaceable and well-provided; much given to Methodism when they have any character; —for the rest, an innocent good-humored people, who all drink home-brewed beer, and have brown loaves of the most excellent home-baked bread. The native peasant village is not generally beautiful, though it might be, were it swept and trimmed; it gives one rather the idea of sluttish stagnancy, —an interesting peep into the Welsh Paradise of Sleepy Hollow. Stones, old kettles, naves of wheels, all kinds of broken litter, with live pigs and etceteras, lie about the street: for, as a rule, no rubbish is removed, but waits patiently the action of mere natural chemistry and accident; if even a house is burnt or falls, you will find it there after half a century, only cloaked by the ever-ready ivy. Sluggish man seems never to have struck a pick into it; his new hut is built close by on ground not encumbered, and the old stones are still left lying.

This is the ordinary Welsh village; but there are exceptions, where people of more cultivated tastes have been led to settle, and Llanblethian is one of the more signal of these. A decidedly cheerful group of human homes, the greater part of them indeed belonging to persons of refined habits; trimness, shady shelter, whitewash, neither conveniency nor decoration has been neglected here. Its effect from the distance on the eastward is very pretty: you see it like a little sleeping cataract of white houses, with trees overshadowing and fringing it; and there the cataract hangs, and does not rush away from you.

John Sterling spent his next five years in this locality. He did not again see it for a quarter of a century; but retained, all his life, a lively remembrance of it; and, just in the end of his twenty-first year, among his earliest printed pieces, we find an elaborate and diffuse description of it and its relations to him, —part of which piece, in spite of its otherwise insignificant quality, may find place here: —

"The fields on which I first looked, and the sands which were marked by my earliest footsteps, are completely lost to my memory; and of those ancient walls among which I began to breathe, I retain no recollection more clear than the outlines of a cloud in a moonless sky. But of L——, the village where I afterwards lived, I persuade myself that every line and hue is more deeply and accurately fixed than those of any spot I have since beheld, even though borne in upon the heart by the association of the strongest feelings.

"My home was built upon the slope of a hill, with a little orchard stretching down before it, and a garden rising behind. At a considerable distance beyond and beneath the orchard, a rivulet flowed through meadows and turned a mill; while, above the garden, the summit of the hill was crowned by a few gray rocks, from which a yew-tree grew, solitary and bare. Extending at each side of the orchard, toward the brook, two scattered patches of cottages lay nestled among their gardens; and beyond this streamlet and the little mill and bridge, another slight eminence arose, divided into green fields, tufted and bordered with copsewood, and crested by a ruined castle, contemporary, as was said, with the Conquest. I know not whether these things in truth made up a prospect of much beauty. Since I was eight years old, I have never seen them; but I well know that no landscape I have since beheld, no picture of Claude or Salvator, gave me half the impression of living, heartfelt, perfect beauty which fills my mind when I think of that green valley, that sparkling rivulet, that broken fortress of dark antiquity, and that hill with its aged yew and breezy summit, from which I have so often looked over the broad stretch of verdure beneath it, and the country-town, and church-tower, silent and white beyond.

"In that little town there was, and I believe is, a school where the elements of human knowledge were communicated to me, for some hours of every day, during a considerable time. The path to it lay across the rivulet and past the mill; from which point we could either journey through the fields below the old castle, and the wood which surrounded it, or along a road at the other side of the ruin, close to the gateway of which it passed. The former track led through two or three beautiful fields, the sylvan domain of the keep on one hand, and the brook on the other; while an oak or two, like giant warders advanced from the wood, broke the sunshine of the green with a soft and graceful shadow. How often, on my way to school, have I stopped beneath the tree to collect the fallen acorns; how often run down to the stream to pluck a branch of the hawthorn which hung over the water! The road which passed the castle joined, beyond these fields, the path which traversed them. It took, I well remember, a certain solemn and mysterious interest from the ruin. The shadow of the archway, the discolorations of time on all the walls, the dimness of the little thicket which encircled it, the traditions of its immeasurable age, made St. Quentin's Castle a wonderful and awful fabric in the imagination of a child; and long after I last saw its mouldering roughness, I never read of fortresses, or heights, or spectres, or banditti, without connecting them with the one ruin of my childhood.

"It was close to this spot that one of the few adventures occurred which marked, in my mind, my boyish days with importance. When loitering beyond the castle, on the way to school, with a brother somewhat older than myself, who was uniformly my champion and protector, we espied a round sloe high up in the hedge-row. We determined to obtain it; and I do not remember whether both of us, or only my brother, climbed the tree. However, when the prize was all but reached, —and no alchemist ever looked more eagerly for the moment of projection which was to give him immortality and omnipotence, —a gruff voice startled us with an oath, and an order to desist; and I well recollect looking back, for long after, with terror to the vision of an old and ill-tempered farmer, armed with a bill-hook, and vowing our decapitation; nor did I subsequently remember without triumph the eloquence whereby alone, in my firm belief, my brother and myself had been rescued from instant death.

"At the entrance of the little town stood an old gateway, with a pointed arch and decaying battlements. It gave admittance to the street which contained the church, and which terminated in another street, the principal one in the town of C— —. In this was situated the school to which I daily wended. I cannot now recall to mind the face of its good conductor, nor of any of his scholars; but I have before me a strong general image of the interior of his establishment. I remember the reverence with which I was wont to carry to his seat a well-thumbed duodecimo, the *History of Greece* by Oliver Goldsmith. I remember the mental agonies I endured in attempting to master the art and mystery of penmanship; a craft in which, alas, I remained too short a time under Mr. R— — to become as great a proficient as he made his other scholars, and which my awkwardness has prevented me from attaining in any considerable perfection under my various subsequent pedagogues. But that which has left behind it a brilliant trait of light was the exhibition of what are called 'Christmas pieces;' things unknown in aristocratic seminaries, but constantly used at the comparatively humble academy which supplied the best knowledge of reading, writing, and arithmetic to be attained in that remote neighborhood.

"The long desks covered from end to end with those painted masterpieces, the Life of Robinson Crusoe, the Hunting of Chevy-Chase, the History of Jack the Giant-Killer, and all the little eager faces and trembling hands bent over these, and filling them up with some choice quotation, sacred or profane; —no, the galleries of art, the theatrical exhibitions, the reviews and processions, —which are only not childish because they are practiced and admired by men instead of children, —all the pomps and vanities of great cities, have shown me no revelation of glory such as did that crowded school-room the week before the Christmas holidays. But these were the splendors of life. The truest and the strongest feelings do not connect themselves with any scenes of gorgeous and gaudy magnificence; they are bound up in the remembrances of home.

"The narrow orchard, with its grove of old apple-trees against one of which I used to lean, and while I brandished a beanstalk, roar out with Fitzjames, —

> 'Come one, come all; this rock shall fly
> From its firm base as soon as I! ' —

while I was ready to squall at the sight of a cur, and run valorously away from a casually approaching cow; the field close beside it, where I rolled about in summer among the hay; the brook in which, despite of maid and mother, I waded by the hour; the garden where I sowed flower-seeds, and then turned up the ground again and planted potatoes, and then rooted out the potatoes to insert acorns and apple-pips, and at last, as may be supposed, reaped neither roses, nor potatoes, nor oak-trees, nor apples; the grass-plots on which I played among those with whom I never can play nor work again: all these are places and employments, —and, alas, playmates, —such as, if it were worth while to weep at all, it would be worth weeping that I enjoy no longer.

"I remember the house where I first grew familiar with peacocks; and the mill-stream into which I once fell; and the religious awe wherewith I heard, in the warm twilight, the psalm-singing around the house of the Methodist miller; and the door-post against which I discharged my brazen artillery; I remember the window by which I sat while my mother taught me French; and the patch of garden which I dug for— But her name is best left blank; it was indeed writ in water. These recollections are to me like the wealth of a departed friend, a mournful treasure. But the public has heard enough of them; to it they are worthless: they are a coin which only circulates at its true value between the different periods of an individual's existence, and good for nothing but to keep up a commerce between boyhood and manhood. I have for years looked forward to the possibility of visiting L— —; but I am told that it is a changed village; and not only has man been at work, but the old yew on the hill has fallen, and scarcely a low stump remains of the tree which I delighted in childhood to think might have furnished bows for the Norman archers. "[3]

In Cowbridge is some kind of free school, or grammar-school, of a certain distinction; and this to Captain Sterling was probably a motive for settling in the neighborhood of it with his children. Of this however, as it turned out, there was no use made: the Sterling family, during its continuance in those parts, did not need more than a primary school. The worthy master who presided over these Christmas galas, and had the honor to teach John Sterling his reading and writing, was an elderly Mr. Reece of Cowbridge, who still (in 1851) survives, or lately did; and is still remembered by his old pupils as a worthy, ingenious and kindly man, "who wore drab breeches and white stockings. " Beyond the Reece sphere of tuition John Sterling did not go in this locality.

In fact the Sterling household was still fluctuating; the problem of a task for Edward Sterling's powers, and of anchorage for his affairs in any sense, was restlessly struggling to solve itself, but was still a good way from being solved. Anthony, in revisiting these scenes with John in 1839, mentions going to the spot "where we used to stand with our Father, looking out for the arrival of the London mail: " a little chink through which is disclosed to us a big restless section of a human life. The Hill of Welsh Llanblethian, then, is like the mythic Caucasus in its degree (as indeed all hills and habitations where men sojourn are); and here too, on a small scale, is a Prometheus Chained! Edward Sterling, I can well understand, was a man to tug at the chains that held him idle in those the prime of his years; and to ask restlessly, yet not in anger and remorse, so much as in hope, locomotive speculation, and ever-new adventure and attempt, Is there no task nearer my own natural size, then? So he looks out from the Hill-side "for the arrival of the London mail; " thence hurries into Cowbridge to the Post-office; and has a wide web, of threads and gossamers, upon his loom, and many shuttles flying, in this world.

By the Marquis of Bute's appointment he had, very shortly after his arrival in that region, become Adjutant of the Glamorganshire Militia, "Local Militia, " I suppose; and was, in this way, turning his military capabilities to some use. The office involved pretty frequent absences, in Cardiff and elsewhere. This doubtless was a welcome outlet, though a small one. He had also begun to try writing, especially on public subjects; a much more copious outlet, —which indeed, gradually widening itself, became the final solution for him. Of the year 1811 we have a Pamphlet of his, entitled *Military Reform*; this is the second edition, "dedicated to the Duke of Kent; " the first appears to have come out the year before, and had thus attained a certain notice, which of course was encouraging. He now furthermore opened a correspondence with the *Times* Newspaper; wrote to it, in 1812, a series of Letters under the signature *Vetus*: voluntary Letters I suppose, without payment or pre-engagement, one successful Letter calling out another; till *Vetus* and his doctrines came to be a distinguishable entity, and the business amounted to something. Out of my own earliest Newspaper reading, I can remember the name *Vetus*, as a kind of editorial hacklog on which able-editors were wont to chop straw now and then. Nay the Letters were collected and reprinted; both this first series, of 1812, and then a second of next year: two very thin, very dim-colored cheap octavos; stray copies of which still exist, and may one day become distillable into a drop of History (should such be wanted of our poor "Scavenger Age" in time coming), though the reading of them has long ceased in this generation. [4] The first series, we perceive, had even gone to a second edition. The tone, wherever one timidly glances into this extinct cockpit, is trenchant and emphatic: the name of *Vetus*, strenuously fighting there, had become considerable in the talking political world; and, no doubt, was especially of mark, as that of a writer who might otherwise be important, with the proprietors of the *Times*. The connection continued: widened and deepened itself, —in a slow tentative manner; passing naturally from voluntary into remunerated: and indeed proving more and more to be the true ultimate arena, and battle-field and seed-field, for the exuberant impetuosities and faculties of this man.

What the *Letters of Vetus* treated of I do not know; doubtless they ran upon Napoleon, Catholic Emancipation, true methods of national defence, of effective foreign Anti-gallicism, and of domestic ditto; which formed the staple of editorial speculation at that time. I have heard in general that Captain Sterling, then and afterwards, advocated "the Marquis of Wellesley's policy; " but that also, what it was, I have forgotten, and the world has been willing to forget. Enough, the heads of the *Times* establishment, perhaps already the Marquis of Wellesley and other important persons, had their eye on this writer; and it began to be surmised by him that here at last was the career he had been seeking.

Accordingly, in 1814, when victorious Peace unexpectedly arrived; and the gates of the Continent after five-and-twenty years of fierce closure were suddenly thrown open; and the hearts of all English and European men awoke staggering as if from a nightmare suddenly removed, and ran hither and thither, —Edward Sterling also determined on a new adventure, that of crossing to Paris, and trying what might lie in store for him. For curiosity, in its idler sense, there was evidently pabulum enough. But he had hopes moreover of learning much that might perhaps avail him afterwards; —hopes withal, I have understood, of getting to be Foreign Correspondent of the *Times* Newspaper, and so adding to his income in the mean while. He left Llanblethian in May; dates from Dieppe the 27th of that month. He lived in occasional contact with Parisian notabilities (all of them except Madame de Stael forgotten now), all summer, diligently surveying his ground; —returned for his family, who were still in Wales but ready to move, in the beginning of August; took them immediately across with him; a house in the neighborhood of Paris, in the pleasant village of Passy at once town and country, being now ready; and so, under foreign skies, again set up his household there.

Here was a strange new "school" for our friend John now in his eighth year! Out of which the little Anthony and he drank doubtless at all pores, vigorously as they had done in no school before. A change total and immediate. Somniferous green Llanblethian has suddenly been blotted out; presto, here are wakeful Passy and the noises of paved Paris instead. Innocent ingenious Mr. Reece in drab breeches and white stockings, he with his mild Christmas galas and peaceable rules of Dilworth and Butterworth, has given place to such a saturnalia of panoramic, symbolic and other teachers and monitors, addressing all the five senses at once. Who John's express tutors were, at Passy, I never heard; nor indeed, especially in his case, was it much worth inquiring. To him and to all of us, the expressly appointed schoolmasters and schoolings we get are as nothing, compared with the unappointed incidental and continual ones, whose school-hours are all the days and nights of our existence, and whose lessons, noticed or unnoticed, stream in upon us with every breath we draw. Anthony says they attended a French school, though only for about three months; and he well remembers the last scene of it, "the boys shouting *Vive l'Empereur* when Napoleon came back. "

Of John Sterling's express schooling, perhaps the most important feature, and by no means a favorable one to him, was the excessive fluctuation that prevailed in it. Change of scene, change of teacher, *both* express and implied, was incessant with him; and gave his young life a nomadic character, —which surely, of all the adventitious tendencies that could have been impressed upon him, so volatile, swift and airy a being as him, was the one he needed least. His gentle pious-hearted Mother, ever watching over him in all outward changes, and assiduously keeping human pieties and good affections alive in him, was probably the best counteracting element in his lot. And on the whole, have we not all to run our chance in that respect; and take, the most victoriously we can, such schooling as pleases to be attainable in our year and place? Not very victoriously, the most of us! A wise well-calculated breeding of a young genial soul in this world, or alas of any young soul in it, lies fatally over the horizon in these epochs! —This French scene of things, a grand school of its sort, and also a perpetual banquet for the young soul, naturally captivated John Sterling; he said afterwards, "New things and experiences here were poured upon his mind and sense, not in streams, but in a Niagara cataract. " This too, however, was but a scene; lasted only some six or seven months; and in the spring of the next year terminated as abruptly as any of the rest could do.

For in the spring of the next year, Napoleon abruptly emerged from Elba; and set all the populations of the world in motion, in a strange manner; —set the Sterling household afloat, in particular; the big European tide rushing into all smallest creeks, at Passy and elsewhere. In brief, on the 20th of March, 1815, the family had to shift, almost to fly, towards home and the sea-coast; and for a day or two were under apprehension of being detained and not reaching home. Mrs. Sterling, with her children and effects, all in one big carriage with two horses, made the journey to Dieppe; in perfect safety, though in continual tremor: here they were joined by Captain Sterling, who had stayed behind at Paris to see the actual advent of Napoleon, and to report what the aspect of affairs was, "Downcast looks of citizens, with fierce saturnalian acclaim of soldiery: " after which they proceeded together to London without farther apprehension; —there to witness, in due time, the tar-barrels of Waterloo, and other phenomena that followed.

Captain Sterling never quitted London as a residence any more; and indeed was never absent from it, except on autumnal or other excursions of a few weeks, till the end of his life. Nevertheless his course there was as yet by no means clear; nor had his relations with the heads of the *Times*, or with other high heads, assumed a form which could be called definite, but were hanging as a cloudy maze of possibilities, firm substance not yet divided from shadow. It continued so for some years. The Sterling household shifted twice or thrice to new streets or localities, —Russell Square or Queen Square, Blackfriars Road, and longest at the Grove, Blackheath, — before the vapors of Wellesley promotions and such like slowly sank as useless precipitate, and the firm rock, which was definite employment, ending in lucrative co-proprietorship and more and more important connection with the *Times* Newspaper, slowly disclosed itself.

These changes of place naturally brought changes in John Sterling's schoolmasters: nor were domestic tragedies wanting, still more important to him. New brothers and sisters had been born; two little brothers more, three little sisters he had in all; some of whom came to their eleventh year beside him, some passed away in their second or fourth: but from his ninth to his sixteenth year they all died; and in 1821 only Anthony and John were left. [5] How many tears, and passionate pangs, and soft infinite regrets; such as are appointed to all mortals! In one year, I find, indeed in one half-year, he lost three little playmates, two of them within one month. His own age was not yet quite twelve. For one of these three, for little Edward, his next younger, who died now at the age of nine, Mr. Hare records that John copied out, in large school-hand, a *History of Valentine and Orson*, to beguile the poor child's sickness, which ended in death soon, leaving a sad cloud on John.

Of his grammar and other schools, which, as I said, are hardly worth enumerating in comparison, the most important seems to have been a Dr. Burney's at Greenwich; a large day-schoo] and boarding-school, where Anthony and John gave their attendance for a year or two (1818-19) from Blackheath. "John frequently did themes for the boys, " says Anthony, "and for myself when I was aground. " His progress in all school learning was certain to be rapid, if he even moderately took to it. A lean, tallish, loose-made boy of twelve; strange alacrity, rapidity and joyous eagerness looking out of his eyes, and of all his ways and movements. I have a Picture of him at this stage; a little portrait, which carries its verification with it. In manhood too, the chief expression of his eyes and physiognomy was what I might call alacrity, cheerful rapidity. You could see, here looked forth a soul which was winged; which dwelt in hope and action, not in hesitation or fear. Anthony says, he was "an affectionate and gallant kind of boy, adventurous and generous, daring to a singular degree. " Apt enough withal to be "petulant now and then; " on the whole, "very self-willed; " doubtless not a little discursive in his thoughts and ways, and "difficult to manage. "

I rather think Anthony, as the steadier, more substantial boy, was the Mother's favorite; and that John, though the quicker and cleverer, perhaps cost her many anxieties. Among the Papers given me, is an old browned half-sheet in stiff school hand, unpunctuated, occasionally ill spelt, —John Sterling's earliest remaining Letter, — which gives record of a crowning escapade of his, the first and the last of its kind; and so may be inserted here. A very headlong adventure on the boy's part; so hasty and so futile, at once audacious and impracticable; emblematic of much that befell in the history of the man!

"To Mrs. Sterling, Blackheath.

"21st September, 1818.

"DEAR MAMMA, —I am now at Dover, where I arrived this morning about seven o'clock. When you thought I was going to church, I went down the Kent Road, and walked on till I came to Gravesend, which is upwards of twenty miles from Blackheath; at about seven o'clock in the evening, without having eat anything the whole time. I applied to an inkeeper (*sic*) there, pretending that I had served a haberdasher in London, who left of (*sic*) business, and turned me away. He believed me; and got me a passage in the coach here, for I said that I had an Uncle here, and that my Father and Mother were dead; —when I wandered about the quays for some time, till I met Captain Keys, whom I asked to give me a passage to Boulogne; which he promised to do, and took me home to breakfast with him: but Mrs. Keys questioned me a good deal; when I not being able to make my story good, I was obliged to confess to her that I had run away from you. Captain Keys says that he will keep me at his house till you answer my letter.

"J. STERLING. "

Anthony remembers the business well; but can assign no origin to it, —some penalty, indignity or cross put suddenly on John, which the hasty John considered unbearable. His Mother's inconsolable weeping, and then his own astonishment at such a culprit's being forgiven, are all that remain with Anthony. The steady historical style of the young runaway of twelve, narrating merely, not in the least apologizing, is also noticeable.

This was some six months after his little brother Edward's death; three months after that of Hester, his little sister next in the family series to him: troubled days for the poor Mother in that small household on Blackheath, as there are for mothers in so many households in this world! I have heard that Mrs. Sterling passed much of her time alone, at this period. Her husband's pursuits, with his Wellesleys and the like, often carrying him into Town and detaining him late there, she would sit among her sleeping children, such of them as death had still spared, perhaps thriftily plying her needle, full of mournful affectionate night-thoughts, —apprehensive too, in her tremulous heart, that the head of the house might have fallen among robbers in his way homeward.

CHAPTER IV.
UNIVERSITIES: GLASGOW; CAMBRIDGE.

At a later stage, John had some instruction from a Dr. Waite at Blackheath; and lastly, the family having now removed into Town, to Seymour Street in the fashionable region there, he "read for a while with Dr. Trollope, Master of Christ's Hospital; " which ended his school history.

In this his ever-changing course, from Reece at Cowbridge to Trollope in Christ's, which was passed so nomadically, under ferulas of various color, the boy had, on the whole, snatched successfully a fair share of what was going. Competent skill in construing Latin, I think also an elementary knowledge of Greek; add ciphering to a small extent, Euclid perhaps in a rather imaginary condition; a swift but not very legible or handsome penmanship, and the copious prompt habit of employing it in all manner of unconscious English prose composition, or even occasionally in verse itself: this, or something like this, he had gained from his grammar-schools: this is the most of what they offer to the poor young soul in general, in these indigent times. The express schoolmaster is not equal to much at present, —while the *un*express, for good or for evil, is so busy with a poor little fellow! Other departments of schooling had been infinitely more productive, for our young friend, than the gerund-grinding one. A voracious reader I believe he all along was, —had "read the whole Edinburgh Review" in these boyish years, and out of the circulating libraries one knows not what cartloads; wading like Ulysses towards his palace "through infinite dung. " A voracious observer and participator in all things he likewise all along was; and had had his sights, and reflections, and sorrows and adventures, from Kaimes Castle onward, —and had gone at least to Dover on his own score. *Puer bonae spei,* as the school-albums say; a boy of whom much may be hoped? Surely, in many senses, yes. A frank veracity is in him, truth and courage, as the basis of all; and of wild gifts and graces there is abundance. I figure him a brilliant, swift, voluble, affectionate and pleasant creature; out of whom, if it were not that symptoms of delicate health already show themselves, great things might be made. Promotions at least, especially in this country and epoch of parliaments and eloquent palavers, are surely very possible for such a one!

Being now turned of sixteen, and the family economics getting yearly more propitious and flourishing, he, as his brother had already been, was sent to Glasgow University, in which city their Mother had connections. His brother and he were now all that remained of the young family; much attached to one another in their College years as afterwards. Glasgow, however, was not properly their College scene: here, except that they had some tuition from Mr. Jacobson, then a senior fellow-student, now (1851) the learned editor of St. Basil, and Regius Professor of Divinity in Oxford, who continued ever afterwards a valued intimate of John's, I find nothing special recorded of them. The Glasgow curriculum, for John especially, lasted but one year; who, after some farther tutorage from Mr. Jacobson or Dr. Trollope, was appointed for a more ambitious sphere of education.

In the beginning of his nineteenth year, "in the autumn of 1824, " he went to Trinity College, Cambridge. His brother Anthony, who had already been there a year, had just quitted this Establishment, and entered on a military life under good omens; I think, at Dublin under the Lord Lieutenant's patronage, to whose service he was, in some capacity, attached. The two brothers, ever in company hitherto, parted roads at this point; and, except on holiday visits and by frequent correspondence, did not again live together; but they continued in a true fraternal attachment while life lasted, and I believe never had any even temporary estrangement, or on either side a cause for such. The family, as I said, was now, for the last three years, reduced to these two; the rest of the young ones, with their laughter and their sorrows, all gone. The parents otherwise were prosperous in outward circumstances; the Father's position more and more developing itself into affluent security, an agreeable circle of acquaintance, and a certain real influence, though of a peculiar sort, according to his gifts for work in this world.

Sterling's Tutor at Trinity College was Julius Hare, now the distinguished Archdeacon of Lewes: —who soon conceived a great esteem for him, and continued ever afterwards, in looser or closer connection, his loved and loving friend. As the Biographical and Editorial work above alluded to abundantly evinces. Mr. Hare celebrates the wonderful and beautiful gifts, the sparkling ingenuity, ready logic, eloquent utterance, and noble generosities and pieties of his pupil; —records in particular how once, on a sudden alarm of fire in some neighboring College edifice while his lecture was proceeding, all hands rushed out to help; how the undergraduates instantly formed themselves in lines from the fire to the river, and in swift continuance kept passing buckets as was needful, till the enemy was visibly fast yielding, —when Mr. Hare, going along the line, was astonished to find Sterling, at the river-end of it, standing up to his waist in water, deftly dealing with the buckets as they came and went. You in the river, Sterling; you with your coughs, and dangerous tendencies of health! —"Somebody must be in it, " answered Sterling; "why not I, as well as another? " Sterling's friends may remember many traits of that kind. The swiftest in all things, he was apt to be found at the head of the column, whithersoever the march might be; if towards any brunt of danger, there was he surest to be at the head; and of himself and his peculiar risks or impediments he was negligent at all times, even to an excessive and plainly unreasonable degree.

Mr. Hare justly refuses him the character of an exact scholar, or technical proficient at any time in either of the ancient literatures. But he freely read in Greek and Latin, as in various modern languages; and in all fields, in the classical as well, his lively faculty of recognition and assimilation had given him large booty in proportion to his labor. One cannot under any circumstances conceive of Sterling as a steady dictionary philologue, historian, or archaeologist; nor did he here, nor could he well, attempt that course. At the same time, Greek and the Greeks being here before him, he could not fail to gather somewhat from it, to take some hue and shape from it. Accordingly there is, to a singular extent, especially in his early writings, a certain tinge of Grecism and Heathen classicality traceable in him; —Classicality, indeed, which does not satisfy one's sense as real or truly living, but which glitters with a certain genial, if perhaps almost meretricious half-*japannish* splendor, —greatly distinguishable from mere gerund-grinding, and death in longs and shorts. If Classicality mean the practical conception, or attempt to conceive, what human life was in the epoch called classical, —perhaps few or none of Sterling's contemporaries in that Cambridge establishment carried away more of available Classicality than even he.

But here, as in his former schools, his studies and inquiries, diligently prosecuted I believe, were of the most discursive wide-flowing character; not steadily advancing along beaten roads towards College honors, but pulsing out with impetuous irregularity now on this tract, now on that, towards whatever spiritual Delphi might promise to unfold the mystery of this world, and announce to him what was, in our new day, the authentic message of the gods. His speculations, readings, inferences, glances and conclusions were doubtless sufficiently encyclopedic; his grand tutors the multifarious set of Books he devoured. And perhaps, —as is the singular case in most schools and educational establishments of this unexampled epoch, —it was not the express set of arrangements in this or any extant University that could essentially forward him, but only the implied and silent ones; less in the prescribed "course of study, " which seems to tend no-whither, than—if you will consider it—in the generous (not ungenerous) rebellion against said prescribed course, and the voluntary spirit of endeavor and adventure excited thereby, does help lie for a brave youth in such places. Curious to consider. The fagging, the illicit boating, and the things *forbidden* by the schoolmaster, —these, I often notice in my Eton acquaintances, are the things that have done them good; these, and not their inconsiderable or considerable knowledge of the Greek accidence almost at all! What is Greek accidence, compared to Spartan discipline, if it can be had? That latter is a real and grand attainment. Certainly, if rebellion is unfortunately needful, and you can rebel in a generous manner, several things may be acquired in that operation, —rigorous mutual fidelity, reticence, steadfastness, mild stoicism, and other virtues far transcending your Greek accidence. Nor can the unwisest "prescribed course of study" be considered quite useless, if it have incited you to try nobly on all sides for a course of your own. A singular condition of Schools and High-schools, which have come down, in their strange old clothes and "courses of study, " from the monkish ages into this highly unmonkish one; —tragical condition, at which the intelligent observer makes deep pause!

One benefit, not to be dissevered from the most obsolete University still frequented by young ingenuous living souls, is that of manifold collision and communication with the said young souls; which, to every one of these coevals, is undoubtedly the most important branch of breeding for him. In this point, as the learned Huber has insisted, [6] the two English Universities, —their studies otherwise being granted to be nearly useless, and even ill done of their kind, — far excel all other Universities: so valuable are the rules of human behavior which from of old have tacitly established themselves there; so manful, with all its sad drawbacks, is the style of English character, "frank, simple, rugged and yet courteous, " which has tacitly but imperatively got itself sanctioned and prescribed there. Such, in full sight of Continental and other Universities, is Huber's opinion. Alas, the question of University Reform goes deep at present; deep as the world; —and the real University of these new epochs is yet a great way from us! Another judge in whom I have confidence declares further, That of these two Universities, Cambridge is decidedly the more catholic (not Roman catholic, but Human catholic) in its tendencies and habitudes; and that in fact, of all the miserable Schools and High-schools in the England of these years, he, if reduced to choose from them, would choose Cambridge as a place of culture for the young idea. So that, in these bad circumstances, Sterling had perhaps rather made a hit than otherwise?

Sterling at Cambridge had undoubtedly a wide and rather genial circle of comrades; and could not fail to be regarded and beloved by many of them. Their life seems to have been an ardently speculating and talking one; by no means excessively restrained within limits; and, in the more adventurous heads like Sterling's, decidedly tending towards the latitudinarian in most things. They had among them a Debating Society called The Union; where on stated evenings was much logic, and other spiritual fencing and ingenuous collision, —probably of a really superior quality in that kind; for not a few of the then disputants have since proved themselves men of parts, and attained distinction in the intellectual walks of life. Frederic Maurice, Richard Trench, John Kemble, Spedding, Venables, Charles Buller, Richard Milnes and others: —I have heard that in speaking and arguing, Sterling was the acknowledged chief in this Union Club; and that "none even came near him, except the late Charles Buller, " whose distinction in this and higher respects was also already notable.

The questions agitated seem occasionally to have touched on the political department, and even on the ecclesiastical. I have heard one trait of Sterling's eloquence, which survived on the wings of grinning rumor, and had evidently borne upon Church Conservatism in some form: "Have they not, "—or perhaps it was, Has she (the Church) not, —"a black dragoon in every parish, on good pay and rations, horse-meat and man's-meat, to patrol and battle for these things? " The "black dragoon, " which naturally at the moment ruffled the general young imagination into stormy laughter, points towards important conclusions in respect to Sterling at this time. I conclude he had, with his usual alacrity and impetuous daring, frankly adopted the anti-superstitious side of things; and stood scornfully prepared to repel all aggressions or pretensions from the opposite quarter. In short, that he was already, what afterwards there is no doubt about his being, at all points a Radical, as the name or nickname then went. In other words, a young ardent soul looking with hope and joy into a world which was infinitely beautiful to him, though overhung with falsities and foul cobwebs as world never was before; overloaded, overclouded, to the zenith and the nadir of it, by incredible uncredited traditions, solemnly sordid hypocrisies, and beggarly deliriums old and new; which latter class of objects it was clearly the part of every noble heart to expend all its lightnings and energies in burning up without delay, and sweeping into their native Chaos out of such a Cosmos as this. Which process, it did not then seem to him could be very difficult; or attended with much other than heroic joy, and enthusiasm of victory or of battle, to the gallant operator, in his part of it. This was, with modifications such as might be, the humor and creed of College Radicalism five-and-twenty years ago. Rather horrible at that time; seen to be not so horrible now, at least to have grown very universal, and to need no concealment now. The natural humor and attitude, we may well regret to say, —and honorable not dishonorable, for a brave young soul such as Sterling's, in those years in those localities!

I do not find that Sterling had, at that stage, adopted the then prevalent Utilitarian theory of human things. But neither, apparently, had he rejected it; still less did he yet at all denounce it with the damnatory vehemence we were used to in him at a later period. Probably he, so much occupied with the negative side of things, had not yet thought seriously of any positive basis for his world; or asked himself, too earnestly, What, then, is the noble rule of living for a man? In this world so eclipsed and scandalously overhung with fable and hypocrisy, what is the eternal fact, on which a man may front the Destinies and the Immensities? The day for such questions, sure enough to come in his case, was still but coming. Sufficient for this day be the work thereof; that of blasting into merited annihilation the innumerable and immeasurable recognized deliriums, and extirpating or coercing to the due pitch those legions of "black dragoons, " of all varieties and purposes, who patrol, with horse-meat and man's-meat, this afflicted earth, so hugely to the detriment of it.

Sterling, it appears, after above a year of Trinity College, followed his friend Maurice into Trinity Hall, with the intention of taking a degree in Law; which intention, like many others with him, came to nothing; and in 1827 he left Trinity Hall and Cambridge altogether; here ending, after two years, his brief University life.

CHAPTER V.
A PROFESSION.

Here, then, is a young soul, brought to the years of legal majority, furnished from his training-schools with such and such shining capabilities, and ushered on the scene of things to inquire practically, What he will do there? Piety is in the man, noble human valor, bright intelligence, ardent proud veracity; light and fire, in none of their many senses, wanting for him, but abundantly bestowed: a kingly kind of man; —whose "kingdom, " however, in this bewildered place and epoch of the world will probably be difficult to find and conquer!

For, alas, the world, as we said, already stands convicted to this young soul of being an untrue, unblessed world; its high dignitaries many of them phantasms and players'-masks; its worthships and worships unworshipful: from Dan to Beersheba, a mad world, my masters. And surely we may say, and none will now gainsay, this his idea of the world at that epoch was nearer to the fact than at most other epochs it has been. Truly, in all times and places, the young ardent soul that enters on this world with heroic purpose, with veracious insight, and the yet unclouded "inspiration of the Almighty" which has given us our intelligence, will find this world a very mad one: why else is he, with his little outfit of heroisms and inspirations, come hither into it, except to make it diligently a little saner? Of him there would have been no need, had it been quite sane. This is true; this will, in all centuries and countries, be true.

And yet perhaps of no time or country, for the last two thousand years, was it *so* true as here in this waste-weltering epoch of Sterling's and ours. A world all rocking and plunging, like that old Roman one when the measure of its iniquities was full; the abysses, and subterranean and supernal deluges, plainly broken loose; in the wild dim-lighted chaos all stars of Heaven gone out. No star of Heaven visible, hardly now to any man; the pestiferous fogs, and foul exhalations grown continual, have, except on the highest mountaintops, blotted out all stars: will-o'-wisps, of various course and color, take the place of stars. Over the wild-surging chaos, in the leaden air, are only sudden glares of revolutionary lightning; then mere darkness, with philanthropistic phosphorescences, empty meteoric lights; here and there an ecclesiastical luminary still hovering, hanging on to its old quaking fixtures, pretending still to be a Moon or Sun, —though visibly it is but a Chinese lantern made of *paper* mainly, with candle-end foully dying in the heart of it. Surely as mad a world as you could wish!

If you want to make sudden fortunes in it, and achieve the temporary hallelujah of flunkies for yourself, renouncing the perennial esteem of wise men; if you can believe that the chief end of man is to collect about him a bigger heap of gold than ever before, in a shorter time than ever before, you will find it a most handy and every way furthersome, blessed and felicitous world. But for any other human aim, I think you will find it not furthersome. If you in any way ask practically, How a noble life is to be led in it? you will be luckier than Sterling or I if you get any credible answer, or find any made road whatever. Alas, it is even so. Your heart's question, if it be of that sort, most things and persons will answer with a "Nonsense! Noble life is in Drury Lane, and wears yellow boots. You fool, compose yourself to your pudding! " —Surely, in these times, if ever in any, the young heroic soul entering on life, so opulent, full of sunny hope, of noble valor and divine intention, is tragical as well as beautiful to us.

Of the three learned Professions none offered any likelihood for Sterling. From the Church his notions of the "black dragoon, " had there been no other obstacle, were sufficient to exclude him. Law he had just renounced, his own Radical philosophies disheartening him, in face of the ponderous impediments, continual up-hill struggles and formidable toils inherent in such a pursuit: with Medicine he had never been in any contiguity, that he should dream of it as a course for him. Clearly enough the professions were unsuitable; they to him, he to them. Professions, built so largely on speciosity instead of performance; clogged, in this bad epoch, and defaced under such suspicions of fatal imposture, were hateful not lovable to the young radical soul, scornful of gross profit, and intent on ideals and human noblenesses. Again, the professions, were they never so perfect and veracious, will require slow steady pulling, to which this individual young radical, with his swift, far-darting brilliancies, and nomadic desultory ways, is of all men the most averse and unfitted. No profession could, in any case, have well gained the early love of Sterling. And perhaps withal the most tragic element of his life is even this, That there now was none to which he could fitly, by those wiser than himself, have been bound and constrained, that he might learn to love it. So swift, light-limbed and fiery an Arab courser ought, for all manner of reasons, to have been trained to saddle and harness. Roaming at full gallop over the heaths, —especially when your heath was London, and English and European life, in the nineteenth century, —he suffered much, and did comparatively little. I have known few creatures whom it was more wasteful to send forth with the bridle thrown up, and to set to steeple-hunting instead of running on highways! But it is the lot of many such, in this dislocated time, —Heaven mend it! In a better time there will be other "professions" than those three extremely cramp, confused and indeed almost obsolete ones: professions, if possible, that are true, and do *not* require you at the threshold to constitute yourself an impostor. Human association, —which will mean discipline, vigorous wise subordination and co-ordination, —is so unspeakably important. Professions, "regimented human pursuits, " how many of honorable and manful might be possible for men; and which should *not*, in their results to society, need to stumble along, in such an unwieldy futile manner, with legs swollen into such enormous elephantiasis and no go at all in them! Men will one day think of the force they squander in every generation, and the fatal damage they encounter, by this neglect.

The career likeliest for Sterling, in his and the world's circumstances, would have been what is called public life: some secretarial, diplomatic or other official training, to issue if possible in Parliament as the true field for him. And here, beyond question, had the gross material conditions been allowed, his spiritual capabilities were first-rate. In any arena where eloquence and argument was the point, this man was calculated to have borne the bell from all competitors. In lucid ingenious talk and logic, in all manner of brilliant utterance and tongue-fence, I have hardly known his fellow. So ready lay his store of knowledge round him, so perfect was his ready utterance of the same, —in coruscating wit, in jocund drollery, in compact articulated clearness or high poignant emphasis, as the case required, —he was a match for any man in argument before a crowd of men. One of the most supple-wristed, dexterous, graceful and successful fencers in that kind. A man, as Mr. Hare has said, "able to argue with four or five at once; " could do the parrying all round, in a succession swift as light, and plant his hits wherever a chance offered. In Parliament, such a soul put into a body of the due toughness might have carried it far. If ours is to be called, as I hear some call it, the Talking Era, Sterling of all men had the talent to excel in it.

Probably it was with some vague view towards chances in this direction that Sterling's first engagement was entered upon; a brief connection as Secretary to some Club or Association into which certain public men, of the reforming sort, Mr. Crawford (the Oriental Diplomatist and Writer), Mr. Kirkman Finlay (then Member for Glasgow), and other political notabilities had now formed themselves, —with what specific objects I do not know, nor with what result if any. I have heard vaguely, it was "to open the trade to India. " Of course they intended to stir up the public mind into co-operation, whatever their goal or object was: Mr. Crawford, an intimate in the Sterling household, recognized the fine literary gift of John; and might think it a lucky hit that he had caught such a Secretary for three hundred pounds a year. That was the salary agreed upon; and for some months actually worked for and paid; Sterling becoming for the time an intimate and almost an inmate in Mr. Crawford's circle, doubtless not without results to himself beyond the secretarial work and pounds sterling: so much is certain. But neither the Secretaryship nor the Association itself had any continuance; nor can I now learn accurately more of it than what is here stated; —in which vague state it must vanish from Sterling's history again, as it in great measure did from his life. From himself in after-years I never heard mention of it; nor were his pursuits connected afterwards with those of Mr. Crawford, though the mutual good-will continued unbroken.

In fact, however splendid and indubitable Sterling's qualifications for a parliamentary life, there was that in him withal which flatly put a negative on any such project. He had not the slow steady-pulling diligence which is indispensable in that, as in all important pursuits and strenuous human competitions whatsoever. In every sense, his momentum depended on velocity of stroke, rather than on weight of metal; "beautifulest sheet-lightning, " as I often said, "not to be condensed into thunder-bolts. " Add to this, —what indeed is perhaps but the same phenomenon in another form, —his bodily frame was thin, excitable, already manifesting pulmonary symptoms; a body which the tear and wear of Parliament would infallibly in few months have wrecked and ended. By this path there was clearly no mounting. The far-darting, restlessly coruscating soul, equips beyond all others to shine in the Talking Era, and lead National Palavers with their *spolia opima* captive, is imprisoned in a fragile hectic body which quite forbids the adventure. "*Es ist dafur gesorgt, *" says Goethe, "Provision has been made that the trees do not grow into the sky; "—means are always there to stop them short of the sky.

CHAPTER VI.
LITERATURE: THE ATHENAEUM.

Of all forms of public life, in the Talking Era, it was clear that only one completely suited Sterling, —the anarchic, nomadic, entirely aerial and unconditional one, called Literature. To this all his tendencies, and fine gifts positive and negative, were evidently pointing; and here, after such brief attempting or thoughts to attempt at other posts, he already in this same year arrives. As many do, and ever more must do, in these our years and times. This is the chaotic haven of so many frustrate activities; where all manner of good gifts go up in far-seen smoke or conflagration; and whole fleets, that might have been war-fleets to conquer kingdoms, are *consumed* (too truly, often), amid "fame" enough, and the admiring shouts of the vulgar, which is always fond to see fire going on. The true Canaan and Mount Zion of a Talking Era must ever be Literature: the extraneous, miscellaneous, self-elected, indescribable *Parliamentum*, or Talking Apparatus, which talks by books and printed papers.

A literary Newspaper called *The Athenaeum*, the same which still subsists, had been founded in those years by Mr. Buckingham; James Silk Buckingham, who has since continued notable under various figures. Mr. Buckingham's *Athenaeum* had not as yet got into a flourishing condition; and he was willing to sell the copyright of it for a consideration. Perhaps Sterling and old Cambridge friends of his had been already writing for it. At all events, Sterling, who had already privately begun writing a Novel, and was clearly looking towards Literature, perceived that his gifted Cambridge friend, Frederic Maurice, was now also at large in a somewhat similar situation; and that here was an opening for both of them, and for other gifted friends. The copyright was purchased for I know not what sum, nor with whose money, but guess it may have been Sterling's, and no great sum; —and so, under free auspices, themselves their own captains, Maurice and he spread sail for this new voyage of adventure into all the world. It was about the end of 1828 that readers of periodical literature, and quidnuncs in those departments, began to report the appearance, in a Paper called the *Athenaeum, of* writings showing a superior brilliancy, and height of aim; one or perhaps two slight specimens of which came into my own hands, in my remote corner, about that time, and were duly recognized by me, while the authors were still far off and hidden behind deep veils.

Some of Sterling's best Papers from the *Athenaeum* have been published by Archdeacon Hare: first-fruits by a young man of twenty-two; crude, imperfect, yet singularly beautiful and attractive; which will still testify what high literary promise lay in him. The ruddiest glow of young enthusiasm, of noble incipient spiritual manhood reigns over them; once more a divine Universe unveiling itself in gloom and splendor, in auroral firelight and many-tinted shadow, full of hope and full of awe, to a young melodious pious heart just arrived upon it. Often enough the delineation has a certain flowing completeness, not to be expected from so young an artist; here and there is a decided felicity of insight; everywhere the point of view adopted is a high and noble one, and the result worked out a result to be sympathized with, and accepted so far as it will go. Good reading still, those Papers, for the less-furnished mind, —thrice-excellent reading compared with what is usually going. For the rest, a grand melancholy is the prevailing impression they leave; —partly as if, while the surface was so blooming and opulent, the heart of them was still vacant, sad and cold. Here is a beautiful mirage, in the dry wilderness; but you cannot quench your thirst there! The writer's heart is indeed still too vacant, except of beautiful shadows and reflexes and resonances; and is far from joyful, though it wears commonly a smile.

In some of the Greek delineations (*The Lycian Painter*, for example), we have already noticed a strange opulence of splendor, characterizable as half-legitimate, half-meretricious, —a splendor hovering between the raffaelesque and the japannish. What other things Sterling wrote there, I never knew; nor would he in any mood, in those later days, have told you, had you asked. This period of his life he always rather accounted, as the Arabs do the idolatrous times before Mahomet's advent, the "period of darkness."

CHAPTER VII.
REGENT STREET.

On the commercial side the *Athenaeum* still lacked success; nor was like to find it under the highly uncommercial management it had now got into. This, by and by, began to be a serious consideration. For money is the sinews of Periodical Literature almost as much as of war itself; without money, and under a constant drain of loss, Periodical Literature is one of the things that cannot be carried on. In no long time Sterling began to be practically sensible of this truth, and that an unpleasant resolution in accordance with it would be necessary. By him also, after a while, the *Athenaeum* was transferred to other hands, better fitted in that respect; and under these it did take vigorous root, and still bears fruit according to its kind.

For the present, it brought him into the thick of London Literature, especially of young London Literature and speculation; in which turbid exciting element he swam and revelled, nothing loath, for certain months longer, —a period short of two years in all. He had lodgings in Regent Street: his Father's house, now a flourishing and stirring establishment, in South Place, Knightsbridge, where, under the warmth of increasing revenue and success, miscellaneous cheerful socialities and abundant speculations, chiefly political (and not John's kind, but that of the *Times* Newspaper and the Clubs), were rife, he could visit daily, and yet be master of his own studies and pursuits. Maurice, Trench, John Mill, Charles Buller: these, and some few others, among a wide circle of a transitory phantasmal character, whom he speedily forgot and cared not to remember, were much about him; with these he in all ways employed and disported himself: a first favorite with them all.

No pleasanter companion, I suppose, had any of them. So frank, open, guileless, fearless, a brother to all worthy souls whatsoever. Come when you might, here is he open-hearted, rich in cheerful fancies, in grave logic, in all kinds of bright activity. If perceptibly or imperceptibly there is a touch of ostentation in him, blame it not; it is so innocent, so good and childlike. He is still fonder of jingling publicly, and spreading on the table, your big purse of opulences than his own. Abrupt too he is, cares little for big-wigs and garnitures; perhaps laughs more than the real fun he has would order; but of arrogance there is no vestige, of insincerity or of ill-nature none. These must have been pleasant evenings in Regent

Street, when the circle chanced to be well adjusted there. At other times, Philistines would enter, what we call bores, dullards, Children of Darkness; and then, —except in a hunt of dullards, and a *bore-baiting*, which might be permissible, —the evening was dark. Sterling, of course, had innumerable cares withal; and was toiling like a slave; his very recreations almost a kind of work. An enormous activity was in the man; —sufficient, in a body that could have held it without breaking, to have gone far, even under the unstable guidance it was like to have!

Thus, too, an extensive, very variegated circle of connections was forming round him. Besides his *Athenaeum* work, and evenings in Regent Street and elsewhere, he makes visits to country-houses, the Bullers' and others; converses with established gentlemen, with honorable women not a few; is gay and welcome with the young of his own age; knows also religious, witty, and other distinguished ladies, and is admiringly known by them. On the whole, he is already locomotive; visits hither and thither in a very rapid flying manner. Thus I find he had made one flying visit to the Cumberland Lake-region in 1828, and got sight of Wordsworth; and in the same year another flying one to Paris, and seen with no undue enthusiasm the Saint-Simonian Portent just beginning to preach for itself, and France in general simmering under a scum of impieties, levities, Saint-Simonisms, and frothy fantasticalities of all kinds, towards the boiling-over which soon made the Three Days of July famous. But by far the most important foreign home he visited was that of Coleridge on the Hill of Highgate, —if it were not rather a foreign shrine and Dodona-Oracle, as he then reckoned, —to which (onwards from 1828, as would appear) he was already an assiduous pilgrim. Concerning whom, and Sterling's all-important connection with him, there will be much to say anon.

Here, from this period, is a Letter of Sterling's, which the glimpses it affords of bright scenes and figures now sunk, so many of them, sorrowfully to the realm of shadows, will render interesting to some of my readers. To me on the mere Letter, not on its contents alone, there is accidentally a kind of fateful stamp. A few months after Charles Buller's death, while his loss was mourned by many hearts, and to his poor Mother all light except what hung upon his memory had gone out in the world, a certain delicate and friendly hand, hoping to give the poor bereaved lady a good moment, sought out this Letter of Sterling's, one morning, and called, with intent to read it to her: —alas, the poor lady had herself fallen suddenly into the languors of death, help of another grander sort now close at hand; and to her this Letter was never read!

On "Fanny Kemble, " it appears, there is an Essay by Sterling in the *Athenaeum* of this year: "16th December, 1829. " Very laudatory, I conclude. He much admired her genius, nay was thought at one time to be vaguely on the edge of still more chivalrous feelings. As the Letter itself may perhaps indicate.

"To Anthony Sterling, Esq., 24th Regiment, Dublin.
"KNIGHTSBRIDGE, 10th Nov., 1829.

"MY DEAR ANTHONY, —Here in the Capital of England and of Europe, there is less, so far as I hear, of movement and variety than in your provincial Dublin, or among the Wicklow Mountains. We have the old prospect of bricks and smoke, the old crowd of busy stupid faces, the old occupations, the old sleepy amusements; and the latest news that reaches us daily has an air of tiresome, doting antiquity. The world has nothing for it but to exclaim with Faust, "Give me my youth again. " And as for me, my month of Cornish amusement is over; and I must tie myself to my old employments. I have not much to tell you about these; but perhaps you may like to hear of my expedition to the West.

"I wrote to Polvellan (Mr. Buller's) to announce the day on which I intended to be there, so shortly before setting out, that there was no time to receive an answer; and when I reached Devonport, which is fifteen or sixteen miles from my place of destination, I found a letter from Mrs. Buller, saying that she was coming in two days to a Ball at Plymouth, and if I chose to stay in the mean while and look about me, she would take me back with her. She added an introduction to a relation of her husband's, a certain Captain Buller of the Rifles, who was with the Depot there, —a pleasant person, who I believe had been acquainted with Charlotte, [7] or at least had seen her. Under his superintendence—...

"On leaving Devonport with Mrs. Buller, I went some of the way by water, up the harbor and river; and the prospects are certainly very beautiful; to say nothing of the large ships, which I admire almost as much as you, though without knowing so much about them. There is a great deal of fine scenery all along the road to Looe; and the House itself, a very unpretending Gothic cottage, stands beautifully among trees, hills and water, with the sea at the distance of a quarter of a mile.

"And here, among pleasant, good-natured, well-informed and clever people, I spent an idle month. I dined at one or two Corporation dinners; spent a few days at the old Mansion of Mr. Buller of Morval, the patron of West Looe; and during the rest of the time, read, wrote, played chess, lounged, and ate red mullet (he who has not done this has not begun to live); talked of cookery to the philosophers, and of metaphysics to Mrs. Buller; and altogether cultivated indolence, and developed the faculty of nonsense with considerable pleasure and unexampled success. Charles Buller you know: he has just come to town, but I have not yet seen him. Arthur, his younger brother, I take to be one of the handsomest men in England; and he too has considerable talent. Mr. Buller the father is rather a clever man of sense, and particularly good-natured and gentlemanly; and his wife, who was a renowned beauty and queen of Calcutta, has still many striking and delicate traces of what she was. Her conversation is more brilliant and pleasant than that of any one I know; and, at all events, I am bound to admire her for the kindness with which she patronizes me. I hope that, some day or other, you may be acquainted with her.

"I believe I have seen no one in London about whom you would care to hear, —unless the fame of Fanny Kemble has passed the Channel, and astonished the Irish Barbarians in the midst of their bloody-minded politics. Young Kemble, whom you have seen, is in Germany: but I have the happiness of being also acquainted with his sister, the divine Fanny; and I have seen her twice on the stage, and three or four times in private, since my return from Cornwall. I had seen some beautiful verses of hers, long before she was an actress; and her conversation is full of spirit and talent. She never was taught to act at all; and though there are many faults in her performance of Juliet, there is more power than in any female playing I ever saw, except Pasta's Medea. She is not handsome, rather short, and by no means delicately formed; but her face is marked, and the eyes are brilliant, dark, and full of character. She has far more ability than she ever can display on the stage; but I have no doubt that, by practice and self-culture, she will be a far finer actress at least than any one since Mrs. Siddons. I was at Charles Kemble's a few evenings ago, when a drawing of Miss Kemble, by Sir Thomas Lawrence, was brought in; and I have no doubt that you will shortly see, even in Dublin, an engraving of her from it, very unlike the caricatures that have hitherto appeared. I hate the stage; and but for her, should very likely never have gone to a theatre again. Even as it is, the annoyance is much more than the pleasure; but I suppose I must go to see her in every character in which she acts. If Charlotte cares for plays, let me know, and I will write in more detail about this new Melpomene. I fear there are very few subjects on which I can say anything that will in the least interest her.

"Ever affectionately yours,
"J. STERLING. "

Sterling and his circle, as their ardent speculation and activity fermented along, were in all things clear for progress, liberalism; their politics, and view of the Universe, decisively of the Radical sort. As indeed that of England then was, more than ever; the crust of old hide-bound Toryism being now openly cracking towards some incurable disruption, which accordingly ensued as the Reform Bill before long. The Reform Bill already hung in the wind. Old hide-bound Toryism, long recognized by all the world, and now at last obliged to recognize its very self, for an overgrown Imposture, supporting itself not by human reason, but by flunky blustering and brazen lying, superadded to mere brute force, could be no creed for young Sterling and his friends. In all things he and they were liberals, and, as was natural at this stage, democrats; contemplating root-and-branch innovation by aid of the hustings and ballot-box. Hustings and ballot-box had speedily to vanish out of Sterling's thoughts: but the character of root-and-branch innovator, essentially of "Radical Reformer, " was indelible with him, and under all forms could be traced as his character through life.

For the present, his and those young people's aim was: By democracy, or what means there are, be all impostures put down. Speedy end to Superstition, —a gentle one if you can contrive it, but an end. What can it profit any mortal to adopt locutions and imaginations which do not correspond to fact; which no sane mortal can deliberately adopt in his soul as true; which the most orthodox of mortals can only, and this after infinite essentially *impious* effort to put out the eyes of his mind, persuade himself to "believe that he believes"? Away with it; in the name of God, come out of it, all true men!

Piety of heart, a certain reality of religious faith, was always Sterling's, the gift of nature to him which he would not and could not throw away; but I find at this time his religion is as good as altogether Ethnic, Greekish, what Goethe calls the Heathen form of religion. The Church, with her articles, is without relation to him. And along with obsolete spiritualisms, he sees all manner of obsolete thrones and big-wigged temporalities; and for them also can prophesy, and wish, only a speedy doom. Doom inevitable, registered in Heaven's Chancery from the beginning of days, doom unalterable as the pillars of the world; the gods are angry, and all nature groans, till this doom of eternal justice be fulfilled.

With gay audacity, with enthusiasm tempered by mockery, as is the manner of young gifted men, this faith, grounded for the present on democracy and hustings operations, and giving to all life the aspect of a chivalrous battle-field, or almost of a gay though perilous tournament, and bout of "A hundred knights against all comers, " — was maintained by Sterling and his friends. And in fine, after whatever loud remonstrances, and solemn considerations, and such shaking of our wigs as is undoubtedly natural in the case, let us be just to it and him. We shall have to admit, nay it will behoove us to see and practically know, for ourselves and him and others, that the essence of this creed, in times like ours, was right and not wrong. That, however the ground and form of it might change, essentially it was the monition of his natal genius to this as it is to every brave man; the behest of all his clear insight into this Universe, the message of Heaven through him, which he could not suppress, but was inspired and compelled to utter in this world by such methods as he had. There for him lay the first commandment; *this* is what it would have been the unforgivable sin to swerve from and desert: the treason of treasons for him, it were there; compared with which all other sins are venial!

The message did not cease at all, as we shall see; the message was ardently, if fitfully, continued to the end: but the methods, the tone and dialect and all outer conditions of uttering it, underwent most important modifications!

CHAPTER VIII.
COLERIDGE.

Coleridge sat on the brow of Highgate Hill, in those years, looking down on London and its smoke-tumult, like a sage escaped from the inanity of life's battle; attracting towards him the thoughts of innumerable brave souls still engaged there. His express contributions to poetry, philosophy, or any specific province of human literature or enlightenment, had been small and sadly intermittent; but he had, especially among young inquiring men, a higher than literary, a kind of prophetic or magician character. He was thought to hold, he alone in England, the key of German and other Transcendentalisms; knew the sublime secret of believing by "the reason" what "the understanding" had been obliged to fling out as incredible; and could still, after Hume and Voltaire had done their best and worst with him, profess himself an orthodox Christian, and say and print to the Church of England, with its singular old rubrics and surplices at Allhallowtide, *Esto perpetua*. A sublime man; who, alone in those dark days, had saved his crown of spiritual manhood; escaping from the black materialisms, and revolutionary deluges, with "God, Freedom, Immortality" still his: a king of men. The practical intellects of the world did not much heed him, or carelessly reckoned him a metaphysical dreamer: but to the rising spirits of the young generation he had this dusky sublime character; and sat there as a kind of *Magus*, girt in mystery and enigma; his Dodona oak-grove (Mr. Gilman's house at Highgate) whispering strange things, uncertain whether oracles or jargon.

The Gilmans did not encourage much company, or excitation of any sort, round their sage; nevertheless access to him, if a youth did reverently wish it, was not difficult. He would stroll about the pleasant garden with you, sit in the pleasant rooms of the place, — perhaps take you to his own peculiar room, high up, with a rearward view, which was the chief view of all. A really charming outlook, in fine weather. Close at hand, wide sweep of flowery leafy gardens, their few houses mostly hidden, the very chimney-pots veiled under blossomy umbrage, flowed gloriously down hill; gloriously issuing in wide-tufted undulating plain-country, rich in all charms of field and town. Waving blooming country of the brightest green; dotted all over with handsome villas, handsome groves; crossed by roads and human traffic, here inaudible or heard only as a musical hum: and behind all swam, under olive-tinted haze, the illimitable limitary ocean of London, with its domes and steeples definite in the sun, big Paul's and the many memories attached to it hanging high over all. Nowhere, of its kind, could you see a grander prospect on a bright summer day, with the set of the air going southward, —southward, and so draping with the city-smoke not you but the city. Here for hours would Coleridge talk, concerning all conceivable or inconceivable things; and liked nothing better than to have an intelligent, or failing that, even a silent and patient human listener. He distinguished himself to all that ever heard him as at least the most surprising talker extant in this world, —and to some small minority, by no means to all, as the most excellent.

The good man, he was now getting old, towards sixty perhaps; and gave you the idea of a life that had been full of sufferings; a life heavy-laden, half-vanquished, still swimming painfully in seas of manifold physical and other bewilderment. Brow and head were round, and of massive weight, but the face was flabby and irresolute. The deep eyes, of a light hazel, were as full of sorrow as of inspiration; confused pain looked mildly from them, as in a kind of mild astonishment. The whole figure and air, good and amiable otherwise, might be called flabby and irresolute; expressive of weakness under possibility of strength. He hung loosely on his limbs, with knees bent, and stooping attitude; in walking, he rather shuffled than decisively steps; and a lady once remarked, he never could fix which side of the garden walk would suit him best, but continually shifted, in corkscrew fashion, and kept trying both. A heavy-laden, high-aspiring and surely much-suffering man. His voice, naturally soft and good, had contracted itself into a plaintive snuffle and singsong; he spoke as if preaching, —you would have said, preaching earnestly and also hopelessly the weightiest things. I still recollect his "object" and "subject, " terms of continual recurrence in the Kantean province; and how he sang and snuffled them into "om-m-mject" and "sum-m-mject, " with a kind of solemn shake or quaver, as he rolled along. No talk, in his century or in any other, could be more surprising.

Sterling, who assiduously attended him, with profound reverence, and was often with him by himself, for a good many months, gives a record of their first colloquy. [8] Their colloquies were numerous, and he had taken note of many; but they are all gone to the fire, except this first, which Mr. Hare has printed, —unluckily without date. It contains a number of ingenious, true and half-true observations, and is of course a faithful epitome of the things said;

but it gives small idea of Coleridge's way of talking; —this one feature is perhaps the most recognizable, "Our interview lasted for three hours, during which he talked two hours and three quarters. " Nothing could be more copious than his talk; and furthermore it was always, virtually or literally, of the nature of a monologue; suffering no interruption, however reverent; hastily putting aside all foreign additions, annotations, or most ingenuous desires for elucidation, as well-meant superfluities which would never do. Besides, it was talk not flowing any-whither like a river, but spreading every-whither in inextricable currents and regurgitations like a lake or sea; terribly deficient in definite goal or aim, nay often in logical intelligibility; *what* you were to believe or do, on any earthly or heavenly thing, obstinately refusing to appear from it. So that, most times, you felt logically lost; swamped near to drowning in this tide of ingenious vocables, spreading out boundless as if to submerge the world.

To sit as a passive bucket and be pumped into, whether you consent or not, can in the long-run be exhilarating to no creature; how eloquent soever the flood of utterance that is descending. But if it be withal a confused unintelligible flood of utterance, threatening to submerge all known landmarks of thought, and drown the world and you! —I have heard Coleridge talk, with eager musical energy, two stricken hours, his face radiant and moist, and communicate no meaning whatsoever to any individual of his hearers, —certain of whom, I for one, still kept eagerly listening in hope; the most had long before given up, and formed (if the room were large enough) secondary humming groups of their own. He began anywhere: you put some question to him, made some suggestive observation: instead of answering this, or decidedly setting out towards answer of it, he would accumulate formidable apparatus, logical swim-bladders, transcendental life-preservers and other precautionary and vehiculatory gear, for setting out; perhaps did at last get under way, —but was swiftly solicited, turned aside by the glance of some radiant new game on this hand or that, into new courses; and ever into new; and before long into all the Universe, where it was uncertain what game you would catch, or whether any.

His talk, alas, was distinguished, like himself, by irresolution: it disliked to he troubled with conditions, abstinences, definite fulfilments; —loved to wander at its own sweet will, and make its auditor and his claims and humble wishes a mere passive bucket for itself! He had knowledge about many things and topics, much curious reading; but generally all topics led him, after a pass or two, into the high seas of theosophic philosophy, the hazy infinitude of Kantean transcendentalism, with its "sum-m-mjects " and " om-m-mjects. " Sad enough; for with such indolent impatience of the claims and ignorances of others, he had not the least talent for explaining this or anything unknown to them; and you swam and fluttered in the mistiest wide unintelligible deluge of things, for most part in a rather profitless uncomfortable manner.

Glorious islets, too, I have seen rise out of the haze; but they were few, and soon swallowed in the general element again. Balmy sunny islets, islets of the blest and the intelligible: —on which occasions those secondary humming groups would all cease humming, and hang breathless upon the eloquent words; till once your islet got wrapt in the mist again, and they could recommence humming. Eloquent artistically expressive words you always had; piercing radiances of a most subtle insight came at intervals; tones of noble pious sympathy, recognizable as pious though strangely colored, were never wanting long: but in general you could not call this aimless, cloud-capt, cloud-based, lawlessly meandering human discourse of reason by the name of "excellent talk, " but only of "surprising; " and were reminded bitterly of Hazlitt's account of it: "Excellent talker, very, —if you let him start from no premises and come to no conclusion. " Coleridge was not without what talkers call wit, and there were touches of prickly sarcasm in him, contemptuous enough of the world and its idols and popular dignitaries; he had traits even of poetic humor: but in general he seemed deficient in laughter; or indeed in sympathy for concrete human things either on the sunny or on the stormy side. One right peal of concrete laughter at some convicted flesh-and-blood absurdity, one burst of noble indignation at some injustice or depravity, rubbing elbows with us on this solid Earth, how strange would it have been in that Kantean haze-world, and how infinitely cheering amid its vacant air-castles and dim-melting ghosts and shadows! None such ever came. His life had been an abstract thinking and dreaming, idealistic, passed amid the ghosts of defunct bodies and of unborn ones. The moaning singsong of that theosophico-metaphysical monotony left on you, at last, a very dreary feeling.

In close colloquy, flowing within narrower banks, I suppose he was more definite and apprehensible; Sterling in after-times did not complain of his unintelligibility, or imputed it only to the abtruse high nature of the topics handled. Let us hope so, let us try to believe so! There is no doubt but Coleridge could speak plain words on things plain: his observations and responses on the trivial matters that occurred were as simple as the commonest man's, or were even distinguished by superior simplicity as well as pertinency. "Ah, your tea is too cold, Mr. Coleridge! " mourned the good Mrs. Gilman once, in her kind, reverential and yet protective manner, handing him a very tolerable though belated cup. —"It's better than I deserve! " snuffled he, in a low hoarse murmur, partly courteous, chiefly pious, the tone of which still abides with me: "It's better than I deserve! "

But indeed, to the young ardent mind, instinct with pious nobleness, yet driven to the grim deserts of Radicalism for a faith, his speculations had a charm much more than literary, a charm almost religious and prophetic. The constant gist of his discourse was lamentation over the sunk condition of the world; which he recognized to be given up to Atheism and Materialism, full of mere sordid misbeliefs, mispursuits and misresults. All Science had become mechanical; the science not of men, but of a kind of human beavers. Churches themselves had died away into a godless mechanical condition; and stood there as mere Cases of Articles, mere Forms of Churches; like the dried carcasses of once swift camels, which you find left withering in the thirst of the universal desert, —ghastly portents for the present, beneficent ships of the desert no more. Men's souls were blinded, hebetated; and sunk under the influence of Atheism and Materialism, and Hume and Voltaire: the world for the present was as an extinct world, deserted of God, and incapable of well-doing till it changed its heart and spirit. This, expressed I think with less of indignation and with more of long-drawn querulousness, was always recognizable as the ground-tone: —in which truly a pious young heart, driven into Radicalism and the opposition party, could not but recognize a too sorrowful truth; and ask of the Oracle, with all earnestness, What remedy, then?

The remedy, though Coleridge himself professed to see it as in sunbeams, could not, except by processes unspeakably difficult, be described to you at all. On the whole, those dead Churches, this dead English Church especially, must be brought to life again. Why not? It was not dead; the soul of it, in this parched-up body, was tragically asleep only. Atheistic Philosophy was true on its side, and Hume and Voltaire could on their own ground speak irrefragably for themselves against any Church: but lift the Church and them into a higher sphere. Of argument, *they* died into inanition, the Church revivified itself into pristine florid vigor, —became once more a living ship of the desert, and invincibly bore you over stock and stone. But how, but how! By attending to the "reason" of man, said Coleridge, and duly chaining up the "understanding" of man: the *Vernunft* (Reason) and *Verstand* (Understanding) of the Germans, it all turned upon these, if you could well understand them, —which you couldn't. For the rest, Mr. Coleridge had on the anvil various Books, especially was about to write one grand Book *On the Logos*, which would help to bridge the chasm for us. So much appeared, however: Churches, though proved false (as you had imagined), were still true (as you were to imagine): here was an Artist who could burn you up an old Church, root and branch; and then as the Alchemists professed to do with organic substances in general, distil you an "Astral Spirit" from the ashes, which was the very image of the old burnt article, its air-drawn counterpart, —this you still had, or might get, and draw uses from, if you could. Wait till the Book on the Logos were done; —alas, till your own terrene eyes, blind with conceit and the dust of logic, were purged, subtilized and spiritualized into the sharpness of vision requisite for discerning such an "om-m-mject. "—The ingenuous young English head, of those days, stood strangely puzzled by such revelations; uncertain whether it were getting inspired, or getting infatuated into flat imbecility; and strange effulgence, of new day or else of deeper meteoric night, colored the horizon of the future for it.

Let me not be unjust to this memorable man. Surely there was here, in his pious, ever-laboring, subtle mind, a precious truth, or prefigurement of truth; and yet a fatal delusion withal. Prefigurement that, in spite of beaver sciences and temporary spiritual hebetude and cecity, man and his Universe were eternally divine; and that no past nobleness, or revelation of the divine, could or would ever be lost to him. Most true, surely, and worthy of all acceptance. Good also to do what you can with old Churches and practical Symbols of the Noble: nay quit not the burnt ruins of them while you find there is still gold to be dug there. But, on the whole, do not think you can, by logical alchemy, distil astral spirits from them; or if you could, that said astral spirits, or defunct logical phantasms, could serve you in anything. What the light of your mind, which is the direct inspiration of the Almighty, pronounces incredible, —that, in God's name, leave uncredited; at your peril do not try believing that. No subtlest hocus-pocus of "reason" versus "understanding" will avail for that feat; —and it is terribly perilous to try it in these provinces!

The truth is, I now see, Coleridge's talk and speculation was the emblem of himself: in it as in him, a ray of heavenly inspiration struggled, in a tragically ineffectual degree, with the weakness of flesh and blood. He says once, he "had skirted the howling deserts of Infidelity; " this was evident enough: but he had not had the courage, in defiance of pain and terror, to press resolutely across said deserts to the new firm lands of Faith beyond; he preferred to create logical fata-morganas for himself on this hither side, and laboriously solace himself with these.

To the man himself Nature had given, in high measure, the seeds of a noble endowment; and to unfold it had been forbidden him. A subtle lynx-eyed intellect, tremulous pious sensibility to all good and all beautiful; truly a ray of empyrean light; —but embedded in such weak laxity of character, in such indolences and esuriences as had made strange work with it. Once more, the tragic story of a high endowment with an insufficient will. An eye to discern the divineness of the Heaven's spendors and lightnings, the insatiable wish to revel in their godlike radiances and brilliances; but no heart to front the scathing terrors of them, which is the first condition of your conquering an abiding place there. The courage necessary for him, above all things, had been denied this man. His life, with such ray of the empyrean in it, was great and terrible to him; and he had not valiantly grappled with it, he had fled from it; sought refuge in vague daydreams, hollow compromises, in opium, in theosophic metaphysics. Harsh pain, danger, necessity, slavish harnessed toil, were of all things abhorrent to him. And so the empyrean element, lying smothered under the terrene, and yet inextinguishable there, made sad writhings. For pain, danger, difficulty, steady slaving toil, and other highly disagreeable behests of destiny, shall in nowise be shirked by any brightest mortal that will approve himself loyal to his mission in this world; nay precisely the higher he is, the deeper will be the disagreeableness, and the detestability to flesh and blood, of the tasks laid on him; and the heavier too, and more tragic, his penalties if he neglect them.

For the old Eternal Powers do live forever; nor do their laws know any change, however we in our poor wigs and church-tippets may attempt to read their laws. To *steal* into Heaven, —by the modern method, of sticking ostrich-like your head into fallacies on Earth, equally as by the ancient and by all conceivable methods, —is forever forbidden. High-treason is the name of that attempt; and it continues to be punished as such. Strange enough: here once more was a kind of Heaven-scaling Ixion; and to him, as to the old one, the just gods were very stern! The ever-revolving, never-advancing Wheel (of a kind) was his, through life; and from his Cloud-Juno did not he too procreate strange Centaurs, spectral Puseyisms, monstrous illusory Hybrids, and ecclesiastical Chimeras, —which now roam the earth in a very lamentable manner!

CHAPTER IX.
SPANISH EXILES.

This magical ingredient thrown into the wild caldron of such a mind, which we have seen occupied hitherto with mere Ethnicism, Radicalism and revolutionary tumult, but hungering all along for something higher and better, was sure to be eagerly welcomed and imbibed, and could not fail to produce important fermentations there. Fermentations; important new directions, and withal important new perversions, in the spiritual life of this man, as it has since done in the lives of so many. Here then is the new celestial manna we were all in quest of? This thrice-refined pabulum of transcendental moonshine? Whoso eateth thereof, —yes, what, on the whole, will *he* probably grow to?

Sterling never spoke much to me of his intercourse with Coleridge; and when we did compare notes about him, it was usually rather in the way of controversial discussion than of narrative. So that, from my own resources, I can give no details of the business, nor specify anything in it, except the general fact of an ardent attendance at Highgate continued for many months, which was impressively known to all Sterling's friends; and am unable to assign even the limitary dates, Sterling's own papers on the subject having all been destroyed by him. Inferences point to the end of 1828 as the beginning of this intercourse; perhaps in 1829 it was at the highest point; and already in 1830, when the intercourse itself was about to terminate, we have proof of the influences it was producing, —in the Novel of *Arthur Coningsby*, then on hand, the first and only Book that Sterling ever wrote. His writings hitherto had been sketches, criticisms, brief essays; he was now trying it on a wider scale; but not yet with satisfactory results, and it proved to be his only trial in that form.

He had already, as was intimated, given up his brief proprietorship of the *Athenaeum*; the commercial indications, and state of sales and of costs, peremptorily ordering him to do so; the copyright went by sale or gift, I know not at what precise date, into other fitter hands; and with the copyright all connection on the part of Sterling. To *Athenaeum* Sketches had now (in 1829-30) succeeded *Arthur Coningsby*, a Novel in three volumes; indicating (when it came to light, a year or two afterwards) equally hasty and much more ambitious aims in Literature; —giving strong evidence, too, of internal spiritual revulsions going painfully forward, and in particular of the impression Coleridge was producing on him. Without and within, it was a wild tide of things this ardent light young soul was afloat upon, at present; and his outlooks into the future, whether for his spiritual or economic fortunes, were confused enough.

Among his familiars in this period, I might have mentioned one Charles Barton, formerly his fellow-student at Cambridge, now an amiable, cheerful, rather idle young fellow about Town; who led the way into certain new experiences, and lighter fields, for Sterling. His Father, Lieutenant-General Barton of the Life-guards, an Irish landlord, I think in Fermanagh County, and a man of connections about Court, lived in a certain figure here in Town; had a wife of fashionable habits, with other sons, and also daughters, bred in this sphere. These, all of them, were amiable, elegant and pleasant people; —such was especially an eldest daughter, Susannah Barton, a stately blooming black-eyed young woman, attractive enough in form and character; full of gay softness, of indolent sense and enthusiasm; about Sterling's own age, if not a little older. In this house, which opened to him, more decisively than his Father's, a new stratum of society, and where his reception for Charles's sake and his own was of the kindest, he liked very well to be; and spent, I suppose, many of his vacant half-hours, lightly chatting with the elders or the youngsters, —doubtless with the young lady too, though as yet without particular intentions on either side.

Nor, with all the Coleridge fermentation, was democratic Radicalism by any means given up; —though how it was to live if the Coleridgean moonshine took effect, might have been an abtruse question. Hitherto, while said moonshine was but taking effect, and coloring the outer surface of things without quite penetrating into the heart, democratic Liberalism, revolt against superstition and oppression, and help to whosoever would revolt, was still the grand element in Sterling's creed; and practically he stood, not ready only, but full of alacrity to fulfil all its behests. We heard long since of the "black dragoons, "—whom doubtless the new moonshine had considerably silvered-over into new hues, by this time; —but here now, while Radicalism is tottering for him and threatening to crumble, comes suddenly the grand consummation and explosion of Radicalism in his life; whereby, all at once, Radicalism exhausted and ended itself, and appeared no more there.

In those years a visible section of the London population, and conspicuous out of all proportion to its size or value, was a small knot of Spaniards, who had sought shelter here as Political Refugees. "Political Refugees: " a tragic succession of that class is one of the possessions of England in our time. Six-and-twenty years ago, when I first saw London, I remember those unfortunate Spaniards among the new phenomena. Daily in the cold spring air, under skies so unlike their own, you could see a group of fifty or a hundred stately tragic figures, in proud threadbare cloaks; perambulating, mostly with closed lips, the broad pavements of Euston Square and the regions about St. Pancras new Church. Their lodging was chiefly in Somers Town, as I understood: and those open pavements about St. Pancras Church were the general place of rendezvous. They spoke little or no English; knew nobody, could employ themselves on nothing, in this new scene. Old steel-gray heads, many of them; the shaggy, thick, blue-black hair of others struck you; their brown complexion, dusky look of suppressed fire, in general their tragic condition as of caged Numidian lions.

That particular Flight of Unfortunates has long since fled again, and vanished; and new have come and fled. In this convulsed revolutionary epoch, which already lasts above sixty years, what tragic flights of such have we not seen arrive on the one safe coast which is open to them, as they get successively vanquished, and chased into exile to avoid worse! Swarm after swarm, of ever-new complexion, from Spain as from other countries, is thrown off, in those ever-recurring paroxysms; and will continue to be thrown off. As there could be (suggests Linnaeus) a "flower-clock, " measuring the hours of the day, and the months of the year, by the kinds of flowers that go to sleep and awaken, that blow into beauty and fade into dust: so in the great Revolutionary Horologe, one might mark the years and epochs by the successive kinds of exiles that walk London streets, and, in grim silent manner, demand pity from us and reflections from us. —This then extant group of Spanish Exiles was the Trocadero swarm, thrown off in 1823, in the Riego and Quirogas quarrel. These were they whom Charles Tenth had, by sheer force, driven from their constitutionalisms and their Trocadero fortresses, —Charles Tenth, who himself was soon driven out, manifoldly by sheer force; and had to head his own swarm of fugitives; and has now himself quite vanished, and given place to others. For there is no end of them; propelling and propelled! —

Of these poor Spanish Exiles, now vegetating about Somers Town, and painfully beating the pavement in Euston Square, the acknowledged chief was General Torrijos, a man of high qualities and fortunes, still in the vigor of his years, and in these desperate circumstances refusing to despair; with whom Sterling had, at this time, become intimate.

CHAPTER X.
TORRIJOS.

Torrijos, who had now in 1829 been here some four or five years, having come over in 1824, had from the first enjoyed a superior reception in England. Possessing not only a language to speak, which few of the others did, but manifold experiences courtly, military, diplomatic, with fine natural faculties, and high Spanish manners tempered into cosmopolitan, he had been welcomed in various circles of society; and found, perhaps he alone of those Spaniards, a certain human companionship among persons of some standing in this country. With the elder Sterlings, among others, he had made acquaintance; became familiar in the social circle at South Place, and was much esteemed there. With Madam Torrijos, who also was a person of amiable and distinguished qualities, an affectionate friendship grew up on the part of Mrs. Sterling, which ended only with the death of these two ladies. John Sterling, on arriving in London from his University work, naturally inherited what he liked to take up of this relation: and in the lodgings in Regent Street, and the democratico-literary element there, Torrijos became a very prominent, and at length almost the central object.

The man himself, it is well known, was a valiant, gallant man; of lively intellect, of noble chivalrous character: fine talents, fine accomplishments, all grounding themselves on a certain rugged veracity, recommended him to the discerning. He had begun youth in the Court of Ferdinand; had gone on in Wellington and other arduous, victorious and unvictorious, soldierings; familiar in camps and council-rooms, in presence-chambers and in prisons. He knew romantic Spain; —he was himself, standing withal in the vanguard of Freedom's fight, a kind of living romance. Infinitely interesting to John Sterling, for one.

It was to Torrijos that the poor Spaniards of Somers Town looked mainly, in their helplessness, for every species of help. Torrijos, it was hoped, would yet lead them into Spain and glorious victory there; meanwhile here in England, under defeat, he was their captain and sovereign in another painfully inverse sense. To whom, in extremity, everybody might apply. When all present resources failed, and the exchequer was quite out, there still remained Torrijos. Torrijos has to find new resources for his destitute patriots, find loans, find Spanish lessons for them among his English friends: in all which charitable operations, it need not be said, John Sterling was his foremost man; zealous to empty his own purse for the object; impetuous in rushing hither or thither to enlist the aid of others, and find lessons or something that would do. His friends, of course, had to assist; the Bartons, among others, were wont to assist; —and I have heard that the fair Susan, stirring up her indolent enthusiasm into practicality, was very successful in finding Spanish lessons, and the like, for these distressed men. Sterling and his friends were yet new in this business; but Torrijos and the others were getting old in it? —and doubtless weary and almost desperate of it. They had now been seven years in it, many of them; and were asking, When will the end be?

Torrijos is described as a man of excellent discernment: who knows how long he had repressed the unreasonable schemes of his followers, and turned a deaf ear to the temptings of fallacious hope? But there comes at length a sum-total of oppressive burdens which is intolerable, which tempts the wisest towards fallacies for relief. These weary groups, pacing the Euston-Square pavements, had often said in their despair, "Were not death in battle better? Here are we slowly mouldering into nothingness; there we might reach it rapidly, in flaming splendor. Flame, either of victory to Spain and us, or of a patriot death, the sure harbinger of victory to Spain. Flame fit to kindle a fire which no Ferdinand, with all his Inquisitions and Charles Tenths, could put out. " Enough, in the end of 1829, Torrijos himself had yielded to this pressure; and hoping against hope, persuaded himself that if he could but land in the South of Spain with a small patriot band well armed and well resolved, a band carrying fire in its heart, —then Spain, all inflammable as touchwood, and groaning indignantly under its brutal tyrant, might blaze wholly into flame round him, and incalculable victory be won. Such was his conclusion; not sudden, yet surely not deliberate either, —desperate rather, and forced on by circumstances. He thought with himself that, considering Somers Town and considering Spain, the terrible chance was worth trying; that this big game of Fate, go how it might, was one which the omens credibly declared he and these poor Spaniards ought to play.

His whole industries and energies were thereupon bent towards starting the said game; and his thought and continual speech and song now was, That if he had a few thousand pounds to buy arms, to freight a ship and make the other preparations, he and these poor gentlemen, and Spain and the world, were made men and a saved

Spain and world. What talks and consultations in the apartment in Regent Street, during those winter days of 1829-30; setting into open conflagration the young democracy that was wont to assemble there! Of which there is now left next to no remembrance. For Sterling never spoke a word of this affair in after-days, nor was any of the actors much tempted to speak. We can understand too well that here were young fervid hearts in an explosive condition; young rash heads, sanctioned by a man's experienced head. Here at last shall enthusiasm and theory become practice and fact; fiery dreams are at last permitted to realize themselves; and now is the time or never! — How the Coleridge moonshine comported itself amid these hot telluric flames, or whether it had not yet begun to play there (which I rather doubt), must be left to conjecture.

Mr. Hare speaks of Sterling "sailing over to St. Valery in an open boat along with others, " upon one occasion, in this enterprise; —in the *final* English scene of it, I suppose. Which is very possible. Unquestionably there was adventure enough of other kinds for it, and running to and fro with all his speed on behalf of it, during these months of his history! Money was subscribed, collected: the young Cambridge democrats were all ablaze to assist Torrijos; nay certain of them decided to go with him, —and went. Only, as yet, the funds were rather incomplete. And here, as I learn from a good hand, is the secret history of their becoming complete. Which, as we are upon the subject, I had better give. But for the following circumstance, they had perhaps never been completed; nor had the rash enterprise, or its catastrophe, so influential on the rest of Sterling's life, taken place at all.

A certain Lieutenant Robert Boyd, of the Indian Army, an Ulster Irishman, a cousin of Sterling's, had received some affront, or otherwise taken some disgust in that service; had thrown up his commission in consequence; and returned home, about this time, with intent to seek another course of life. Having only, for outfit, these impatient ardors, some experience in Indian drill exercise, and five thousand pounds of inheritance, he found the enterprise attended with difficulties; and was somewhat at a loss how to dispose of himself. Some young Ulster comrade, in a partly similar situation, had pointed out to him that there lay in a certain neighboring creek of the Irish coast, a worn-out royal gun-brig condemned to sale, to be had dog-cheap: this he proposed that they two, or in fact Boyd with his five thousand pounds, should buy; that they should refit and arm and man it; —and sail a-privateering "to the Eastern Archipelago, " Philippine Isles, or I know not where; and *so* conquer the golden fleece.

Boyd naturally paused a little at this great proposal; did not quite reject it; came across, with it and other fine projects and impatiences fermenting in his head, to London, there to see and consider. It was in the months when the Torrijos enterprise was in the birth-throes; crying wildly for capital, of all things. Boyd naturally spoke of his projects to Sterling, —of his gun-brig lying in the Irish creek, among others. Sterling naturally said, "If you want an adventure of the Sea-king sort, and propose to lay your money and your life into such a game, here is Torrijos and Spain at his back; here is a golden fleece to conquer, worth twenty Eastern Archipelagoes. "—Boyd and Torrijos quickly met; quickly bargained. Boyd's money was to go in purchasing, and storing with a certain stock of arms and etceteras, a small ship in the Thames, which should carry Boyd with Torrijos and the adventurers to the south coast of Spain; and there, the game once played and won, Boyd was to have promotion enough, —"the colonelcy of a Spanish cavalry regiment, " for one express thing. What exact share Sterling had in this negotiation, or whether he did not even take the prudent side and caution Boyd to be wary I know not; but it was he that brought the parties together; and all his friends knew, in silence, that to the end of his life he painfully remembered that fact.

And so a ship was hired, or purchased, in the Thames; due furnishings began to be executed in it; arms and stores were gradually got on board; Torrijos with his Fifty picked Spaniards, in the mean while, getting ready. This was in the spring of 1830. Boyd's 5000 pounds was the grand nucleus of finance; but vigorous subscription was carried on likewise in Sterling's young democratic circle, or wherever a member of it could find access; not without considerable result, and with a zeal that may be imagined. Nay, as above hinted, certain of these young men decided, not to give their money only, but themselves along with it, as democratic volunteers and soldiers of progress; among whom, it need not be said, Sterling intended to be foremost. Busy weeks with him, those spring ones of the year 1830! Through this small Note, accidentally preserved to us, addressed to his friend Barton, we obtain a curious glance into the subterranean workshop: —

"To Charles Barton, Esq., Dorset Sq., Regent's Park.
[No date; apparently March or February, 1830.]

"MY DEAR CHARLES, —I have wanted to see you to talk to you about my Foreign affairs. If you are going to be in London for a few days, I believe you can be very useful to me, at a considerable expense and trouble to yourself, in the way of buying accoutrements; *inter alia*, a sword and a saddle, —not, you will understand, for my own use.

"Things are going on very well, but are very, even frightfully near; only be quiet! Pray would you, in case of necessity, take a free passage to Holland, next week or the week after; stay two or three days, and come back, all expenses paid? If you write to B—— at Cambridge, tell him above all things to hold his tongue. If you are near Palace Yard to-morrow before two, pray come to see me. Do not come on purpose; especially as I may perhaps be away, and at all events shall not be there until eleven, nor perhaps till rather later.

"I fear I shall have alarmed your Mother by my irruption. Forgive me for that and all my exactions from you. If the next month were over, I should not have to trouble any one.

"Yours affectionately,
"J. STERLING. "

Busy weeks indeed; and a glowing smithy-light coming through the chinks! —The romance of *Arthur Coningsby* lay written, or half-written, in his desk; and here, in his heart and among his hands, was an acted romance and unknown catastrophes keeping pace with that.

Doubts from the doctors, for his health was getting ominous, threw some shade over the adventure. Reproachful reminiscences of Coleridge and Theosophy were natural too; then fond regrets for Literature and its glories: if you act your romance, how can you also write it? Regrets, and reproachful reminiscences, from Art and Theosophy; perhaps some tenderer regrets withal. A crisis in life had come; when, of innumerable possibilities one possibility was to be elected king, and to swallow all the rest, the rest of course made noise enough, and swelled themselves to their biggest.

Meanwhile the ship was fast getting ready: on a certain day, it was to drop quietly down the Thames; then touch at Deal, and take on board Torrijos and his adventurers, who were to be in waiting and on the outlook for them there. Let every man lay in his accoutrements, then; let every man make his packages, his arrangements and farewells. Sterling went to take leave of Miss Barton. "You are going, then; to Spain? To rough it amid the storms of war and perilous insurrection; and with that weak health of yours; and—we shall never see you more, then! " Miss Barton, all her gayety gone, the dimpling softness become liquid sorrow, and the musical ringing voice one wail of woe, "burst into tears, "—so I have it on authority: —here was one possibility about to be strangled that made unexpected noise! Sterling's interview ended in the offer of his hand, and the acceptance of it; —any sacrifice to get rid of this horrid Spanish business, and save the health and life of a gifted young man so precious to the world and to another!

"Ill-health, " as often afterwards in Sterling's life, when the excuse was real enough but not the chief excuse; "ill-health, and insuperable obstacles and engagements, " had to bear the chief brunt in apologizing: and, as Sterling's actual presence, or that of any Englishman except Boyd and his money, was not in the least vital to the adventure, his excuse was at once accepted. The English connections and subscriptions are a given fact, to be presided over by what English volunteers there are: and as for Englishmen, the fewer Englishmen that go, the larger will be the share of influence for each. The other adventurers, Torrijos among them in due readiness, moved silently one by one down to Deal; Sterling, superintending the naval hands, on board their ship in the Thames, was to see the last finish given to everything in that department; then, on the set evening, to drop down quietly to Deal, and there say *Andad con Dios*, and return.

Behold! Just before the set evening came, the Spanish Envoy at this Court has got notice of what is going on; the Spanish Envoy, and of course the British Foreign Secretary, and of course also the Thames Police. Armed men spring suddenly on board, one day, while Sterling is there; declare the ship seized and embargoed in the King's name; nobody on board to stir till he has given some account of himself in due time and place! Huge consternation, naturally, from stem to stern. Sterling, whose presence of mind seldom forsook him, casts his eye over the River and its craft; sees a wherry, privately signals it, drops rapidly on board of it: "Stop! " fiercely interjects the marine policeman from the ship's deck. —"Why stop? What use have you for me, or I for you? " and the oars begin playing. —"Stop, or I'll shoot you! " cries the marine policeman, drawing a pistol. — "No, you won't. "—"I will! "—"If you do you'll be hanged at the next Maidstone assizes, then; that's all, "—and Sterling's wherry shot rapidly ashore; and out of this perilous adventure.

That same night he posted down to Deal; disclosed to the Torrijos party what catastrophe had come. No passage Spainward from the Thames; well if arrestment do not suddenly come from the Thames! It was on this occasion, I suppose, that the passage in the open boat to St. Valery occurred; —speedy flight in what boat or boats, open or shut, could be got at Deal on the sudden. Sterling himself, according to Hare's authority, actually went with them so far. Enough, they got shipping, as private passengers in one craft or the other; and, by degrees or at once, arrived all at Gibraltar, —Boyd, one or two young democrats of Regent Street, the fifty picked Spaniards, and Torrijos, —safe, though without arms; still in the early part of the year.

CHAPTER XI.
MARRIAGE: ILL-HEALTH; WEST-INDIES.

Sterling's outlooks and occupations, now that his Spanish friends were gone, must have been of a rather miscellaneous confused description. He had the enterprise of a married life close before him; and as yet no profession, no fixed pursuit whatever. His health was already very threatening; often such as to disable him from present activity, and occasion the gravest apprehensions; practically blocking up all important courses whatsoever, and rendering the future, if even life were lengthened and he had any future, an insolubility for him. Parliament was shut, public life was shut: Literature, —if, alas, any solid fruit could lie in literature!

Or perhaps one's health would mend, after all; and many things be better than was hoped! Sterling was not of a despondent temper, or given in any measure to lie down and indolently moan: I fancy he walked briskly enough into this tempestuous-looking future; not heeding too much its thunderous aspects; doing swiftly, for the day, what his hand found to do. *Arthur Coningsby*, I suppose, lay on the anvil at present; visits to Coleridge were now again more possible; grand news from Torrijos might be looked for, though only small yet came: —nay here, in the hot July, is France, at least, all thrown into volcano again! Here are the miraculous Three Days; heralding, in thunder, great things to Torrijos and others; filling with babblement and vaticination the mouths and hearts of all democratic men.

So rolled along, in tumult of chaotic remembrance and uncertain hope, in manifold emotion, and the confused struggle (for Sterling as for the world) to extricate the New from the falling ruins of the Old, the summer and autumn of 1830. From Gibraltar and Torrijos the tidings were vague, unimportant and discouraging: attempt on Cadiz, attempt on the lines of St. Roch, those attempts, or rather resolutions to attempt, had died in the birth, or almost before it. Men blamed Torrijos, little knowing his impediments. Boyd was still patient at his post: others of the young English (on the strength of the subscribed moneys) were said to be thinking of tours, —perhaps in the Sierra Morena and neighboring Quixote regions. From that Torrijos enterprise it did not seem that anything considerable would come.

On the edge of winter, here at home, Sterling was married: "at Christchurch, Marylebone, 2d November, 1830, " say the records. His blooming, kindly and true-hearted Wife had not much money, nor had he as yet any: but friends on both sides were bountiful and hopeful; had made up, for the young couple, the foundations of a modestly effective household; and in the future there lay more substantial prospects. On the finance side Sterling never had anything to suffer. His Wife, though somewhat languid, and of indolent humor, was a graceful, pious-minded, honorable and affectionate woman; she could not much support him in the ever-shifting struggles of his life, but she faithfully attended him in them, and loyally marched by his side through the changes and nomadic pilgrimings, of which many were appointed him in his short course.

Unhappily a few weeks after his marriage, and before any household was yet set up, he fell dangerously ill; worse in health than he had ever yet been: so many agitations crowded into the last few months had been too much for him. He fell into dangerous pulmonary illness, sank ever deeper; lay for many weeks in his Father's house utterly prostrate, his young Wife and his Mother watching over him; friends, sparingly admitted, long despairing of his life. All prospects in this world were now apparently shut upon him.

After a while, came hope again, and kindlier symptoms: but the doctors intimated that there lay consumption in the question, and that perfect recovery was not to be looked for. For weeks he had been confined to bed; it was several months before he could leave his sick-room, where the visits of a few friends had much cheered him. And now when delivered, readmitted to the air of day again, —weak as he was, and with such a liability still lurking in him, —what his young partner and he were to do, or whitherward to turn for a good course of life, was by no means too apparent.

One of his Mother Mrs. Edward Sterling's Uncles, a Coningham from Derry, had, in the course of his industrious and adventurous life, realized large property in the West Indies, —a valuable Sugar-estate, with its equipments, in the Island of St. Vincent; —from which Mrs. Sterling and her family were now, and had been for some years before her Uncle's decease, deriving important benefits. I have heard, it was then worth some ten thousand pounds a year to the parties interested. Anthony Sterling, John, and another a cousin of theirs were ultimately to be heirs, in equal proportions. The old gentleman, always kind to his kindred, and a brave and solid man though somewhat abrupt in his ways, had lately died; leaving a settlement to this effect, not without some intricacies, and almost caprices, in the conditions attached.

This property, which is still a valuable one, was Sterling's chief pecuniary outlook for the distant future. Of course it well deserved taking care of; and if the eye of the master were upon it, of course too (according to the adage) the cattle would fatten better. As the warm climate was favorable to pulmonary complaints, and Sterling's occupations were so shattered to pieces and his outlooks here so waste and vague, why should not he undertake this duty for himself and others?

It was fixed upon as the eligiblest course. A visit to St. Vincent, perhaps a permanent residence there: he went into the project with his customary impetuosity; his young Wife cheerfully consenting, and all manner of new hopes clustering round it. There are the rich tropical sceneries, the romance of the torrid zone with its new skies and seas and lands; there are Blacks, and the Slavery question to be investigated: there are the bronzed Whites and Yellows, and their strange new way of life: by all means let us go and try! — Arrangements being completed, so soon as his strength had sufficiently recovered, and the harsh spring winds had sufficiently abated, Sterling with his small household set sail for St. Vincent; and arrived without accident. His first child, a son Edward, now living and grown to manhood, was born there, "at Brighton in the Island of St. Vincent, " in the fall of that year 1831.

CHAPTER XII.
ISLAND OF ST. VINCENT.

Sterling found a pleasant residence, with all its adjuncts, ready for him, at Colonarie, in this "volcanic Isle" under the hot sun. An interesting Isle: a place of rugged chasms, precipitous gnarled heights, and the most fruitful hollows; shaggy everywhere with luxuriant vegetation; set under magnificent skies, in the mirror of the summer seas; offering everywhere the grandest sudden outlooks and contrasts. His Letters represent a placidly cheerful riding life: a pensive humor, but the thunder-clouds all sleeping in the distance. Good relations with a few neighboring planters; indifference to the noisy political and other agitations of the rest: friendly, by no means romantic appreciation of the Blacks; quiet prosperity economic and domestic: on the whole a healthy and recommendable way of life, with Literature very much in abeyance in it.

He writes to Mr. Hare (date not given): "The landscapes around me here are noble and lovely as any that can be conceived on Earth. How indeed could it be otherwise, in a small Island of volcanic mountains, far within the Tropics, and perpetually covered with the richest vegetation? " The moral aspect of things is by no means so good; but neither is that without its fair features. "So far as I see, the Slaves here are cunning, deceitful and idle; without any great aptitude for ferocious crimes, and with very little scruple at committing others. But I have seen them much only in very favorable circumstances. They are, as a body, decidedly unfit for freedom; and if left, as at present, completely in the hands of their masters, will never become so, unless through the agency of the Methodists. "[9]

In the Autumn came an immense hurricane; with new and indeed quite perilous experiences of West-Indian life. This hasty Letter, addressed to his Mother, is not intrinsically his remarkablest from St. Vincent: but the body of fact delineated in it being so much the greatest, we will quote it in preference. A West-Indian tornado, as John Sterling witnesses it, and with vivid authenticity describes it, may be considered worth looking at.

"*To Mrs. Sterling, South Place, Knightsbridge, London.*
"BRIGHTON, ST. VINCENT, 28th August, 1831.

"MY DEAR MOTHER, — The packet came in yesterday; bringing me some Newspapers, a Letter from my Father, and one from Anthony, with a few lines from you. I wrote, some days ago, a hasty Note to my Father, on the chance of its reaching you through Grenada sooner than any communication by the packet; and in it I spoke of the great misfortune which had befallen this Island and Barbadoes, but from which all those you take an interest in have happily escaped unhurt.

"From the day of our arrival in the West Indies until Thursday the 11th instant, which will long be a memorable day with us, I had been doing my best to get ourselves established comfortably; and I had at last bought the materials for making some additions to the house. But on the morning I have mentioned, all that I had exerted myself to do, nearly all the property both of Susan and myself, and the very house we lived in, were suddenly destroyed by a visitation of Providence far more terrible than any I have ever witnessed.

"When Susan came from her room, to breakfast, at eight o'clock, I pointed out to her the extraordinary height and violence of the surf, and the singular appearance of the clouds of heavy rain sweeping down the valleys before us. At this time I had so little apprehension of what was coming, that I talked of riding down to the shore when the storm should abate, as I had never seen so fierce a sea. In about a quarter of an hour the House-Negroes came in, to close the outside shutters of the windows. They knew that the plantain-trees about the Negro houses had been blown down in the night; and had told the maid-servant Tyrrell, but I had heard nothing of it. A very few minutes after the closing of the windows, I found that the shutters of Tyrrell's room, at the south and commonly the most sheltered end of the House, were giving way. I tried to tie them; but the silk handkerchief which I used soon gave way; and as I had neither hammer, boards nor nails in the house, I could do nothing more to keep out the tempest. I found, in pushing at the leaf of the shutter, that the wind resisted, more as if it had been a stone wall or a mass of iron, than a mere current of air. There were one or two people outside trying to fasten the windows, and I went out to help; but we had no tools at hand: one man was blown down the hill in front of the house, before my face; and the other and myself had great difficulty in getting back again inside the door. The rain on my face and hands felt like so much small shot from a gun. There was great exertion necessary to shut the door of the house.

"The windows at the end of the large room were now giving way; and I suppose it was about nine o'clock, when the hurricane burst them in, as if it had been a discharge from a battery of heavy cannon. The shutters were first forced open, and the wind fastened them back to the wall; and then the panes of glass were smashed by the mere force of the gale, without anything having touched them. Even now I was not at all sure the house would go. My books, I saw, were lost; for the rain poured past the bookcases, as if it had been the Colonarie River. But we carried a good deal of furniture into the passage at the entrance; we set Susan there on a sofa, and the Black Housekeeper was even attempting to get her some breakfast. The house, however, began to shake so violently, and the rain was so searching, that she could not stay there long. She went into her own room and I stayed to see what could be done.

"Under the forepart of the house, there are cellars built of stone, but not arched. To these, however, there was no access except on the outside; and I knew from my own experience that Susan could not have gone a step beyond the door, without being carried away by the storm, and probably killed on the spot. The only chance seemed to be that of breaking through the floor. But when the old Cook and myself resolved on this, we found that we had no instrument with which it would be possible to do it. It was now clear that we had only God to trust in. The front windows were giving way with successive crashes, and the floor shook as you may have seen a carpet on a gusty day in London. I went into our bedroom; where I found Susan, Tyrrell, and a little Colored girl of seven or eight years old; and told them that we should probably not be alive in half an hour. I could have escaped, if I had chosen to go alone, by crawling on the ground either into the kitchen, a separate stone building at no great distance, or into the open fields away from trees or houses; but Susan could not have gone a yard. She became quite calm when she knew the worst; and she sat on my knee in what seemed the safest corner of the room, while every blast was bringing nearer and nearer the moment of our seemingly certain destruction. —

"The house was under two parallel roofs; and the one next the sea, which sheltered the other, and us who were under the other, went off, I suppose about ten o'clock. After my old plan, I will give you a sketch, from which you may perceive how we were situated: —

The *a, a* are the windows that were first destroyed: *b* went next; my books were between the windows *b*, and on the wall opposite to them. The lines *c* and *d* mark the directions of the two roofs; *e* is the room in which we were, and 2 is a plan of it on a larger scale. Look now at 2: *a* is the bed; *c*, *c* the two wardrobes; *b* the corner in which we were. I was sitting in an arm-chair, holding my Wife; and Tyrrell and the little Black child were close to us. We had given up all notion of surviving; and only waited for the fall of the roof to perish together.

"Before long the roof went. Most of the materials, however, were carried clear away: one of the large couples was caught on the bedpost marked *d*, and held fast by the iron spike; while the end of it hung over our heads: had the beam fallen an inch on either side of the bedpost, it must necessarily have crushed us. The walls did not go with the roof; and we remained for half an hour, alternately praying to God, and watching them as they bent, creaked, and shivered before the storm.

"Tyrrell and the child, when the roof was off, made their way through the remains of the partition, to the outer door; and with the help of the people who were looking for us, got into the kitchen. A good while after they were gone, and before we knew anything of their fate, a Negro suddenly came upon us; and the sight of him gave us a hope of safety. When the people learned that we were in danger, and while their own huts were flying about their ears, they crowded to help us; and the old Cook urged them on to our rescue. He made five attempts, after saving Tyrrell, to get to us; and four times he was blown down. The fifth time he, and the Negro we first saw, reached the house. The space they had to traverse was not above twenty yards of level ground, if so much. In another minute or two, the Overseers and a crowd of Negroes, most of whom had come on their hands and knees, were surrounding us; and with their help Susan was carried round to the end of the house; where they broke open the cellar window, and placed her in comparative safety. The force of the hurricane was, by this time, a good deal diminished, or it would have been impossible to stand before it.

"But the wind was still terrific; and the rain poured into the cellars through the floor above. Susan, Tyrrell, and a crowd of Negroes remained under it, for more than two hours: and I was long afraid that the wet and cold would kill her, if she did not perish more violently. Happily we had wine and spirits at hand, and she was much nerved by a tumbler of claret. As soon as I saw her in comparative security, I went off with one of the Overseers down to the Works, where the greater number of the Negroes were collected, that we might see what could be done for them. They were wretched enough, but no one was hurt; and I ordered them a dram apiece, which seemed to give them a good deal of consolation.

"Before I could make my way back, the hurricane became as bad as at first; and I was obliged to take shelter for half an hour in a ruined Negro house. This, however, was the last of its extreme violence. By one o'clock, even the rain had in a great degree ceased; and as only one room of the house, the one marked *f*, was standing, and that rickety, —I had Susan carried in a chair down the hill, to the Hospital; where, in a small paved unlighted room, she spent the next twenty-four hours. She was far less injured than might have been expected from such a catastrophe.

"Next day, I had the passage at the entrance of the house repaired and roofed; and we returned to the ruins of our habitation, still encumbered as they were with the wreck of almost all we were possessed of. The walls of the part of the house next the sea were carried away, in less I think than half an hour after we reached the cellar: when I had leisure to examine the remains of the house, I found the floor strewn with fragments of the building, and with broken furniture; and our books all soaked as completely as if they had been for several hours in the sea.

"In the course of a few days I had the other room, *g*, which is under the same roof as the one saved, rebuilt; and Susan stayed in this temporary abode for a week, —when we left Colonarie, and came to Brighton. Mr. Munro's kindness exceeds all precedent. We shall certainly remain here till my Wife is recovered from her confinement. In the mean while we shall have a new house built, in which we hope to be well settled before Christmas.

"The roof was half blown off the kitchen, but I have had it mended already; the other offices were all swept away. The gig is much injured; and my horse received a wound in the fall of the stable, from which he will not be recovered for some weeks: in the mean time I have no choice but to buy another, as I must go at least once or twice a week to Colonarie, besides business in Town. As to our own comforts, we can scarcely expect ever to recover from the blow that has now stricken us. No money would repay me for the loss of my books, of which a large proportion had been in my hands for so many years that they were like old and faithful friends, and of which many had been given me at different times by the persons in the world whom I most value.

"But against all this I have to set the preservation of our lives, in a way the most awfully providential; and the safety of every one on the Estate. And I have also the great satisfaction of reflecting that all the Negroes from whom any assistance could reasonably be expected, behaved like so many Heroes of Antiquity; risking their lives and limbs for us and our property, while their own poor houses were flying like chaff before the hurricane. There are few White people here who can say as much for their Black dependents; and the force and value of the relation between Master and Slave has been tried by the late calamity on a large scale.

"Great part of both sides of this Island has been laid completely waste. The beautiful wide and fertile Plain called the Charib Country, extending for many miles to the north of Colonarie, and formerly containing the finest sets of works and best dwelling-houses in the Island, is, I am told, completely desolate: on several estates not a roof even of a Negro hut standing. In the embarrassed circumstances of many of the proprietors, the ruin is, I fear, irreparable. —At Colonarie the damage is serious, but by no means desperate. The crop is perhaps injured ten or fifteen per cent. The roofs of several large buildings are destroyed, but these we are already supplying; and the injuries done to the cottages of the Negroes are, by this time, nearly if not quite remedied.

"Indeed, all that has been suffered in St. Vincent appears nothing when compared with the appalling loss of property and of human lives at Barbadoes. There the Town is little but a heap of ruins, and the corpses are reckoned by thousands; while throughout the Island there are not, I believe, ten estates on which the buildings are standing. The Elliotts, from whom we have heard, are living with all their family in a tent; and may think themselves wonderfully saved, when whole families round them were crushed at once beneath their houses. Hugh Barton, the only officer of the Garrison hurt, has broken his arm, and we know nothing of his prospects of recovery. The more horrible misfortune of Barbadoes is partly to be accounted for by the fact of the hurricane having begun there during the night. The flatness of the surface in that Island presented no obstacle to the wind, which must, however, I think have been in itself more furious than with us. No other island has suffered considerably.

"I have told both my Uncle and Anthony that I have given you the details of our recent history; —which are not so pleasant that I should wish to write them again. Perhaps you will be good enough to let them see this, as soon as you and my Father can spare it.... I am ever, dearest Mother,

"Your grateful and affectionate
"JOHN STERLING. "

This Letter, I observe, is dated 28th August, 1831; which is otherwise a day of mark to the world and me, —the Poet Goethe's last birthday. While Sterling sat in the Tropical solitudes, penning this history, little European Weimar had its carriages and state-carriages busy on the streets, and was astir with compliments and visiting-cards, doing its best, as heretofore, on behalf of a remarkable day; and was not, for centuries or tens of centuries, to see the like of it again! —

At Brighton, the hospitable home of those Munros, our friends continued for above two months. Their first child, Edward, as above noticed, was born here, "14th October, 1831; "—and now the poor lady, safe from all her various perils, could return to Colonarie under good auspices.

It was in this year that I first heard definitely of Sterling as a contemporary existence; and laid up some note and outline of him in my memory, as of one whom I might yet hope to know. John Mill, Mrs. Austin and perhaps other friends, spoke of him with great affection and much pitying admiration; and hoped to see him home again, under better omens, from over the seas. As a gifted amiable being, of a certain radiant tenuity and velocity, too thin and rapid and diffusive, in danger of dissipating himself into the vague, or alas into death itself: it was so that, like a spot of bright colors, rather than a portrait with features, he hung occasionally visible in my imagination.

CHAPTER XIII.
A CATASTROPHE.

The ruin of his house had hardly been repaired, when there arrived out of Europe tidings which smote as with a still more fatal hurricane on the four corners of his inner world, and awoke all the old thunders that lay asleep on his horizon there. Tidings, at last of a decisive nature, from Gibraltar and the Spanish democrat adventure. This is what the Newspapers had to report—the catastrophe at once, the details by degrees—from Spain concerning that affair, in the beginning of the new year 1832.

Torrijos, as we have seen, had hitherto accomplished as good as nothing, except disappointment to his impatient followers, and sorrow and regret to himself. Poor Torrijos, on arriving at Gibraltar with his wild band, and coming into contact with the rough fact, had found painfully how much his imagination had deceived him. The fact lay round him haggard and iron-bound; flatly refusing to be handled according to his scheme of it. No Spanish soldiery nor citizenry showed the least disposition to join him; on the contrary the official Spaniards of that coast seemed to have the watchfulest eye on all his movements, nay it was conjectured they had spies in Gibraltar who gathered his very intentions and betrayed them. This small project of attack, and then that other, proved futile, or was abandoned before the attempt. Torrijos had to lie painfully within the lines of Gibraltar, —his poor followers reduced to extremity of impatience and distress; the British Governor too, though not unfriendly to him, obliged to frown. As for the young Cantabs, they, as was said, had wandered a little over the South border of romantic Spain; had perhaps seen Seville, Cadiz, with picturesque views, since not with belligerent ones; and their money being done, had now returned home. So had it lasted for eighteen months.

The French Three Days breaking out had armed the Guerrillero Mina, armed all manner of democratic guerrieros and guerrilleros; and considerable clouds of Invasion, from Spanish exiles, hung minatory over the North and North-East of Spain, supported by the new-born French Democracy, so far as privately possible. These Torrijos had to look upon with inexpressible feelings, and take no hand in supporting from the South; these also he had to see brushed away, successively abolished by official generalship; and to sit within his lines, in the painfulest manner, unable to do anything. The fated, gallant-minded, but too headlong man. At length the British Governor himself was obliged, in official decency and as is thought on repeated remonstrance from his Spanish official neighbors, to signify how indecorous, improper and impossible it was to harbor within one's lines such explosive preparations, once they were discovered, against allies in full peace with us, —the necessity, in fact, there was for the matter ending. It is said, he offered Torrijos and his people passports, and British protection, to any country of the world except Spain: Torrijos did not accept the passports; spoke of going peaceably to this place or to that; promised at least, what he saw and felt to be clearly necessary, that he would soon leave Gibraltar. And he did soon leave it; he and his, Boyd alone of the Englishmen being now with him.

It was on the last night of November, 1831, that they all set forth; Torrijos with Fifty-five companions; and in two small vessels committed themselves to their nigh-desperate fortune. No sentry or official person had noticed them; it was from the Spanish Consul, next morning, that the British Governor first heard they were gone. The British Governor knew nothing of them; but apparently the Spanish officials were much better informed. Spanish guardships, instantly awake, gave chase to the two small vessels, which were making all sail towards Malaga; and, on shore, all manner of troops and detached parties were in motion, to render a retreat to Gibraltar by land impossible.

Crowd all sail for Malaga, then; there perhaps a regiment will join us; there, —or if not, we are but lost! Fancy need not paint a more tragic situation than that of Torrijos, the unfortunate gallant man, in the gray of this morning, first of December, 1831, —his last free morning. Noble game is afoot, afoot at last; and all the hunters have him in their toils. —The guardships gain upon Torrijos; he cannot even reach Malaga; has to run ashore at a place called Fuengirola, not far from that city; —the guardships seizing his vessels, so soon as he is disembarked. The country is all up; troops scouring the coast everywhere: no possibility of getting into Malaga with a party of Fifty-five. He takes possession of a farmstead (Ingles, the place is called); barricades himself there, but is speedily beleaguered with forces hopelessly superior. He demands to treat; is refused all treaty; is granted six hours to consider, shall then either surrender at discretion, or be forced to do it. Of course he *does* it, having no alternative; and enters Malaga a prisoner, all his followers prisoners.

Here had the Torrijos Enterprise, and all that was embarked upon it, finally arrived.

Express is sent to Madrid; express instantly returns; "Military execution on the instant; give them shriving if they want it; that done, fusillade them all. " So poor Torrijos and his followers, the whole Fifty-six of them, Robert Boyd included, meet swift death in Malaga. In such manner rushes down the curtain on them and their affair; they vanish thus on a sudden; rapt away as in black clouds of fate. Poor Boyd, Sterling's cousin, pleaded his British citizenship; to no purpose: it availed only to his dead body, this was delivered to the British Consul for interment, and only this. Poor Madam Torrijos, hearing, at Paris where she now was, of her husband's capture, hurries towards Madrid to solicit mercy; whither also messengers from Lafayette and the French Government were hurrying, on the like errand: at Bayonne, news met the poor lady that it was already all over, that she was now a widow, and her husband hidden from her forever. —Such was the handsel of the new year 1832 for Sterling in his West-Indian solitudes.

Sterling's friends never heard of these affairs; indeed we were all secretly warned not to mention the name of Torrijos in his hearing, which accordingly remained strictly a forbidden subject. His misery over this catastrophe was known, in his own family, to have been immense. He wrote to his Brother Anthony: "I hear the sound of that musketry; it is as if the bullets were tearing my own brain. " To figure in one's sick and excited imagination such a scene of fatal man-hunting, lost valor hopelessly captured and massacred; and to add to it, that the victims are not men merely, that they are noble and dear forms known lately as individual friends: what a Dance of the Furies and wild-pealing Dead-march is this, for the mind of a loving, generous and vivid man! Torrijos getting ashore at Fuengirola; Robert Boyd and others ranked to die on the esplanade at Malaga — Nay had not Sterling, too, been the innocent yet heedless means of Boyd's embarking in this enterprise? By his own kinsman poor Boyd had been witlessly guided into the pitfalls. "I hear the sound of that musketry; it is as if the bullets were tearing my own brain! "

CHAPTER XIV.
PAUSE.

These thoughts dwelt long with Sterling; and for a good while, I fancy, kept possession of the proscenium of his mind; madly parading there, to the exclusion of all else, —coloring all else with their own black hues. He was young, rich in the power to be miserable or otherwise; and this was his first grand sorrow which had now fallen upon him.

An important spiritual crisis, coming at any rate in some form, had hereby suddenly in a very sad form come. No doubt, as youth was passing into manhood in these Tropical seclusions, and higher wants were awakening in his mind, and years and reflection were adding new insight and admonition, much in his young way of thought and action lay already under ban with him, and repentances enough over many things were not wanting. But here on a sudden had all repentances, as it were, dashed themselves together into one grand whirlwind of repentance; and his past life was fallen wholly as into a state of reprobation. A great remorseful misery had come upon him. Suddenly, as with a sudden lightning-stroke, it had kindled into conflagration all the ruined structure of his past life; such ruin had to blaze and flame round him, in the painfulest manner, till it went out in black ashes. His democratic philosophies, and mutinous radicalisms, already falling doomed in his thoughts, had reached their consummation and final condemnation here. It was all so rash, imprudent, arrogant, all that; false, or but half true; inapplicable wholly as a rule of noble conduct; —and it has ended *thus*. Woe on it! Another guidance must be found in life, or life is impossible! —

It is evident, Sterling's thoughts had already, since the old days of the "black dragoon, " much modified themselves. We perceive that, by mere increase of experience and length of time, the opposite and much deeper side of the question, which also has its adamantine basis of truth, was in turn coming into play; and in fine that a Philosophy of Denial, and world illuminated merely by the flames of Destruction, could never have permanently been the resting-place of such a man. Those pilgrimings to Coleridge, years ago, indicate deeper wants beginning to be felt, and important ulterior resolutions becoming inevitable for him. If in your own soul there is any tone of the "Eternal Melodies, " you cannot live forever in those poor outer, transitory grindings and discords; you will have to struggle inwards and upwards, in search of some diviner home for yourself! — Coleridge's prophetic moonshine, Torrijos's sad tragedy: those were important occurrences in Sterling's life. But, on the whole, there was a big Ocean for him, with impetuous Gulf-streams, and a doomed voyage in quest of the Atlantis, *before* either of those arose as lights on the horizon. As important beacon-lights let us count them nevertheless; —signal-dates they form to us, at lowest. We may reckon this Torrijos tragedy the crisis of Sterling's history; the turning-point, which modified, in the most important and by no means wholly in the most favorable manner, all the subsequent stages of it.

Old Radicalism and mutinous audacious Ethnicism having thus fallen to wreck, and a mere black world of misery and remorse now disclosing itself, whatsoever of natural piety to God and man, whatsoever of pity and reverence, of awe and devout hope was in Sterling's heart now awoke into new activity; and strove for some due utterance and predominance. His Letters, in these months, speak of earnest religious studies and efforts; —of attempts by prayer and longing endeavor of all kinds, to struggle his way into the temple, if temple there were, and there find sanctuary. [10] The realities were grown so haggard; life a field of black ashes, if there rose no temple anywhere on it! Why, like a fated Orestes, is man so whipt by the Furies, and driven madly hither and thither, if it is not even that he may seek some shrine, and there make expiation and find deliverance?

In these circumstances, what a scope for Coleridge's philosophy, above all! "If the bottled moonshine *be* actually substance? Ah, could one but believe in a Church while finding it incredible! What is faith; what is conviction, credibility, insight? Can a thing be at once known for true, and known for false? 'Reason, ' 'Understanding: ' is there, then, such an internecine war between these two? It was so Coleridge imagined it, the wisest of existing men! "—No, it is not an easy matter (according to Sir Kenelm Digby), this of getting up your "astral spirit" of a thing, and setting it in action, when the thing itself is well burnt to ashes. Poor Sterling; poor sons of Adam in general, in this sad age of cobwebs, worn-out symbolisms, reminiscences and simulacra! Who can tell the struggles of poor Sterling, and his pathless wanderings through these things! Long afterwards, in speech with his Brother, he compared his case in this time to that of "a young lady who has tragically lost her lover, and is willing to be half-hoodwinked into a convent, or in any noble or quasi-noble way to escape from a world which has become intolerable. "

During the summer of 1832, I find traces of attempts towards Anti-Slavery Philanthropy; shadows of extensive schemes in that direction. Half-desperate outlooks, it is likely, towards the refuge of Philanthropism, as a new chivalry of life. These took no serious hold of so clear an intellect; but they hovered now and afterwards as day-dreams, when life otherwise was shorn of aim; —mirages in the desert, which are found not to be lakes when you put your bucket into them. One thing was clear, the sojourn in St. Vincent was not to last much longer.

Perhaps one might get some scheme raised into life, in Downing Street, for universal Education to the Blacks, preparatory to emancipating them? There were a noble work for a man! Then again poor Mrs. Sterling's health, contrary to his own, did not agree with warm moist climates. And again, &c. &c. These were the outer surfaces of the measure; the unconscious pretexts under which it showed itself to Sterling and was shown by him: but the inner heart and determining cause of it (as frequently in Sterling's life, and in all our lives) was not these. In brief, he had had enough of St. Vincent. The strangling oppressions of his soul were too heavy for him there. Solution lay in Europe, or might lie; not in these remote solitudes of the sea, —where no shrine or saint's well is to be looked for, no communing of pious pilgrims journeying together towards a shrine.

CHAPTER XV.
BONN; HERSTMONCEUX.

After a residence of perhaps fifteen months Sterling quitted St. Vincent, and never returned. He reappeared at his Father's house, to the joy of English friends, in August, 1832; well improved in health, and eager for English news; but, beyond vague schemes and possibilities, considerably uncertain what was next to be done.

After no long stay in this scene, —finding Downing Street dead as stone to the Slave-Education and to all other schemes, —he went across, with his wife and child, to Germany; purposing to make not so much a tour as some loose ramble, or desultory residence in that country, in the Rhineland first of all. Here was to be hoped the picturesque in scenery, which he much affected; here the new and true in speculation, which he inwardly longed for and wanted greatly more; at all events, here as readily as elsewhere might a temporary household be struck up, under interesting circumstances. —I conclude he went across in the Spring of 1833; perhaps directly after *Arthur Coningsby* had got through the press. This Novel, which, as we have said, was begun two or three years ago, probably on his cessation from the *Athenaeum*, and was mainly finished, I think, before the removal to St. Vincent, had by this time fallen as good as obsolete to his own mind; and its destination now, whether to the press or to the fire, was in some sort a matter at once of difficulty and of insignificance to him. At length deciding for the milder alternative, he had thrown in some completing touches here and there, —especially, as I conjecture, a proportion of Coleridgean moonshine at the end; and so sent it forth.

It was in the sunny days, perhaps in May or June of this year, that *Arthur Coningsby* reached my own hand, far off amid the heathy wildernesses; sent by John Mill: and I can still recollect the pleasant little episode it made in my solitude there. The general impression it left on me, which has never since been renewed by a second reading in whole or in part, was the certain prefigurement to myself, more or less distinct, of an opulent, genial and sunny mind, but misdirected, disappointed, experienced in misery; —nay crude and hasty; mistaking for a solid outcome from its woes what was only to me a gilded vacuity. The hero an ardent youth, representing Sterling himself, plunges into life such as we now have it in these anarchic times, with the radical, utilitarian, or mutinous heathen theory, which is the readiest for inquiring souls; finds, by various courses of adventure, utter shipwreck in this; lies broken, very wretched: that is the tragic nodus, or apogee of his life-course. In this mood of mind, he clutches desperately towards some new method (recognizable as Coleridge's) of laying hand again on the old Church, which has hitherto been extraneous and as if non-extant to his way of thought; makes out, by some Coleridgean legerdemain, that there actually is still a Church for him; that this extant Church, which he long took for an extinct shadow, is not such, but a substance; upon which he can anchor himself amid the storms of fate; —and he does so, even taking orders in it, I think. Such could by no means seem to me the true or tenable solution. Here clearly, struggling amid the tumults, was a lovable young fellow-soul; who had by no means yet got to land; but of whom much might be hoped, if he ever did. Some of the delineations are highly pictorial, flooded with a deep ruddy effulgence; betokening much wealth, in the crude or the ripe state. The hope of perhaps, one day, knowing Sterling, was welcome and interesting to me. *Arthur Coningsby*, struggling imperfectly in a sphere high above circulating-library novels, gained no notice whatever in that quarter; gained, I suppose in a few scattered heads, some such recognition as the above; and there rested. Sterling never mentioned the name of it in my hearing, or would hear it mentioned.

In those very days while *Arthur Coningsby* was getting read amid the Scottish moors, "in June, 1833, " Sterling, at Bonn in the Rhine-country, fell in with his old tutor and friend, the Reverend Julius Hare; one with whom he always delighted to communicate, especially on such topics as then altogether occupied him. A man of cheerful serious character, of much approved accomplishment, of perfect courtesy; surely of much piety, in all senses of that word. Mr. Hare had quitted his scholastic labors and distinctions, some time ago; the call or opportunity for taking orders having come; and as Rector of Herstmonceux in Sussex, a place patrimonially and otherwise endeared to him, was about entering, under the best omens, on a new course of life. He was now on his return from Rome, and a visit of some length to Italy. Such a meeting could not but be welcome and important to Sterling in such a mood. They had much earnest conversation, freely communing on the highest matters; especially of Sterling's purpose to undertake the clerical profession, in which course his reverend friend could not but bid him good speed.

It appears, Sterling already intimated his intention to become a clergyman: He would study theology, biblicalities, perfect himself in the knowledge seemly or essential for his new course; —read diligently "for a year or two in some good German University, " then seek to obtain orders: that was his plan. To which Mr. Hare gave his hearty *Euge*; adding that if his own curacy happened then to be vacant, he should be well pleased to have Sterling in that office. So they parted.

"A year or two" of serious reflection "in some good German University, " or anywhere in the world, might have thrown much elucidation upon these confused strugglings and purposings of Sterling's, and probably have spared him some confusion in his subsequent life. But the talent of waiting was, of all others, the one he wanted most. Impetuous velocity, all-hoping headlong alacrity, what we must call rashness and impatience, characterized him in most of his important and unimportant procedures; from the purpose to the execution there was usually but one big leap with him. A few months after Mr. Hare was gone, Sterling wrote that his purposes were a little changed by the late meeting at Bonn; that he now longed to enter the Church straightway: that if the Herstmonceux Curacy was still vacant, and the Rector's kind thought towards him still held, he would instantly endeavor to qualify himself for that office.

Answer being in the affirmative on both heads, Sterling returned to England; took orders, —"ordained deacon at Chichester on Trinity Sunday in 1834" (he never became technically priest): —and so, having fitted himself and family with a reasonable house, in one of those leafy lanes in quiet Herstmonceux, on the edge of Pevensey Level, he commenced the duties of his Curacy.

The bereaved young lady has *taken* the veil, then! Even so. "Life is growing all so dark and brutal; must be redeemed into human, if it will continue life. Some pious heroism, to give a human color to life again, on any terms, "—even on impossible ones!

To such length can transcendental moonshine, cast by some morbidly radiating Coleridge into the chaos of a fermenting life, act magically there, and produce divulsions and convulsions and diseased developments. So dark and abstruse, without lamp or authentic finger-post, is the course of pious genius towards the

Eternal Kingdoms grown. No fixed highway more; the old spiritual highways and recognized paths to the Eternal, now all torn up and flung in heaps, submerged in unutterable boiling mud-oceans of Hypocrisy and Unbelievability, of brutal living Atheism and damnable dead putrescent Cant: surely a tragic pilgrimage for all mortals; Darkness, and the mere shadow of Death, enveloping all things from pole to pole; and in the raging gulf-currents, offering us will-o'-wisps for loadstars, —intimating that there are no stars, nor ever were, except certain Old-Jew ones which have now gone out. Once more, a tragic pilgrimage for all mortals; and for the young pious soul, winged with genius, and passionately seeking land, and passionately abhorrent of floating carrion withal, more tragical than for any! —A pilgrimage we must all undertake nevertheless, and make the best of with our respective means. Some arrive; a glorious few: many must be lost, —go down upon the floating wreck which they took for land. Nay, courage! These also, so far as there was any heroism in them, have bequeathed their life as a contribution to us, have valiantly laid their bodies in the chasm for us: of these also there is no ray of heroism *lost*, —and, on the whole, what else of them could or should be "saved" at any time? Courage, and ever Forward!

Concerning this attempt of Sterling's to find sanctuary in the old Church, and desperately grasp the hem of her garment in such manner, there will at present be many opinions: and mine must be recorded here in flat reproval of it, in mere pitying condemnation of it, as a rash, false, unwise and unpermitted step. Nay, among the evil lessons of his Time to poor Sterling, I cannot but account this the worst; properly indeed, as we may say, the apotheosis, the solemn apology and consecration, of all the evil lessons that were in it to him. Alas, if we did remember the divine and awful nature of God's Truth, and had not so forgotten it as poor doomed creatures never did before, —should we, durst we in our most audacious moments, think of wedding *it* to the World's Untruth, which is also, like all untruths, the Devil's? Only in the world's last lethargy can such things be done, and accounted safe and pious! Fools! "Do you think the Living God is a buzzard idol, " sternly asks Milton, that you dare address Him in this manner? —Such darkness, thick sluggish clouds of cowardice and oblivious baseness, have accumulated on us: thickening as if towards the eternal sleep! It is not now known, what never needed proof or statement before, that Religion is not a doubt; that it is a certainty, —or else a mockery and horror. That none or all of the many things we are in doubt about, and need to have demonstrated and rendered probable, can by any alchemy be made a "Religion" for us; but are and must continue a baleful, quiet or unquiet, Hypocrisy for us; and bring—*salvation*, do we fancy? I think, it is another thing they will bring, and are, on all hands, visibly bringing this good while! —

The time, then, with its deliriums, has done its worst for poor Sterling. Into deeper aberration it cannot lead him; this is the crowning error. Happily, as beseems the superlative of errors, it was a very brief, almost a momentary one. In June, 1834, Sterling dates as installed at Herstmonceux; and is flinging, as usual, his whole soul into the business; successfully so far as outward results could show: but already in September, he begins to have misgivings; and in February following, quits it altogether, —the rest of his life being, in great part, a laborious effort of detail to pick the fragments of it off him, and be free of it in soul as well as in title.

At this the extreme point of spiritual deflexion and depression, when the world's madness, unusually impressive on such a man, has done its very worst with him, and in all future errors whatsoever he will be a little less mistaken, we may close the First Part of Sterling's Life.

PART II.

CHAPTER I.
CURATE.

By Mr. Hare's account, no priest of any Church could more fervently address himself to his functions than Sterling now did. He went about among the poor, the ignorant, and those·that had need of help; zealously forwarded schools and beneficences; strove, with his whole might, to instruct and aid whosoever suffered consciously in body, or still worse unconsciously in mind. He had charged himself to make the Apostle Paul his model; the perils and voyagings and ultimate martyrdom of Christian Paul, in those old ages, on the great scale, were to be translated into detail, and become the practical emblem of Christian Sterling on the coast of Sussex in this new age. "It would be no longer from Jerusalem to Damascus, " writes Sterling, "to Arabia, to Derbe, Lystra, Ephesus, that he would travel: but each house of his appointed Parish would be to him what each of those great cities was, —a place where he would bend his whole being, and spend his heart for the conversion, purification, elevation of those under his influence. The whole man would be forever at work for this purpose; head, heart, knowledge, time, body, possessions, all would be directed to this end. " A high enough model set before one: —how to be realized! —Sterling hoped to realize it, to struggle towards realizing it, in some small degree. This is Mr. Hare's report of him: —

"He was continually devising some fresh scheme for improving the condition of the Parish. His aim was to awaken the minds of the people, to arouse their conscience, to call forth their sense of moral responsibility, to make them feel their own sinfulness, their need of redemption, and thus lead them to a recognition of the Divine Love by which that redemption is offered to us. In visiting them he was diligent in all weathers, to the risk of his own health, which was greatly impaired thereby; and his gentleness and considerate care for the sick won their affection; so that, though his stay was very short, his name is still, after a dozen years, cherished by many. "

How beautiful would Sterling be in all this; rushing forward like a host towards victory; playing and pulsing like sunshine or soft lightning; busy at all hours to perform his part in abundant and superabundant measure! "Of that which it was to me personally, " continues Mr. Hare, "to have such a fellow-laborer, to live constantly in the freest communion with such a friend, I cannot speak. He came to me at a time of heavy affliction, just after I had heard that the Brother, who had been the sharer of all my thoughts and feelings from childhood, had bid farewell to his earthly life at Rome; and thus he seemed given to me to make up in some sort for him whom I had lost. Almost daily did I look out for his usual hour of coming to me, and watch his tall slender form walking rapidly across the hill in front of my window; with the assurance that he was coming to cheer and brighten, to rouse and stir me, to call me up to some height of feeling, or down to some depth of thought. His lively spirit, responding instantaneously to every impulse of Nature and Art; his generous ardor in behalf of whatever is noble and true; his scorn of all meanness, of all false pretences and conventional beliefs, softened as it was by compassion for the victims of those besetting sins of a cultivated age; his never-flagging impetuosity in pushing onward to some unattained point of duty or of knowledge: all this, along with his gentle, almost reverential affectionateness towards his former tutor, rendered my intercourse with him an unspeakable blessing; and time after time has it seemed to me that his visit had been like a shower of rain, bringing down freshness and brightness on a dusty roadside hedge. By him too the recollection of these our daily meetings was cherished till the last. "[11]

There are many poor people still at Herstmonceux who affectionately remember him: Mr. Hare especially makes mention of one good man there, in his young days "a poor cobbler, " and now advanced to a much better position, who gratefully ascribes this outward and the other improvements in his life to Sterling's generous encouragement and charitable care for him. Such was the curate life at Herstmonceux. So, in those actual leafy lanes, on the edge of Pevensey Level, in this new age, did our poor New Paul (on hest of certain oracles) diligently study to comport himself, —and struggle with all his might *not* to be a moonshine shadow of the First Paul.

It was in this summer of 1834, —month of May, shortly after arriving in London, —that I first saw Sterling's Father. A stout broad gentleman of sixty, perpendicular in attitude, rather showily dressed, and of gracious, ingenious and slightly elaborate manners. It was at Mrs. Austin's in Bayswater; he was just taking leave as I entered, so our interview lasted only a moment: but the figure of the man, as Sterling's father, had already an interest for me, and I remember the time well. Captain Edward Sterling, as we formerly called him, had now quite dropt the military title, nobody even of his friends now remembering it; and was known, according to his wish, in political and other circles, as Mr. Sterling, a private gentleman of some figure. Over whom hung, moreover, a kind of mysterious nimbus as the principal or one of the principal writers in the *Times*, which gave an interesting chiaroscuro to his character in society. A potent, profitable, but somewhat questionable position; of which, though he affected, and sometimes with anger, altogether to disown it, and rigorously insisted on the rights of anonymity, he was not unwilling to take the honors too: the private pecuniary advantages were very undeniable; and his reception in the Clubs, and occasionally in higher quarters, was a good deal modelled on the universal belief in it.

John Sterling at Herstmonceux that afternoon, and his Father here in London, would have offered strange contrasts to an eye that had seen them both. Contrasts, and yet concordances. They were two very different-looking men, and were following two very different modes of activity that afternoon. And yet with a strange family likeness, too, both in the men and their activities; the central impulse in each, the faculties applied to fulfil said impulse, not at all dissimilar, —as grew visible to me on farther knowledge.

CHAPTER II.
NOT CURATE.

Thus it went on for some months at Herstmonceux; but thus it could not last. We said there were already misgivings as to health, &c. in September: [12] that was but the fourth month, for it had begun only in June. The like clouds of misgiving, flights of dark vapor, chequering more and more the bright sky of this promised land, rose heavier and rifer month after month; till in February following, that is in the eighth month from starting, the sky had grown quite overshaded; and poor Sterling had to think practically of departure from his promised land again, finding that the goal of his pilgrimage was *not* there. Not there, wherever it may be! March again, therefore; the abiding city, and post at which we can live and die, is still ahead of us, it would appear!

"Ill-health" was the external cause; and, to all parties concerned, to Sterling himself I have no doubt as completely as to any, the one determining cause. Nor was the ill-health wanting; it was there in too sad reality. And yet properly it was not there as the burden; it was there as the last ounce which broke the camel's back. I take it, in this as in other cases known to me, ill-health was not the primary cause but rather the ultimate one, the summing-up of innumerable far deeper conscious and unconscious causes, —the cause which could boldly show itself on the surface, and give the casting vote. Such was often Sterling's way, as one could observe in such cases: though the most guileless, undeceptive and transparent of men, he had a noticeable, almost childlike faculty of self-deception, and usually substituted for the primary determining motive and set of motives, some ultimate ostensible one, and gave that out to himself and others as the ruling impulse for important changes in life. As is the way with much more ponderous and deliberate men; —as is the way, in a degree, with all men!

Enough, in February, 1835, Sterling came up to London, to consult with his physicians, —and in fact in all ways to consider with himself and friends, —what was to be done in regard to this Herstmonceux business. The oracle of the physicians, like that of Delphi, was not exceedingly determinate: but it did bear, what was a sufficiently undeniable fact, that Sterling's constitution, with a tendency to pulmonary ailments, was ill-suited for the office of a preacher; that total abstinence from preaching for a year or two would clearly be the safer course. To which effect he writes to Mr. Hare with a tone of sorrowful agitation; gives up his clerical duties at Herstmonceux; —and never resumed them there or elsewhere. He had been in the Church eight months in all: a brief section of his life, but an important one, which colored several of his subsequent years, and now strangely colors all his years in the memory of some.

This we may account the second grand crisis of his History. Radicalism, not long since, had come to its consummation, and vanished from him in a tragic manner. "Not by Radicalism is the path to Human Nobleness for me! " And here now had English Priesthood risen like a sun, over the waste ruins and extinct volcanoes of his dead Radical world, with promise of new blessedness and healing under its Wings; and this too has soon found itself an illusion: "Not by Priesthood either lies the way, then. Once more, where does the way lie! " —To follow illusions till they burst and vanish is the lot of all new souls who, luckily or lucklessly, are left to their own choice in starting on this Earth. The roads are many; the authentic finger-posts are few, —never fewer than in this era, when in so many senses the waters are out. Sterling of all men had the quickest sense for nobleness, heroism and the human *summum bonum*; the liveliest headlong spirit of adventure and audacity; few gifted living men less stubbornness of perseverance. Illusions, in his chase of the *summum bonum*, were not likely to be wanting; aberrations, and wasteful changes of course, were likely to be many! It is in the history of such vehement, trenchant, far-shining and yet intrinsically light and volatile souls, missioned into this epoch to seek their way there, that we best see what a confused epoch it is.

This clerical aberration, —for such it undoubtedly was in Sterling, — we have ascribed to Coleridge; and do clearly think that had there been no Coleridge, neither had this been, —nor had English Puseyism or some other strange enough universal portents been. Nevertheless, let us say farther that it lay partly in the general bearing of the world for such a man. This battle, universal in our sad epoch of "all old things passing away" against "all things becoming new, " has its summary and animating heart in that of Radicalism against Church; there, as in its flaming core, and point of focal splendor, does the heroic worth that lies in each side of the quarrel most clearly disclose itself; and Sterling was the man, above many, to recognize such worth on both sides. Natural enough, in such a one, that the light of Radicalism having gone out in darkness for him, the opposite splendor should next rise as the chief, and invite his loyalty till it also failed. In one form or the other, such an aberration was not unlikely for him. But an aberration, especially in this form, we may certainly call it. No man of Sterling's veracity, had he clearly consulted his own heart, or had his own heart been capable of clearly responding, and not been dazzled and bewildered by transient fantasies and theosophic moonshine, could have undertaken this function. His heart would have answered: "No, thou canst not. What is incredible to thee, thou shalt not, at thy soul's peril, attempt to believe! —Elsewhither for a refuge, or die here. Go to Perdition if thou must, —but not with a lie in thy mouth; by the Eternal Maker, no! "

Alas, once more! How are poor mortals whirled hither and thither in the tumultuous chaos of our era; and, under the thick smoke-canopy which has eclipsed all stars, how do they fly now after this poor meteor, now after that! —Sterling abandoned his clerical office in February, 1835; having held it, and ardently followed it, so long as we say, —eight calendar months in all.

It was on this his February expedition to London that I first saw Sterling, —at the India House incidentally, one afternoon, where I found him in company with John Mill, whom I happened like himself to be visiting for a few minutes. The sight of one whose fine qualities I had often heard of lately, was interesting enough; and, on the whole, proved not disappointing, though it was the translation of dream into fact, that is of poetry into prose, and showed its unrhymed side withal. A loose, careless-looking, thin figure, in careless dim costume, sat, in a lounging posture, carelessly and copiously talking. I was struck with the kindly but restless swift-glancing eyes, which looked as if the spirits were all out coursing like a pack of merry eager beagles, beating every bush. The brow, rather sloping in form, was not of imposing character, though again the head was longish, which is always the best sign of intellect; the physiognomy in general indicated animation rather than strength.

We talked rapidly of various unmemorable things: I remember coming on the Negroes, and noticing that Sterling's notion on the Slavery Question had not advanced into the stage of mine. In reference to the question whether an "engagement for life, " on just terms, between parties who are fixed in the character of master and servant, as the Whites and the Negroes are, is not really better than one from day to day, —he said with a kindly jeer, "I would have the

90

Negroes themselves consulted as to that! "—and would not in the least believe that the Negroes were by no means final or perfect judges of it. —His address, I perceived, was abrupt, unceremonious; probably not at all disinclined to logic, and capable of dashing in upon you like a charge of Cossacks, on occasion: but it was also eminently ingenious, social, guileless. We did all very well together: and Sterling and I walked westward in company, choosing whatever lanes or quietest streets there were, as far as Knightsbridge where our roads parted; talking on moralities, theological philosophies; arguing copiously, but *except* in opinion not disagreeing

In his notions on such subjects, the expected Coleridge cast of thought was very visible; and he seemed to express it even with exaggeration, and in a fearless dogmatic manner. Identity of sentiment, difference of opinion: these are the known elements of a pleasant dialogue. We parted with the mutual wish to meet again; — which accordingly, at his Father's house and at mine, we soon repeatedly did; and already, in the few days before his return to Herstmonceux, had laid the foundations of a frank intercourse, pointing towards pleasant intimacies both with himself and with his circle, which in the future were abundantly fulfilled. His Mother, essentially and even professedly "Scotch, " took to my Wife gradually with a most kind maternal relation; his Father, a gallant showy stirring gentleman, the Magus of the *Times*, had talk and argument ever ready, was an interesting figure, and more and more took interest in us. We had unconsciously made an acquisition, which grew richer and wholesomer with every new year; and ranks now, seen in the pale moonlight of memory, and must ever rank, among the precious possessions of life.

Sterling's bright ingenuity, and also his audacity, velocity and alacrity, struck me more and more. It was, I think, on the occasion of a party given one of these evenings at his Father's, where I remember John Mill, John Crawford, Mrs. Crawford, and a number of young and elderly figures of distinction, —that a group having formed on the younger side of the room, and transcendentalisms and theologies forming the topic, a number of deep things were said in abrupt conversational style, Sterling in the thick of it. For example, one sceptical figure praised the Church of England, in Hume's phrase, "as a Church tending to keep down fanaticism, " and recommendable for its very indifferency; whereupon a transcendental figure urges him: "You are afraid of the horse's kicking: but will you sacrifice all qualities to being safe from that?

Then get a dead horse. None comparable to that for not kicking in your stable! " Upon which, a laugh; with new laughs on other the like occasions; —and at last, in the fire of some discussion, Sterling, who was unusually eloquent and animated, broke out with this wild phrase, "I could plunge into the bottom of Hell, if I were sure of finding the Devil there and getting him strangled! " Which produced the loudest laugh of all; and had to be repeated, on Mrs. Crawford's inquiry, to the house at large; and, creating among the elders a kind of silent shudder, —though we urged that the feat would really be a good investment of human industry, —checked or stopt these theologic thunders for the evening. I still remember Sterling as in one of his most animated moods that evening. He probably returned to Herstmonceux next day, where he proposed yet to reside for some indefinite time.

Arrived at Herstmonceux, he had not forgotten us. One of his Letters written there soon after was the following, which much entertained me, in various ways. It turns on a poor Book of mine, called *Sartor Resartus*; which was not then even a Book, but was still hanging desolately under bibliopolic difficulties, now in its fourth or fifth year, on the wrong side of the river, as a mere aggregate of Magazine Articles; having at last been slit into that form, and lately completed *so*, and put together into legibility. I suppose Sterling had borrowed it of me. The adventurous hunter spirit which had started such a bemired *Auerochs*, or Urus of the German woods, and decided on chasing that as game, struck me not a little; —and the poor Wood-Ox, so bemired in the forests, took it as a compliment rather: —

"*To Thomas Carlyle, Esq., Chelsea, London.*
"HERSTMONCEUX near BATTLE, 29th May, 1835.

"MY DEAR CARLYLE, —I have now read twice, with care, the wondrous account of Teufelsdrockh and his Opinions; and I need not say that it has given me much to think of. It falls in with the feelings and tastes which were, for years, the ruling ones of my life; but which you will not be angry with me when I say that I am infinitely and hourly thankful for having escaped from. Not that I think of this state of mind as one with which I have no longer any concern. The sense of a oneness of life and power in all existence; and of a boundless exuberance of beauty around us, to which most men are well-nigh dead, is a possession which no one that has ever enjoyed it would wish to lose. When to this we add the deep feeling of the difference between the actual and the ideal in Nature, and still more in Man; and bring in, to explain this, the principle of duty, as that which connects us with a possible Higher State, and sets us in progress towards it, —we have a cycle of thoughts which was the whole spiritual empire of the wisest Pagans, and which might well supply food for the wide speculations and richly creative fancy of Teufelsdrockh, or his prototype Jean Paul.

"How then comes it, we cannot but ask, that these ideas, displayed assuredly with no want of eloquence, vivacity or earnestness, have found, unless I am much mistaken, so little acceptance among the best and most energetic minds in this country? In a country where millions read the Bible, and thousands Shakspeare; where Wordsworth circulates through book-clubs and drawing-rooms; where there are innumerable admirers of your favorite Burns; and where Coleridge, by sending from his solitude the voice of earnest spiritual instruction, came to be beloved, studied and mourned for, by no small or careless school of disciples? —To answer this question would, of course, require more thought and knowledge than I can pretend to bring to it. But there are some points on which I will venture to say a few words.

"In the first place, as to the form of composition, —which may be called, I think, the Rhapsodico-Reflective. In this the *Sartor Resartus* resembles some of the master-works of human invention, which have been acknowledged as such by many generations; and especially the works of Rabelais, Montaigne, Sterne and Swift. There is nothing I know of in Antiquity like it. That which comes nearest is perhaps the Platonic Dialogue. But of this, although there is something of the playful and fanciful on the surface, there is in reality neither in the language (which is austerely determined to its end), nor in the method and progression of the work, any of that headlong self-asserting capriciousness, which, if not discernible in the plan of Teufelsdrockh's Memoirs, is yet plainly to be seen in the structure of the sentences, the lawless oddity, and strange heterogeneous combination and allusion. The principle of this difference, observable often elsewhere in modern literature (for the same thing is to be found, more or less, in many of our most genial works of imagination, —*Don Quixote*, for instance, and the writings of Jeremy Taylor), seems to be that well-known one of the predominant objectivity of the Pagan mind; while among us the subjective has risen into superiority, and brought with it in each individual a multitude of peculiar associations and relations. These, as not explicable from any one *external* principle assumed as a premise by the ancient philosopher, were rejected from the sphere of his aesthetic creation: but to us they all have a value and meaning; being connected by the bond of our own personality and all alike existing in that infinity which is its arena.

"But however this may be, and comparing the Teufelsdrockhean Epopee only with those other modern works, —it is noticeable that Rabelais, Montaigne and Sterne have trusted for the currency of their writings, in a great degree, to the use of obscene and sensual stimulants. Rabelais, besides, was full of contemporary and personal satire; and seems to have been a champion in the great cause of his time, —as was Montaigne also, —that of the right of thought in all competent minds, unrestrained by any outward authority. Montaigne, moreover, contains more pleasant and lively gossip, and more distinct good-humored painting of his own character and daily habits, than any other writer I know. Sterne is never obscure, and never moral; and the costume of his subjects is drawn from the familiar experience of his own time and country: and Swift, again, has the same merit of the clearest perspicuity, joined to that of the most homely, unaffected, forcible English. These points of difference seem to me the chief ones which bear against the success of the *Sartor*. On the other hand, there is in Teufelsdrockh a depth and fervor of feeling, and a power of serious eloquence, far beyond that of any of these four writers; and to which indeed there is nothing at all comparable in any of them, except perhaps now and then, and very imperfectly, in Montaigne.

"Of the other points of comparison there are two which I would chiefly dwell on: and first as to the language. A good deal of this is positively barbarous. 'Environment, ' ' vestural, ' 'stertorous, ' 'visualized, ' 'complected, ' and others to be found I think in the first twenty pages, —are words, so far as I know, without any authority; some of them contrary to analogy: and none repaying by their value the disadvantage of novelty. To these must be added new and erroneous locutions; 'whole other tissues' for *all the other*, and similar uses of the word *whole*; 'orients' for *pearls*; 'lucid' and 'lucent' employed as if they were different in meaning; 'hulls' perpetually for *coverings*, it being a word hardly used, and then only for the husk of a nut; 'to insure a man of misapprehension; ' 'talented, ' a mere newspaper and hustings word, invented, I believe, by O'Connell.

"I must also mention the constant recurrence of some words in a quaint and queer connection, which gives a grotesque and somewhat repulsive mannerism to many sentences. Of these the commonest offender is 'quite; ' which appears in almost every page, and gives at first a droll kind of emphasis; but soon becomes wearisome. 'Nay, ' 'manifold, ' 'cunning enough significance, ' 'faculty' (meaning a man's rational or moral *power*), 'special, ' 'not without, ' haunt the reader as if in some uneasy dream which does not rise to the dignity of nightmare. Some of these strange mannerisms fall under the general head of a singularity peculiar, so far as I know, to Teufelsdrockh. For instance, that of the incessant use of a sort of odd superfluous qualification of his assertions; which seems to give the character of deliberateness and caution to the style, but in time sounds like mere trick or involuntary habit. 'Almost' does more than yeoman's, *almost* slave's service in this way. Something similar may be remarked of the use of the double negative by way of affirmation.

"Under this head, of language, may be mentioned, though not with strict grammatical accuracy, two standing characteristics of the Professor's style, —at least as rendered into English: *First*, the composition of words, such as 'snow-and-rosebloom maiden: ' an attractive damsel doubtless in Germany, but, with all her charms, somewhat uncouth here. 'Life-vision' is another example; and many more might be found. To say nothing of the innumerable cases in which the words are only intelligible as a compound term, though not distinguished by hyphens. Of course the composition of words is sometimes allowable even in English: but the habit of dealing with German seems to have produced, in the pages before us, a prodigious superabundance of this form of expression; which gives harshness and strangeness, where the matter would at all events have been surprising enough. *Secondly*, I object, with the same qualification, to the frequent use of *inversion*; which generally appears as a transposition of the two members of a clause, in a way which would not have been practiced in conversation. It certainly gives emphasis and force, and often serves to point the meaning. But a style may be fatiguing and faulty precisely by being too emphatic, forcible and pointed; and so straining the attention to find its meaning, or the admiration to appreciate its beauty.

"Another class of considerations connects itself with the heightened and plethoric fulness of the style: its accumulation and contrast of imagery; its occasional jerking and almost spasmodic violence; —and above all, the painful subjective excitement, which seems the element and groundwork even of every description of Nature; often taking the shape of sarcasm or broad jest, but never subsiding into calm.

There is also a point which I should think worth attending to, were I planning any similar book: I mean the importance, in a work of imagination, of not too much disturbing in the reader's mind the balance of the New and Old. The former addresses itself to his active, the latter to his passive faculty; and these are mutually dependent, and must coexist in certain proportion, if you wish to combine his sympathy and progressive exertion with willingness and ease of attention. This should be taken into account in forming a style; for of course it cannot be consciously thought of in composing each sentence.

"But chiefly it seems important in determining the plan of a work. If the tone of feeling, the line of speculation are out of the common way, and sure to present some difficulty to the average reader, then it would probably be desirable to select, for the circumstances, drapery and accessories of all kinds, those most familiar, or at least most attractive. A fable of the homeliest purport, and commonest every-day application, derives an interest and charm from its turning on the characters and acts of gods and genii, lions and foxes, Arabs and Affghauns. On the contrary, for philosophic inquiry and truths of awful preciousness, I would select as my personages and interlocutors beings with whose language and 'whereabouts' my readers would be familiar. Thus did Plato in his Dialogues, Christ in his Parables. Therefore it seems doubtful whether it was judicious to make a German Professor the hero of *Sartor*. Berkeley began his *Siris* with tar-water; but what can English readers be expected to make of *Gukguk* by way of prelibation to your nectar and tokay? The circumstances and details do not flash with living reality on the minds of your readers, but, on the contrary, themselves require some of that attention and minute speculation, the whole original stock of which, in the minds of most of them, would not be too much to enable them to follow your views of Man and Nature. In short, there is not a sufficient basis of the common to justify the amount of peculiarity in the work. In a book of science, these considerations would of course be inapplicable; but then the whole shape and coloring of the book must be altered to make it such; and a man who wishes merely to get at the philosophical result, or summary of the whole, will regard the details and illustrations as so much unprofitable surplusage.

"The sense of strangeness is also awakened by the marvellous combinations, in which the work abounds to a degree that the common reader must find perfectly bewildering. This can hardly, however, be treated as a consequence of the *style*; for the style in this respect coheres with, and springs from, the whole turn and tendency of thought. The noblest images are objects of a humorous smile, in a mind which sees itself above all Nature and throned in the arms of an Almighty Necessity; while the meanest have a dignity, inasmuch as they are trivial symbols of the same one life to which the great whole belongs. And hence, as I divine, the startling whirl of incongruous juxtaposition, which of a truth must to many readers seem as amazing as if the Pythia on the tripod should have struck up a drinking-song, or Thersites had caught the prophetic strain of Cassandra.

"All this, of course, appears to me true and relevant; but I cannot help feeling that it is, after all, but a poor piece of quackery to comment on a multitude of phenomena without adverting to the principle which lies at the root, and gives the true meaning to them all. Now this principle I seem to myself to find in the state of mind which is attributed to Teufelsdrockh; in his state of mind, I say, not in his opinions, though these are, in him as in all men, most important, —being one of the best indices to his state of mind. Now what distinguishes him, not merely from the greatest and best men who have been on earth for eighteen hundred years, but from the whole body of those who have been working forwards towards the good, and have been the salt and light of the world, is this: That he does not believe in a God. Do not be indignant, I am blaming no one; —but if I write my thoughts, I must write them honestly.

"Teufelsdrockh does not belong to the herd of sensual and thoughtless men; because he does perceive in all Existence a unity of power; because he does believe that this is a real power external to him and dominant to a certain extent over him, and does not think that he is himself a shadow in a world of shadows. He had a deep feeling of the beautiful, the good and the true; and a faith in their final victory.

"At the same time, how evident is the strong inward unrest, the Titanic heaving of mountain on mountain; the storm-like rushing over land and sea in search of peace. He writhes and roars under his consciousness of the difference in himself between the possible and the actual, the hoped-for and the existent. He feels that duty is the highest law of his own being; and knowing how it bids the waves be stilled into an icy fixedness and grandeur, he trusts (but with a boundless inward misgiving) that there is a principle of order which will reduce all confusion to shape and clearness. But wanting peace himself, his fierce dissatisfaction fixes on all that is weak, corrupt and imperfect around him; and instead of a calm and steady co-operation with all those who are endeavoring to apply the highest ideas as remedies for the worst evils, he holds himself aloof in savage isolation; and cherishes (though he dare not own) a stern joy at the prospect of that Catastrophe which is to turn loose again the elements of man's social life, and give for a time the victory to evil; —in hopes that each new convulsion of the world must bring us nearer to the ultimate restoration of all things; fancying that each may be the last. Wanting the calm and cheerful reliance, which would be the spring of active exertion, he flatters his own distemper by persuading himself that his own age and generation are peculiarly feeble and decayed; and would even perhaps be willing to exchange the restless immaturity of our self-consciousness, and the promise of its long throe-pangs, for the unawakened undoubting simplicity of the world's childhood; of the times in which there was all the evil and horror of our day, only with the difference that conscience had not arisen to try and condemn it. In these longings, if they are Teufelsdrockh's, he seems to forget that, could we go back five thousand years, we should only have the prospect of travelling them again, and arriving at last at the same point at which we stand now.

"Something of this state of mind I may say that I understand; for I have myself experienced it. And the root of the matter appears to me: A want of sympathy with the great body of those who are now endeavoring to guide and help onward their fellow-men. And in what is this alienation grounded? It is, as I believe, simply in the difference on that point: viz. the clear, deep, habitual recognition of a one Living *Personal* God, essentially good, wise, true and holy, the Author of all that exists; and a reunion with whom is the only end of all rational beings. This belief... [*There follow now several pages on "Personal God, " and other abstruse or indeed properly unspeakable matters; these, and a general Postscript of qualifying purport, I will suppress; extracting only the following fractions, as luminous or slightly significant to us:*]

"Now see the difference of Teufelsdrockh's feelings. At the end of book iii. chap. 8, I find these words: 'But whence? O Heaven, whither? Sense knows not; Faith knows not; only that it is through mystery to mystery, from God to God.

'We *are such stuff*
As dreams are made of, and our little life
Is rounded with a sleep. '

And this tallies with the whole strain of his character. What we find everywhere, with an abundant use of the name of God, is the conception of a formless Infinite whether in time or space; of a high inscrutable Necessity, which it is the chief wisdom and virtue to submit to, which is the mysterious impersonal base of all Existence, —shows itself in the laws of every separate being's nature; and for man in the shape of duty. On the other hand, I affirm, we do know whence we come and whither we go! —

... "And in this state of mind, as there is no true sympathy with others, just as little is there any true peace for ourselves. There is indeed possible the unsympathizing factitious calm of Art, which we find in Goethe. But at what expense is it bought? Simply, by abandoning altogether the idea of duty, which is the great witness of our personality. And he attains his inhuman ghastly calmness by reducing the Universe to a heap of material for the idea of beauty to work on! —

... "The sum of all I have been writing as to the connection of our faith in God with our feeling towards men and our mode of action, may of course be quite erroneous: but granting its truth, it would supply the one principle which I have been seeking for, in order to explain the peculiarities of style in your account of Teufelsdrockh and his writings.... The life and works of Luther are the best comment I know of on this doctrine of mine.

"Reading over what I have written, I find I have not nearly done justice to my own sense of the genius and moral energy of the book; but this is what you will best excuse. —Believe me most sincerely and faithfully yours,

"JOHN STERLING. "

Here are sufficient points of "discrepancy with agreement, " here is material for talk and argument enough; and an expanse of free discussion open, which requires rather to be speedily restricted for convenience' sake, than allowed to widen itself into the boundless, as it tends to do! —

In all Sterling's Letters to myself and others, a large collection of which now lies before me, duly copied and indexed, there is, to one that knew his speech as well, a perhaps unusual likeness between the speech and the Letters; and yet, for most part, with a great inferiority on the part of these. These, thrown off, one and all of them, without premeditation, and with most rapid-flowing pen, are naturally as like his speech as writing can well be; this is their grand merit to us: but on the other hand, the want of the living tones, swift looks and motions, and manifold dramatic accompaniments, tells heavily, more heavily than common. What can be done with champagne itself, much more with soda-water, when the gaseous spirit is fled! The reader, in any specimens he may see, must bear this in mind.

Meanwhile these Letters do excel in honesty, in candor and transparency; their very carelessness secures their excellence in this respect. And in another much deeper and more essential respect I must likewise call them excellent, —in their childlike goodness, in the purity of heart, the noble affection and fidelity they everywhere manifest in the writer. This often touchingly strikes a familiar friend in reading them; and will awaken reminiscences (when you have the commentary in your own memory) which are sad and beautiful, and not without reproach to you on occasion. To all friends, and all good causes, this man is true; behind their back as before their face, the same man! —Such traits of the autobiographic sort, from these Letters, as can serve to paint him or his life, and promise not to weary the reader, I must endeavor to select, in the sequel.

CHAPTER III.
BAYSWATER

Sterling continued to reside at Herstmonceux through the spring and summer; holding by the peaceable retired house he still had there, till the vague future might more definitely shape itself, and better point out what place of abode would suit him in his new circumstances. He made frequent brief visits to London; in which I, among other friends, frequently saw him, our acquaintance at each visit improving in all ways. Like a swift dashing meteor he came into our circle; coruscated among us, for a day or two, with sudden pleasant illumination; then again suddenly withdrew, —we hoped, not for long.

I suppose, he was full of uncertainties; but undoubtedly was gravitating towards London. Yet, on the whole, on the surface of him, you saw no uncertainties; far from that: it seemed always rather with peremptory resolutions, and swift express businesses, that he was charged. Sickly in body, the testimony said: but here always was a mind that gave you the impression of peremptory alertness, cheery swift decision, —of a *health* which you might have called exuberant. I remember dialogues with him, of that year; one pleasant dialogue under the trees of the Park (where now, in 1851, is the thing called "Crystal Palace"), with the June sunset flinging long shadows for us; the last of the Quality just vanishing for dinner, and the great night beginning to prophesy of itself. Our talk (like that of the foregoing Letter) was of the faults of my style, of my way of thinking, of my &c. &c. ; all which admonitions and remonstrances, so friendly and innocent, from this young junior-senior, I was willing to listen to, though unable, as usual, to get almost any practical hold of them. As usual, the garments do not fit you, you are lost in the garments, or you cannot get into them at all; this is not your suit of clothes, it must be another's: —alas, these are not your dimensions, these are only the optical angles you subtend; on the whole, you will never get measured in that way! —

Another time, of date probably very contiguous, I remember hearing Sterling preach. It was in some new college-chapel in Somerset-house (I suppose, what is now called King's College); a very quiet small place, the audience student-looking youths, with a few elder people, perhaps mostly friends of the preacher's. The discourse, delivered with a grave sonorous composure, and far surpassing in talent the usual run of sermons, had withal an air of human veracity as I still recollect, and bespoke dignity and piety of mind: but gave me the impression rather of artistic excellence than of unction or inspiration in that kind. Sterling returned with us to Chelsea that day; —and in the afternoon we went on the Thames Putney-ward together, we two with my Wife; under the sunny skies, on the quiet water, and with copious cheery talk, the remembrance of which is still present enough to me.

This was properly my only specimen of Sterling's preaching. Another time, late in the same autumn, I did indeed attend him one evening to some Church in the City, —a big Church behind Cheapside, "built by Wren" as he carefully informed me; —but there, in my wearied mood, the chief subject of reflection was the almost total vacancy of the place, and how an eloquent soul was preaching to mere lamps and prayer-books; and of the sermon I retain no image. It came up in the way of banter, if he ever urged the duty of "Church extension, " which already he very seldom did and at length never, what a specimen we once had of bright lamps, gilt prayer-books, baize-lined pews, Wren-built architecture; and how, in almost all directions, you might have fired a musket through the church, and hit no Christian life. A terrible outlook indeed for the Apostolic laborer in the brick-and-mortar line! —

In the Autumn of this same 1835, he removed permanently to London, whither all summer he had been evidently tending; took a house in Bayswater, an airy suburb, half town, half country, near his Father's, and within fair distance of his other friends and objects; and decided to await there what the ultimate developments of his course might be. His house was in Orme Square, close by the corner of that little place (which has only *three* sides of houses); its windows looking to the east: the Number was, and I believe still is, No. 5. A sufficiently commodious, by no means sumptuous, small mansion; where, with the means sure to him, he could calculate on finding adequate shelter for his family, his books and himself, and live in a decent manner, in no terror of debt, for one thing. His income, I suppose, was not large; but he lived generally a safe distance within it; and showed himself always as a man bountiful in money matters, and taking no thought that way.

His study-room in this house was perhaps mainly the drawing-room; looking out safe, over the little dingy grassplot in front, and the quiet little row of houses opposite, with the huge dust-whirl of

Oxford Street and London far enough ahead of you as background, —as back-curtain, blotting out only *half* your blue hemisphere with dust and smoke. On the right, you had the continuous growl of the Uxbridge Road and its wheels, coming as lullaby not interruption. Leftward and rearward, after some thin belt of houses, lay mere country; bright sweeping green expanses, crowned by pleasant Hampstead, pleasant Harrow, with their rustic steeples rising against the sky. Here on winter evenings, the bustle of removal being all well ended, and family and books got planted in their new places, friends could find Sterling, as they often did, who was delighted to be found by them, and would give and take, vividly as few others, an hour's good talk at any time.

His outlooks, it must be admitted, were sufficiently vague and overshadowed; neither the past nor the future of a too joyful kind. Public life, in any professional form, is quite forbidden; to work with his fellows anywhere appears to be forbidden: nor can the humblest solitary endeavor to work worthily as yet find an arena. How unfold one's little bit of talent; and live, and not lie sleeping, while it is called To-day? As Radical, as Reforming Politician in any public or private form, —not only has this, in Sterling's case, received tragical sentence and execution; but the opposite extreme, the Church whither he had fled, likewise proves abortive: the Church also is not the haven for him at all. What is to be done? Something must be done, and soon, —under penalties. Whoever has received, on him there is an inexorable behest to give. "*Fais ton fait*, Do thy little stroke of work: " this is Nature's voice, and the sum of all the commandments, to each man!

A shepherd of the people, some small Agamemnon after his sort, doing what little sovereignty and guidance he can in his day and generation: such every gifted soul longs, and should long, to be. But how, in any measure, is the small kingdom necessary for Sterling to be attained? Not through newspapers and parliaments, not by rubrics and reading-desks: none of the sceptres offered in the world's market-place, nor none of the crosiers there, it seems, can be the shepherd's-crook for this man. A most cheerful, hoping man; and full of swift faculty, though much lamed, —considerably bewildered too; and tending rather towards the wastes and solitary places for a home; the paved world not being friendly to him hitherto! The paved world, in fact, both on its practical and spiritual side, slams to its doors against him; indicates that he cannot enter, and even must not, —that it will prove a choke-vault, deadly to soul and to body, if he enter. Sceptre, crosier, sheep-crook is none there for him.

There remains one other implement, the resource of all Adam's posterity that are otherwise foiled, —the Pen. It was evident from this point that Sterling, however otherwise beaten about, and set fluctuating, would gravitate steadily with all his real weight towards Literature. That he would gradually try with consciousness to get into Literature; and, on the whole, never quit Literature, which was now all the world for him. Such is accordingly the sum of his history henceforth: such small sum, so terribly obstructed and diminished by circumstances, is all we have realized from him.

Sterling had by no means as yet consciously quitted the clerical profession, far less the Church as a creed. We have seen, he occasionally officiated still in these months, when a friend requested or an opportunity invited. Nay it turned out afterwards, he had, unknown even to his own family, during a good many weeks in the coldest period of next spring, when it was really dangerous for his health and did prove hurtful to it, —been constantly performing the morning service in some Chapel in Bayswater for a young clerical neighbor, a slight acquaintance of his, who was sickly at the time. So far as I know, this of the Bayswater Chapel in the spring of 1836, a feat severely rebuked by his Doctor withal, was his last actual service as a churchman. But the conscious life ecclesiastical still hung visibly about his inner unconscious and real life, for years to come; and not till by slow degrees he had unwinded from him the wrappages of it, could he become clear about himself, and so much as try heartily what his now sole course was. Alas, and he had to live all the rest of his days, as in continual flight for his very existence; "ducking under like a poor unfledged partridge-bird, " as one described it, "before the mower; darting continually from nook to nook, and there crouching, to escape the scythe of Death. " For Literature Proper there was but little left in such a life. Only the smallest broken fractions of his last and heaviest-laden years can poor Sterling be said to have completely lived. His purpose had risen before him slowly in noble clearness; clear at last, —and even then the inevitable hour was at hand.

In those first London months, as always afterwards while it remained physically possible, I saw much of him; loved him, as was natural, more and more; found in him, many ways, a beautiful acquisition to my existence here. He was full of bright speech and argument; radiant with arrowy vitalities, vivacities and ingenuities. Less than any man he gave you the idea of ill-health. Hopeful, sanguine; nay he did not even seem to need definite hope, or much to form any; projecting himself in aerial pulses like an aurora borealis, like a summer dawn, and filling all the world with present brightness for himself and others. Ill-health? Nay you found at last, it was the very excess of *life* in him that brought on disease. This restless play of being, fit to conquer the world, could it have been held and guided, could not be held. It had worn *holes* in the outer case of it, and there found vent for itself, —there, since not otherwise.

In our many promenades and colloquies, which were of the freest, most copious and pleasant nature, religion often formed a topic, and perhaps towards the beginning of our intercourse was the prevailing topic. Sterling seemed much engrossed in matters theological, and led the conversation towards such; talked often about Church, Christianity Anglican and other, how essential the belief in it to man; then, on the other side, about Pantheism and such like; —all in the Coleridge dialect, and with eloquence and volubility to all lengths. I remember his insisting often and with emphasis on what he called a "personal God, " and other high topics, of which it was not always pleasant to give account in the argumentative form, in a loud hurried voice, walking and arguing through the fields or streets. Though of warm quick feelings, very positive in his opinions, and vehemently eager to convince and conquer in such discussions, I seldom or never saw the least anger in him against me or any friend. When the blows of contradiction came too thick, he could with consummate dexterity whisk aside out of their way; prick into his adversary on some new quarter; or gracefully flourishing his weapon, end the duel in some handsome manner. One angry glance I remember in him, and it was but a glance, and gone in a moment. "Flat Pantheism! " urged he once (which he would often enough do about this time), as if triumphantly, of something or other, in the fire of a debate, in my hearing: "It is mere Pantheism, that! " —"And suppose it were Pot-theism? " cried the other: "If the thing is true! " —Sterling did look hurt at such flippant heterodoxy, for a moment. The soul of his own creed, in those days, was far other than this indifference to Pot or Pan in such departments of inquiry.

To me his sentiments for most part were lovable and admirable, though in the logical outcome there was everywhere room for opposition. I admired the temper, the longing towards antique heroism, in this young man of the nineteenth century; but saw not how, except in some German-English empire of the air, he was ever to realize it on those terms. In fact, it became clear to me more and more that here was nobleness of heart striving towards all nobleness; here was ardent recognition of the worth of Christianity, for one thing; but no belief in it at all, in my sense of the word belief, —no belief but one definable as mere theoretic moonshine, which would never stand the wind and weather of fact. Nay it struck me farther that Sterling's was not intrinsically, nor had ever been in the highest or chief degree, a devotional mind. Of course all excellence in man, and worship as the supreme excellence, was part of the inheritance of this gifted man: but if called to define him, I should say, Artist not Saint was the real bent of his being. He had endless admiration, but intrinsically rather a deficiency of reverence in comparison. Fear, with its corollaries, on the religious side, he appeared to have none, nor ever to have had any.

In short, it was a strange enough symptom to me of the bewildered condition of the world, to behold a man of this temper, and of this veracity and nobleness, self-consecrated here, by free volition and deliberate selection, to be a Christian Priest; and zealously struggling to fancy himself such in very truth. Undoubtedly a singular present fact; —from which, as from their point of intersection, great perplexities and aberrations in the past, and considerable confusions in the future might be seen ominously radiating. Happily our friend, as I said, needed little hope. To-day with its activities was always bright and rich to him. His unmanageable, dislocated, devastated world, spiritual or economical, lay all illuminated in living sunshine, making it almost beautiful to his eyes, and gave him no hypochondria. A richer soul, in the way of natural outfit for felicity, for joyful activity in this world, so far as his strength would go, was nowhere to be met with.

The Letters which Mr. Hare has printed, Letters addressed, I imagine, mostly to himself, in this and the following year or two, give record of abundant changeful plannings and laborings, on the part of Sterling; still chiefly in the theological department. Translation from Tholuck, from Schleiermacher; treatise on this thing, then on that, are on the anvil: it is a life of abstruse vague speculations, singularly cheerful and hopeful withal, about Will, Morals, Jonathan Edwards, Jewhood, Manhood, and of Books to be written on these topics. Part of which adventurous vague plans, as the Translation from Tholuck, he actually performed; other greater part, merging always into wider undertakings, remained plan merely. I remember he talked often about Tholuck, Schleiermacher, and others of that stamp; and looked disappointed, though full of good nature, at my obstinate indifference to them and their affairs.

His knowledge of German Literature, very slight at this time, limited itself altogether to writers on Church matters, —Evidences, Counter-Evidences, Theologies and Rumors of Theologies; by the Tholucks, Schleiermachers, Neanders, and I know not whom. Of the true sovereign souls of that Literature, the Goethes, Richters, Schillers, Lessings, he had as good as no knowledge; and of Goethe in particular an obstinate misconception, with proper abhorrence appended, —which did not abate for several years, nor quite abolish itself till a very late period. Till, in a word, he got Goethe's works fairly read and studied for himself! This was often enough the course with Sterling in such cases. He had a most swift glance of recognition for the worthy and for the unworthy; and was prone, in his ardent decisive way, to put much faith in it. "Such a one is a worthless idol; not excellent, only sham-excellent: " here, on this negative side especially, you often had to admire how right he was; —often, but not quite always. And he would maintain, with endless ingenuity, confidence and persistence, his fallacious spectrum to be a real image. However, it was sure to come all right in the end. Whatever real excellence he might misknow, you had but to let it stand before him, soliciting new examination from him: none surer than he to recognize it at last, and to pay it all his dues, with the arrears and interest on them. Goethe, who figures as some absurd high-stalking hollow play-actor, or empty ornamental clock-case of an "Artist" so-called, in the Tale of the *Onyx Ring*, was in the throne of Sterling's intellectual world before all was done; and the theory of "Goethe's want of feeling, " want of &c. &c. appeared to him also abundantly contemptible and forgettable.

Sterling's days, during this time as always, were full of occupation, cheerfully interesting to himself and others; though, the wrecks of theology so encumbering him, little fruit on the positive side could come of these labors. On the negative side they were productive; and there also, so much of encumbrance requiring removal, before fruit could grow, there was plenty of labor needed. He looked happy as well as busy; roamed extensively among his friends, and loved to have them about him, —chiefly old Cambridge comrades now settling into occupations in the world; —and was felt by all friends, by myself as by few, to be a welcome illumination in the dim whirl of things. A man of altogether social and human ways; his address everywhere pleasant and enlivening. A certain smile of thin but genuine laughter, we might say, hung gracefully over all he said and did; —expressing gracefully, according to the model of this epoch, the stoical pococurantism which is required of the cultivated Englishman. Such laughter in him was not deep, but neither was it false (as lamentably happens often); and the cheerfulness it went to symbolize was hearty and beautiful, —visible in the silent unsymbolized state in a still gracefuler fashion.

Of wit, so far as rapid lively intellect produces wit, he had plenty, and did not abuse his endowment that way, being always fundamentally serious in the purport of his speech: of what we call humor, he had some, though little; nay of real sense for the ludicrous, in any form, he had not much for a man of his vivacity; and you remarked that his laugh was limited in compass, and of a clear but not rich quality. To the like effect shone something, a kind of childlike half-embarrassed shimmer of expression, on his fine vivid countenance; curiously mingling with its ardors and audacities. A beautiful childlike soul! He was naturally a favorite in conversation, especially with all who had any funds for conversing: frank and direct, yet polite and delicate withal, —though at times too he could crackle with his dexterous petulancies, making the air all like needles round you; and there was no end to his logic when you excited it; no end, unless in some form of silence on your part. Elderly men of reputation I have sometimes known offended by him: for he took a frank way in the matter of talk; spoke freely out of him, freely listening to what others spoke, with a kind of "hail fellow well met" feeling; and carelessly measured a men much less by his reputed account in the bank of wit, or in any other bank, than by what the man had to show for himself in the shape of real spiritual cash on the occasion. But withal there was ever a fine element of natural courtesy in Sterling; his deliberate demeanor to acknowledged superiors was fine and graceful; his apologies and the like, when in a fit of repentance he felt commanded to apologize, were full of naivete, and very pretty and ingenuous.

His circle of friends was wide enough; chiefly men of his own standing, old College friends many of them; some of whom have now become universally known. Among whom the most important to him was Frederic Maurice, who had not long before removed to the Chaplaincy of Guy's Hospital here, and was still, as he had long been, his intimate and counsellor. Their views and articulate opinions, I suppose, were now fast beginning to diverge; and these went on diverging far enough: but in their kindly union, in their perfect trustful familiarity, precious to both parties, there never was the least break, but a steady, equable and duly increasing current to the end. One of Sterling's commonest expeditions, in this time, was a sally to the other side of London Bridge: "Going to Guy's to-day. " Maurice, in a year or two, became Sterling's brother-in-law; wedded Mrs. Sterling's younger sister, —a gentle excellent female soul; by whom the relation was, in many ways, strengthened and beautified for Sterling and all friends of the parties. With the Literary notabilities I think he had no acquaintance; his thoughts indeed still tended rather towards a certain class of the Clerical; but neither had he much to do with these; for he was at no time the least of a tuft-hunter, but rather had a marked natural indifference to *tufts*.

The Rev. Mr. Dunn, a venerable and amiable Irish gentleman, "distinguished, " we were told, "by having refused a bishopric: " and who was now living, in an opulent enough retirement, amid his books and philosophies and friends, in London, —is memorable to me among this clerical class: one of the mildest, beautifulest old men I have ever seen, —"like Fenelon, " Sterling said: his very face, with its kind true smile, with its look of suffering cheerfulness and pious wisdom, was a sort of benediction. It is of him that Sterling writes, in the Extract which Mr. Hare, modestly reducing the name to an initial "Mr. D., " has given us: [13] "Mr. Dunn, for instance; the defect of whose Theology, compounded as it is of the doctrine of the Greek Fathers, of the Mystics and of Ethical Philosophers, consists, —if I may hint a fault in one whose holiness, meekness and fervor would have made him the beloved disciple of him whom Jesus loved, —in an insufficient apprehension of the reality and depth of Sin. " A characteristic "defect" of this fine gentle soul. On Mr. Dunn's death, which occurred two or three years later, Stirling gave, in some veiled yet transparent form, in *Blackwood's Magazine,* an affectionate and eloquent notice of him; which, stript of the veil, was excerpted into the Newspapers also. [14]

Of Coleridge there was little said. Coleridge was now dead, not long since; nor was his name henceforth much heard in Sterling's circle; though on occasion, for a year or two to come, he would still assert his transcendent admiration, especially if Maurice were by to help. But he was getting into German, into various inquiries and sources of knowledge new to him, and his admirations and notions on many things were silently and rapidly modifying themselves.

So, amid interesting human realities, and wide cloud-canopies of uncertain speculation, which also had their interests and their rainbow-colors to him, and could not fail in his life just now, did Sterling pass his year and half at Bayswater. Such vaporous speculations were inevitable for him at present; but it was to be hoped they would subside by and by, and leave the sky clear. All this was but the preliminary to whatever work might lie in him: — and, alas, much other interruption lay between him and that.

CHAPTER V.
TO MADEIRA.

Sterling's dubieties as to continuing at Bordeaux were quickly decided. The cholera in France, the cholera in Nice, the— In fact his moorings were now loose; and having been fairly at sea, he never could anchor himself here again. Very shortly after this Letter, he left Belsito again (for good, as it proved); and returned to England with his household, there to consider what should next be done.

On my return from Scotland, that year, perhaps late in September, I remember finding him lodged straitly but cheerfully, and in happy humor, in a little cottage on Blackheath; whither his Father one day persuaded me to drive out with him for dinner. Our welcome, I can still recollect, was conspicuously cordial; the place of dinner a kind of upper room, half garret and full of books, which seemed to be John's place of study. From a shelf, I remember also, the good soul took down a book modestly enough bound in three volumes, lettered on the back Carlyle's *French Revolution*, which had been published lately; this he with friendly banter bade me look at as a first symptom, small but significant, that the book was not to die all at once. "One copy of it at least might hope to last the date of sheep-leather, " I admitted, —and in my then mood the little fact was welcome. Our dinner, frank and happy on the part of Sterling, was peppered with abundant jolly satire from his Father: before tea, I took myself away; towards Woolwich, I remember, where probably there was another call to make, and passage homeward by steamer: Sterling strode along with me a good bit of road in the bright sunny evening, full of lively friendly talk, and altogether kind and amiable; and beautifully sympathetic with the loads he thought he saw on *me*, forgetful of his own. We shook hands on the road near the foot of Shooter's Hill: —at which point dim oblivious clouds rush down; and of small or great I remember nothing more in my history or his for some time.

Besides running much about among friends, and holding counsels for the management of the coming winter, Sterling was now considerably occupied with Literature again; and indeed may be said to have already definitely taken it up as the one practical pursuit left for him. Some correspondence with *Blackwood's Magazine* was opening itself, under promising omens: now, and more and more henceforth, he began to look on Literature as his real employment, after all; and was prosecuting it with his accustomed loyalty and ardor. And he continued ever afterwards, in spite of such fitful circumstances and uncertain outward fluctuations as his were sure of being, to prosecute it steadily with all the strength he had.

One evening about this time, he came down to us, to Chelsea, most likely by appointment and with stipulation for privacy; and read, for our opinion, his Poem of the *Sexton's Daughter*, which we now first heard of. The judgment in this house was friendly, but not the most encouraging. We found the piece monotonous, cast in the mould of Wordsworth, deficient in real human fervor or depth of melody, dallying on the borders of the infantile and "goody-good; "—in fact, involved still in the shadows of the surplice, and inculcating (on hearsay mainly) a weak morality, which he would one day find not to be moral at all, but in good part maudlin-hypocritical and immoral. As indeed was to be said still of most of his performances, especially the poetical; a sickly *shadow* of the parish-church still hanging over them, which he could by no means recognize for sickly. *Imprimatur* nevertheless was the concluding word, —with these grave abatements, and rhadamanthine admonitions. To all which Sterling listened seriously and in the mildest humor. His reading, it might have been added, had much hurt the effect of the piece: a dreary pulpit or even conventicle manner; that flattest moaning hoo-hoo of predetermined pathos, with a kind of rocking canter introduced by way of intonation, each stanza the exact fellow Of the other, and the dull swing of the rocking-horse duly in each; — no reading could be more unfavorable to Sterling's poetry than his own. Such a mode of reading, and indeed generally in a man of such vivacity the total absence of all gifts for play-acting or artistic mimicry in any kind, was a noticeable point.

After much consultation, it was settled at last that Sterling should go to Madeira for the winter. One gray dull autumn afternoon, towards the middle of October, I remember walking with him to the eastern Dock region, to see his ship, and how the final preparations in his own little cabin were proceeding there. A dingy little ship, the deck crowded with packages, and bustling sailors within eight-and-forty hours of lifting anchor; a dingy chill smoky day, as I have said withal, and a chaotic element and outlook, enough to make a friend's heart sad. I admired the cheerful careless humor and brisk activity of Sterling, who took the matter all on the sunny side, as he was wont in such cases. We came home together in manifold talk: he accepted with the due smile my last contribution to his sea-equipment, a sixpenny box of German lucifers purchased on the sudden in St. James's Street, fit to be offered with laughter or with tears or with both; he was to leave for Portsmouth almost immediately, and there go on board. Our next news was of his safe arrival in the temperate Isle. Mrs. Sterling and the children were left at Knightsbridge; to pass this winter with his Father and Mother.

At Madeira Sterling did well: improved in health; was busy with much Literature; and fell in with society which he could reckon pleasant. He was much delighted with the scenery of the place; found the climate wholesome to him in a marked degree; and, with good news from home, and kindly interests here abroad, passed no disagreeable winter in that exile. There was talking, there was writing, there was hope of better health; he rode almost daily, in cheerful busy humor, along those fringed shore-roads: —beautiful leafy roads and horse-paths; with here and there a wild cataract and bridge to look at; and always with the soft sky overhead, the dead volcanic mountain on one hand, and broad illimitable sea spread out on the other. Here are two Letters which give reasonably good account of him: —

> *"To Thomas Carlyle, Esq., Chelsea, London.*
> "FUNCHAL, MADEIRA, 16th November, 1837.

"MY DEAR CARLYLE, —I have been writing a good many letters all in a batch, to go by the same opportunity; and I am thoroughly weary of writing the same things over and over again to different people. My letter to you therefore, I fear, must have much of the character of remainder-biscuit. But you will receive it as a proof that I do not wish you to forget me, though it may be useless for any other purpose.

"I reached this on the 2d, after a tolerably prosperous voyage, deformed by some days of sea-sickness, but otherwise not to be complained of. I liked my twenty fellow-passengers far better than I expected; —three or four of them I like much, and continue to see frequently. The Island too is better than I expected: so that my Barataria at least does not disappoint me. The bold rough mountains, with mist about their summits, verdure below, and a bright sun over all, please me much; and I ride daily on the steep and narrow paved roads, which no wheels ever journeyed on. The Town is clean, and there its merits end: but I am comfortably lodged; with a large and pleasant sitting-room to myself. I have met with much kindness; and see all the society I want, —though it is not quite equal to that of London, even excluding Chelsea.

"I have got about me what Books I brought out; and have read a little, and done some writing for *Blackwood*, —all, I have the pleasure to inform you, prose, nay extremely prose. I shall now be more at leisure; and hope to get more steadily to work; though I do not know what I shall begin upon. As to reading, I have been looking at *Goethe*, especially the *Life*, —much as a shying horse looks at a post. In truth, I am afraid of him. I enjoy and admire him so much, and feel I could so easily be tempted to go along with him. And yet I have a deeply rooted and old persuasion that he was the most splendid of anachronisms. A thoroughly, nay intensely Pagan Life, in an age when it is men's duty to be Christian. I therefore never take him up without a kind of inward check, as if I were trying some forbidden spell; while, on the other hand, there is so infinitely much to be learnt from him, and it is so needful to understand the world we live in, and our own age, and especially its greatest minds, that I cannot bring myself to burn my books as the converted Magicians did, or sink them as did Prospero. There must, as I think, have been some prodigious defect in his mind, to let him hold such views as his about women and some other things; and in another respect, I find so much coldness and hollowness as to the highest truths, and feel so strongly that the Heaven he looks up to is but a vault of ice, —that these two indications, leading to the same conclusion, go far to convince me he was a profoundly immoral and irreligious spirit, with as rare faculties of intelligence as ever belonged to any one. All this may be mere *goody* weakness and twaddle, on my part: but it is a persuasion that I cannot escape from; though I should feel the doing so to be a deliverance from a most painful load. If you could help me, I heartily wish you would. I never take him up without high admiration, or lay him down without real sorrow for what he chose to be.

"I have been reading nothing else that you would much care for. Southey's *Amadis* has amused me; and Lyell's *Geology* interested me. The latter gives one the same sort of bewildering view of the abysmal extent of Time that Astronomy does of Space. I do not think I shall take your advice as to learning Portuguese. It is said to be very ill spoken here; and assuredly it is the most direful series of nasal twangs I ever heard. One gets on quite well with English.

"The people here are, I believe, in a very low condition; but they do not appear miserable. I am told that the influence of the priests makes the peasantry all Miguelites; but it is said that nobody wants any more revolutions. There is no appearance of riot or crime; and they are all extremely civil. I was much interested by learning that Columbus once lived here, before he found America and fame. I have been to see a deserted *quinta* (country-house), where there is a great deal of curious old sculpture, in relief, upon the masonry; many of the figures, which are nearly as large as life, representing soldiers clad and armed much as I should suppose those of Cortez were. There are no buildings about the Town, of the smallest pretensions to beauty or charm of any kind. On the whole, if Madeira were one's world, life would certainly rather tend to stagnate; but as a temporary refuge, a niche in an old ruin where one is sheltered from the shower, it has great merit. I am more comfortable and contented than I expected to be, so far from home and from everybody I am closely connected with: but, of course, it is at best a tolerable exile.

"Tell Mrs. Carlyle that I have written, since I have been here, and am going to send to *Blackwood*, a humble imitation of her *Watch and Canary-Bird*, entitled *The Suit of Armor and the Skeleton*. [15] I am conscious that I am far from having reached the depth and fulness of despair and mockery which distinguish the original! But in truth there is a lightness of tone about her style, which I hold to be invaluable: where she makes hairstrokes, I make blotches. I have a vehement suspicion that my Dialogue is an entire failure; but I cannot be plagued with it any longer. Tell her I will not send her messages, but will write to her soon. —Meanwhile I am affectionately hers and yours,

"JOHN STERLING. "

The next is to his Brother-in-law; and in a still hopefuler tone: —

"*To Charles Barton, Esq.* [16]
FUNCHAL, MADEIRA, 3d March, 1838.

"MY DEAR CHARLES, —I have often been thinking of you and your whereabouts in Germany, and wishing I knew more about you; and at last it occurred to me that you might perhaps have the same wish about me, and that therefore I should do well to write to you.

"I have been here exactly four months, having arrived on the 2d of November, —my wedding-day; and though you perhaps may not think it a compliment to Susan, I have seldom passed four months more cheerfully and agreeably. I have of course felt my absence from my family, and missed the society of my friends; for there is not a person here whom I knew before I left England. But, on the whole, I have been in good health, and actively employed. I have a good many agreeable and valuable acquaintances, one or two of whom I hope I may hereafter reckon as friends. The weather has generally been fine, and never cold; and the scenery of the Island is of a beauty which you unhappy Northern people can have little conception of.

"It consists of a great mass of volcanic mountains, covered in their lower parts with cottages, vines and patches of vegetables. When you pass through, or over the central ridge, and get towards the North, there are woods of trees, of the laurel kind, covering the wild steep slopes, and forming some of the strangest and most beautiful prospects I have ever seen. Towards the interior, the forms of the hills become more abrupt, and loftier; and give the notion of very recent volcanic disturbances, though in fact there has been nothing of the kind since the discovery of the Island by Europeans. Among these mountains, the dark deep precipices, and narrow ravines with small streams at the bottom; the basaltic knobs and ridges on the summits; and the perpetual play of mist and cloud around them, under this bright sun and clear sky, —form landscapes which you would thoroughly enjoy, and which I much wish I could give you a notion of. The Town is on the south, and of course the sheltered side of the Island; perfectly protected from the North and East; although we have seen sometimes patches of bright snow on the dark peaks in the distance. It is a neat cheerful place; all built of gray stone, but having many of the houses colored white or red. There is not a really handsome building in it, but there is a general aspect of comfort and solidity. The shops are very poor. The English do not mix at all with the Portuguese. The Bay is a very bad anchorage; but is wide, bright and cheerful; and there are some picturesque points—one a small black island—scattered about it.

"I lived till a fortnight ago in lodgings, having two rooms, one a very good one; and paying for everything fifty-six dollars a month, the dollar being four shillings and twopence. This you will see is dear; but I could make no better arrangement, for there is an unusual affluence of strangers this year. I have now come to live with a friend, a Dr. Calvert, in a small house of our own, where I am much more comfortable, and live greatly cheaper. He is a friend of Mrs. Percival's; about my age, an Oriel man, and a very superior person. I think the chances are, we shall go home together.... I cannot tell you of all the other people I have become familiar with; and shall only mention in addition Bingham Baring, eldest son of Lord Ashburton, who was here for some weeks on account of a dying brother, and whom I saw a great deal of. He is a pleasant, very good-natured and rather clever man; Conservative Member for North Staffordshire.

"During the first two months I was here, I rode a great deal about the Island, having a horse regularly; and was much in agreeable company, seeing a great deal of beautiful scenery. Since then, the weather has been much more unsettled, though not cold; and I have gone about less, as I cannot risk the being wet. But I have spent my time pleasantly, reading and writing. I have written a good many things for *Blackwood*; one of which, the *Armor and the Skeleton*, I see is printed in the February Number. I have just sent them a long Tale, called the *Onyx Ring*, which cost me a good deal of trouble; and the extravagance of which, I think, would amuse you; but its length may prevent its appearance in *Blackwood*. If so, I think I should make a volume of it. I have also written some poems, and shall probably publish the *Sexton's Daughter* when I return.

"My health goes on most favorably. I have had no attack of the chest this spring; which has not happened to me since the spring before we went to Bonn; and I am told, if I take care, I may roll along for years. But I have little hope of being allowed to spend the four first months of any year in England; and the question will be, Whether to go at once to Italy, by way of Germany and Switzerland, with my family, or to settle with them in England, perhaps at Hastings, and go abroad myself when it may be necessary. I cannot decide till I return; but I think the latter the most probable.

"To my dear Charles I do not like to use the ordinary forms of ending a letter, for they are very inadequate to express my sense of your long and most unvarying kindness; but be assured no one living could say with more sincerity that he is ever affectionately yours,

"JOHN STERLING. "

Other Letters give occasionally views of the shadier side of things: dark broken weather, in the sky and in the mind; ugly clouds covering one's poor fitful transitory prospect, for a time, as they might well do in Sterling's case. Meanwhile we perceive his literary business is fast developing itself; amid all his confusions, he is never idle long. Some of his best Pieces—the Onyx *Ring*, for one, as we perceive—were written here this winter. Out of the turbid whirlpool of the days he strives assiduously to snatch what he can.

Sterling's communications with *Blackwood's Magazine* had now issued in some open sanction of him by Professor Wilson, the distinguished presiding spirit of that Periodical; a fact naturally of high importance to him under the literary point of view. For Wilson, with his clear flashing eye and great genial heart, had at once recognized Sterling; and lavished stormily, in his wild generous way, torrents of praise on him in the editorial comments: which undoubtedly was one of the gratefulest literary baptisms, by fire or by water, that could befall a soul like Sterling's. He bore it very gently, being indeed past the age to have his head turned by anybody's praises: nor do I think the exaggeration that was in these eulogies did him any ill whatever; while surely their generous encouragement did him much good, in his solitary struggle towards new activity under such impediments as his. *Laudari a laudato*; to be called noble by one whom you and the world recognize as noble: this great satisfaction, never perhaps in such a degree before or after had now been vouchsafed to Sterling; and was, as I compute, an important fact for him. He proceeded on his pilgrimage with new energy, and felt more and more as if authentically consecrated to the same.

The *Onyx Ring*, a curious Tale, with wild improbable basis, but with a noble glow of coloring and with other high merits in it, a Tale still worth reading, in which, among the imaginary characters, various friends of Sterling's are shadowed forth, not always in the truest manner, came out in *Blackwood* in the winter of this year. Surely a very high talent for painting, both of scenery and persons, is visible in this Fiction; the promise of a Novel such as we have few. But there wants maturing, wants purifying of clear from unclear; —properly there want patience and steady depth. The basis, as we said, is wild and loose; and in the details, lucent often with fine color, and dipt in beautiful sunshine, there are several things mis*seen*, untrue, which is the worst species of mispainting. Witness, as Sterling himself would have by and by admitted, the "empty clockcase" (so we called it) which he has labelled Goethe, —which puts all other untruths in the Piece to silence.

One of the great alleviations of his exile at Madeira he has already celebrated to us: the pleasant circle of society he fell into there. Great luck, thinks Sterling in this voyage; as indeed there was: but he himself, moreover, was readier than most men to fall into pleasant circles everywhere, being singularly prompt to make the most of any circle. Some of his Madeira acquaintanceships were really good; and one of them, if not more, ripened into comradeship and friendship for him. He says, as we saw, "The chances are, Calvert and I will come home together."

Among the English in pursuit of health, or in flight from fatal disease, that winter, was this Dr. Calvert; an excellent ingenious cheery Cumberland gentleman, about Sterling's age, and in a deeper stage of ailment, this not being his first visit to Madeira: he, warmly joining himself to Sterling, as we have seen, was warmly received by him; so that there soon grew a close and free intimacy between them; which for the next three years, till poor Calvert ended his course, was a leading element in the history of both. Companionship in incurable malady, a touching bond of union, was by no means purely or chiefly a companionship in misery in their case. The sunniest inextinguishable cheerfulness shone, through all manner of clouds, in both. Calvert had been travelling physician in some family of rank, who had rewarded him with a pension, shielding his own ill-health from one sad evil. Being hopelessly gone in pulmonary disorder, he now moved about among friendly climates and places, seeking what alleviation there might be; often spending his summers in the house of a sister in the environs of London; an insatiable rider on his little brown pony; always, wherever you might meet him, one of the cheeriest of men. He had plenty of speculation too, clear glances of all kinds into religious, social, moral concerns; and pleasantly incited Sterling's outpourings on such subjects. He could report of fashionable persons and manners, in a fine human Cumberland manner; loved art, a great collector of drawings; he had endless help and ingenuity; and was in short every way a very human, lovable, good and nimble man, —the laughing blue eyes of him, the clear cheery soul of him, still redolent of the fresh Northern breezes and transparent Mountain streams. With this Calvert, Sterling formed a natural intimacy; and they were to each other a great possession, mutually enlivening many a dark day during the next three years. They did come home together this spring; and subsequently made several of these health-journeys in partnership.

CHAPTER VI.
LITERATURE: THE STERLING CLUB.

In spite of these wanderings, Sterling's course in life, so far as his poor life could have any course or aim beyond that of screening itself from swift death, was getting more and more clear to him; and he pursued it diligently, in the only way permitted him, by hasty snatches, in the intervals of continual fluctuation, change of place and other interruption.

Such, once for all, were the conditions appointed him. And it must be owned he had, with a most kindly temper, adjusted himself to these; nay you would have said, he loved them; it was almost as if he would have chosen them as the suitablest. Such an adaptation was there in him of volition to necessity: —for indeed they both, if well seen into, proceeded from one source. Sterling's bodily disease was the expression, under physical conditions, of the too vehement life which, under the moral, the intellectual and other aspects, incessantly struggled within him. Too vehement; —which would have required a frame of oak and iron to contain it: in a thin though most wiry body of flesh and bone, it incessantly "wore holes, " and so found outlet for itself. He could take no rest, he had never learned that art; he was, as we often reproached him, fatally incapable of sitting still. Rapidity, as of pulsing auroras, as of dancing lightnings: rapidity in all forms characterized him. This, which was his bane, in many senses, being the real origin of his disorder, and of such continual necessity to move and change, —was also his antidote, so far as antidote there might be; enabling him to love change, and to snatch, as few others could have done, from the waste chaotic years, all tumbled into ruin by incessant change, what hours and minutes of available turned up. He had an incredible facility of labor. He flashed with most piercing glance into a subject; gathered it up into organic utterability, with truly wonderful despatch, considering the success and truth attained; and threw it on paper with a swift felicity, ingenuity, brilliancy and general excellence, of which, under such conditions of swiftness, I have never seen a parallel. Essentially an *improviser* genius; as his Father too was, and of admirable completeness he too, though under a very different form.

If Sterling has done little in Literature, we may ask, What other man than he, in such circumstances, could have done anything? In virtue of these rapid faculties, which otherwise cost him so dear, he has built together, out of those wavering boiling quicksands of his few later years, a result which may justly surprise us. There is actually some result in those poor Two Volumes gathered from him, such as they are; he that reads there will not wholly lose his time, nor rise with a malison instead of a blessing on the writer. Here actually is a real seer-glance, of some compass, into the world of our day; blessed glance, once more, of an eye that is human; truer than one of a thousand, and beautifully capable of making others see with it. I have known considerable temporary reputations gained, considerable piles of temporary guineas, with loud reviewing and the like to match, on a far less basis than lies in those two volumes. Those also, I expect, will be held in memory by the world, one way or other, till the world has extracted all its benefit from them. Graceful, ingenious and illuminative reading, of their sort, for all manner of inquiring souls. A little verdant flowery island of poetic intellect, of melodious human verity; sunlit island founded on the rocks; —which the enormous circumambient continents of mown reed-grass and floating lumber, with *their* mountain-ranges of ejected stable-litter however alpine, cannot by any means or chance submerge: nay, I expect, they will not even quite hide it, this modest little island, from the well-discerning; but will float past it towards the place appointed for them, and leave said island standing. *Allah kereem,* say the Arabs! And of the English also some still know that there is a, difference in the material of mountains! —

As it is this last little result, the amount of his poor and ever-interrupted literary labor, that henceforth forms the essential history of Sterling, we need not dwell at too much length on the foreign journeys, disanchorings, and nomadic vicissitudes of household, which occupy his few remaining years, and which are only the disastrous and accidental arena of this. He had now, excluding his early and more deliberate residence in the West Indies, made two flights abroad, once with his family, once without, in search of health. He had two more, in rapid succession, to make, and many more to meditate; and in the whole from Bayswater to the end, his family made no fewer than five complete changes of abode, for his sake. But these cannot be accepted as in any sense epochs in his life: the one last epoch of his life was that of his internal change towards Literature as his work in the world; and we need not linger much on these, which are the mere outer accidents of that, and had no distinguished influence in modifying that.

Friends still hoped the unrest of that brilliant too rapid soul would abate with years. Nay the doctors sometimes promised, on the physical side, a like result; prophesying that, at forty-five or some mature age, the stress of disease might quit the lungs, and direct itself to other quarters of the system. But no such result was appointed for us; neither forty-five itself, nor the ameliorations promised then, were ever to be reached. Four voyages abroad, three of them without his family, in flight from death; and at home, for a like reason, five complete shiftings of abode: in such wandering manner, and not otherwise, had Sterling to continue his pilgrimage till it ended.

Once more I must say, his cheerfulness throughout was wonderful. A certain grimmer shade, coming gradually over him, might perhaps be noticed in the concluding years; not impatience properly, yet the consciousness how much he needed patience; something more caustic in his tone of wit, more trenchant and indignant occasionally in his tone of speech: but at no moment was his activity bewildered or abated, nor did his composure ever give way. No; both his activity and his composure he bore with him, through all weathers, to the final close; and on the whole, right manfully he walked his wild stern way towards the goal, and like a Roman wrapt his mantle round him when he fell. —Let us glance, with brevity, at what he saw and suffered in his remaining pilgrimings and chargings; and count up what fractions of spiritual fruit he realized to us from them.

Calvert and he returned from Madeira in the spring of 1838. Mrs. Sterling and the family had lived in Knightsbridge with his Father's people through the winter: they now changed to Blackheath, or ultimately Hastings, and he with them, coming up to London pretty often; uncertain what was to be done for next winter. Literature went on briskly here: *Blackwood* had from him, besides the *Onyx Ring* which soon came out with due honor, assiduous almost monthly contributions in prose and verse. The series called *Hymns of a Hermit* was now going on; eloquent melodies, tainted to me with something of the same disease as the *Sexton's Daughter*, though perhaps in a less degree, considering that the strain was in a so much higher pitch. Still better, in clear eloquent prose, the series of detached thoughts, entitled *Crystals from a Cavern*; of which the set of fragments, generally a little larger in compass, called *Thoughts and Images*, and again those called *Sayings and Essayings*, [17] are properly continuations. Add to which, his friend John Mill had now charge of a Review, *The London and Westminster* its name; wherein Sterling's assistance, ardently desired, was freely afforded, with satisfaction to both parties, in this and the following years. An Essay on *Montaigne*, with the notes and reminiscences already spoken of, was Sterling's first contribution here; then one on *Simonides*: [18] both of the present season.

On these and other businesses, slight or important, he was often running up to London; and gave us almost the feeling of his being resident among us. In order to meet the most or a good many of his friends at once on such occasions, he now furthermore contrived the scheme of a little Club, where monthly over a frugal dinner some reunion might take place; that is, where friends of his, and withal such friends of theirs as suited, —and in fine, where a small select company definable as persons to whom it was pleasant to talk together, —might have a little opportunity of talking. The scheme was approved by the persons concerned: I have a copy of the Original Regulations, probably drawn up by Sterling, a very solid lucid piece of economics; and the List of the proposed Members, signed "James Spedding, Secretary, " and dated "8th August, 1838. "[19] The Club grew; was at first called the *Anonymous Club*; then, after some months of success, in compliment to the founder who had now left us again, the *Sterling Club*; —under which latter name, it once lately, for a time, owing to the Religious Newspapers, became rather famous in the world! In which strange circumstances the name was again altered, to suit weak brethren; and the Club still subsists, in a sufficiently flourishing though happily once more a private condition. That is the origin and genesis of poor Sterling's Club; which, having honestly paid the shot for itself at Will's Coffee-house or elsewhere, rashly fancied its bits of affairs were quite settled; and once little thought of getting into Books of History with them! —

But now, Autumn approaching, Sterling had to quit Clubs, for matters of sadder consideration. A new removal, what we call "his third peregrinity, " had to be decided on; and it was resolved that Rome should be the goal of it, the journey to be done in company with Calvert, whom also the Italian climate might be made to serve instead of Madeira. One of the liveliest recollections I have, connected with the *Anonymous Club*, is that of once escorting Sterling, after a certain meeting there, which I had seen only towards the end, and now remember nothing of, —except that, on breaking up, he proved to be encumbered with a carpet-bag, and could not at once find a cab for Knightsbridge. Some small bantering hereupon, during the instants of embargo. But we carried his carpet-bag, slinging it on my stick, two or three of us alternately, through dusty vacant streets, under the gaslights and the stars, towards the surest cab-stand; still jesting, or pretending to jest, he and we, not in the mirthfulest manner; and had (I suppose) our own feelings about the poor Pilgrim, who was to go on the morrow, and had hurried to meet us in this way, as the last thing before leaving England.

CHAPTER VII.
ITALY.

The journey to Italy was undertaken by advice of Sir James Clark, reckoned the chief authority in pulmonary therapeutics; who prophesied important improvements from it, and perhaps even the possibility henceforth of living all the year in some English home. Mrs. Sterling and the children continued in a house avowedly temporary, a furnished house at Hastings, through the winter. The two friends had set off for Belgium, while the due warmth was still in the air. They traversed Belgium, looking well at pictures and such objects; ascended the Rhine; rapidly traversed Switzerland and the Alps; issuing upon Italy and Milan, with immense appetite for pictures, and time still to gratify themselves in that pursuit, and be deliberate in their approach to Rome. We will take this free-flowing sketch of their passage over the Alps; written amid "the rocks of Arona, " —Santo Borromeo's country, and poor little Mignon's! The "elder Perdonnets" are opulent Lausanne people, to whose late son Sterling had been very kind in Madeira the year before: —

"*To Mrs. Sterling, Knightsbridge, London.*
"ARONA on the LAGO MAGGIORE, 8th Oct., 1838.

"MY DEAR MOTHER, —I bring down the story of my proceedings to the present time since the 29th of September. I think it must have been after that day that I was at a great breakfast at the elder Perdonnets', with whom I had declined to dine, not choosing to go out at night.... I was taken by my hostess to see several pretty pleasure-grounds and points of view in the neighborhood; and latterly Calvert was better, and able to go with us. He was in force again, and our passports were all settled so as to enable us to start on the morning of the 2d, after taking leave of our kind entertainer with thanks for her infinite kindness.

"We reached St. Maurice early that evening; having had the Dent du Midi close to us for several hours; glittering like the top of a silver teapot, far up in the sky. Our course lay along the Valley of the Rhone; which is considered one of the least beautiful parts of Switzerland, and perhaps for this reason pleased us, as we had not been prepared to expect much. We saw, before reaching the foot of the Alpine pass at Brieg, two rather celebrated Waterfalls; the one the Pissevache, which has no more beauty than any waterfall one hundred or two hundred feet high must necessarily have: the other, near Tourtemagne, is much more pleasing, having foliage round it, and being in a secluded dell. If you buy a Swiss Waterfall, choose this one.

"Our second day took us through Martigny to Sion, celebrated for its picturesque towers upon detached hills, for its strong Romanism and its population of *cretins*, —that is, maimed idiots having the *goitre*. It looked to us a more thriving place than we expected. They are building a great deal; among other things, a new Bishop's Palace and a new Nunnery, —to inhabit either of which *ex officio* I feel myself very unsuitable. From Sion we came to Brieg; a little village in a nook, close under an enormous mountain and glacier, where it lies like a molehill, or something smaller, at the foot of a haystack. Here also we slept; and the next day our voiturier, who had brought us from Lausanne, started with us up the Simplon Pass; helped on by two extra horses.

"The beginning of the road was rather cheerful; having a good deal of green pasturage, and some mountain villages; but it soon becomes dreary and savage in aspect, and but for our bright sky and warm air, would have been truly dismal. However, we gained gradually a distinct and near view of several large glaciers; and reached at last the high and melancholy valleys of the Upper Alps; where even the pines become scanty, and no sound is heard but the wheels of one's carriage, except when there happens to be a storm or an avalanche, neither of which entertained us. There is, here and there, a small stream of water pouring from the snow; but this is rather a monotonous accompaniment to the general desolation than an interruption of it. The road itself is certainly very good, and impresses one with a strong notion of human power. But the common descriptions are much exaggerated; and many of what the Guide-Books call 'galleries' are merely parts of the road supported by a wall built against the rock, and have nothing like a roof above them. The 'stupendous bridges, ' as they are called, might be packed, a dozen together, into one arch of London Bridge; and they are seldom even very striking from the depth below. The roadway is excellent, and kept in the best order. On the whole, I am very glad to have travelled the most famous road in Europe, and to have had delightful weather for doing so, as indeed we have had ever since we left Lausanne. The Italian descent is greatly more remarkable than the other side.

"We slept near the top, at the Village of Simplon, in a very fair and well-warmed inn, close to a mountain stream, which is one of the great ornaments of this side of the road. We have here passed into a region of granite, from that of limestone, and what is called gneiss. The valleys are sharper and closer, —like cracks in a hard and solid mass; —and there is much more of the startling contrast of light and shade, as well as more angular boldness of outline; to all which the more abundant waters add a fresh and vivacious interest. Looking back through one of these abysmal gorges, one sees two torrents dashing together, the precipice and ridge on one side, pitch-black with shade; and that on the other all flaming gold; while behind rises, in a huge cone, one of the glacier summits of the chain. The stream at one's feet rushes at a leap some two hundred feet down, and is bordered with pines and beeches, struggling through a ruined world of clefts and boulders. I never saw anything so much resembling some of the *Circles* described by Dante. From Simplon we made for Duomo d'Ossola; having broken out, as through the mouth of a mine, into green and fertile valleys full of vines and chestnuts, and white villages, —in short, into sunshine and Italy.

"At this place we dismissed our Swiss voiturier, and took an Italian one; who conveyed us to Omegna on the Lake of Orta; a place little visited by English travellers, but which fully repaid us the trouble of going there. We were lodged in a simple and even rude Italian inn; where they cannot speak a word of French; where we occupied a barn-like room, with a huge chimney fit to lodge a hundred ghosts, whom we expelled by dint of a hot woodfire. There were two beds, and as it happened good ones, in this strange old apartment; which was adorned by pictures of Architecture, and by Heads of Saints, better than many at the Royal Academy Exhibition, and which one paid nothing for looking at. The thorough Italian character of the whole scene amused us, much more than Meurice's at Paris would have done; for we had voluble, commonplace good-humor, with the aspect and accessories of a den of banditti.

"To-day we have seen the Lake of Orta, have walked for some miles among its vineyards and chestnuts; and thence have come, by Baveno, to this place; —having seen by the way, I believe, the most beautiful part of the Lago Maggiore, and certainly the most cheerful, complete and extended example of fine scenery I have ever fallen in with. Here we are, much to my wonder, —for it seems too good to be true, —fairly in Italy; and as yet my journey has been a pleasanter and more instructive, and in point of health a more successful one, than I at all imagined possible. Calvert and I go on as well as can be. I let him have his way about natural science, and he only laughs benignly when he thinks me absurd in my moral speculations. My only regrets are caused by my separation from my family and friends, and by the hurry I have been living in, which has prevented me doing any work, —and compelled me to write to you at a good deal faster rate than the *vapore* moves on the Lago Maggiore. It will take me to-morrow to Sesto Calende, whence we go to Varese. We shall not be at Milan for some days. Write thither, if you are kind enough to write at all, till I give you another address. Love to my Father.

"Your affectionate son,
"JOHN STERLING. "

Omitting Milan, Florence nearly all, and much about "Art, " Michael Angelo, and other aerial matters, here are some select terrestrial glimpses, the fittest I can find, of his progress towards Rome: —

To his Mother.

"*Lucca, Nov. 27th*, 1838. —I had dreams, like other people, before I came here, of what the Lombard Lakes must be; and the week I spent among them has left me an image, not only more distinct, but far more warm, shining and various, and more deeply attractive in innumerable respects, than all I had before conceived of them. And so also it has been with Florence; where I spent three weeks: enough for the first hazy radiant dawn of sympathy to pass away; yet constantly adding an increase of knowledge and of love, while I examined, and tried to understand, the wonderful minds that have left behind them there such abundant traces of their presence.... On Sunday, the day before I left Florence, I went to the highest part of the Grand Duke's Garden of Boboli, which commands a view of most of the City, and of the vale of the Arno to the westward; where, as we had been visited by several rainy days, and now at last had a very fine one, the whole prospect was in its highest beauty. The mass of buildings, chiefly on the other side of the River, is sufficient to fill the eye, without perplexing the mind by vastness like that of London; and its name and history, its outline and large and picturesque buildings, give it grandeur of a higher order than that of mere multitudinous extent. The Hills that border the Valley of the Arno are also very pleasing and striking to look upon; and the view of the rich Plain, glimmering away into blue distance, covered with

128

an endless web of villages and country-houses, is one of the most delightful images of human well-being I have ever seen....

"Very shortly before leaving Florence, I went through the house of Michael Angelo; which is still possessed by persons of the same family, descendants, I believe, of his Nephew. There is in it his 'first work in marble, ' as it is called; and a few drawings, —all with the stamp of his enginery upon them, which was more powerful than all the steam in London.... On the whole, though I have done no work in Florence that can be of any use or pleasure to others, except my Letters to my Wife, —I leave it with the certainty of much valuable knowledge gained there, and with a most pleasant remembrance of the busy and thoughtful days I owe to it.

"We left Florence before seven yesterday morning [26th November] for this place; travelling on the northern side of the Arno, by Prato, Pistoia, Pescia. We tried to see some old frescos in a Church at Prato; but found the Priests all about, saying mass; and of course did not venture to put our hands into a hive where the bees were buzzing and on the wing. Pistoia we only coasted. A little on one side of it, there is a Hill, the first on the road from Florence; which we walked up, and had a very lively and brilliant prospect over the road we had just travelled, and the town of Pistoia. Thence to this place the whole land is beautiful, and in the highest degree prosperous, —in short, to speak metaphorically, all dotted with Leghorn bonnets, and streaming with olive-oil. The girls here are said to employ themselves chiefly in platting straw, which is a profitable employment; and the slightness and quiet of the work are said to be much more favorable to beauty than the coarser kinds of labor performed by the country-women elsewhere. Certain it is that I saw more pretty women in Pescia, in the hour I spent there, than I ever before met with among the same numbers of the 'phare sect. ' Wherefore, as a memorial of them, I bought there several Legends of Female Saints and Martyrs, and of other Ladies quite the reverse, and held up as warnings; all of which are written in *ottava rima*, and sold for three halfpence apiece. But unhappily I have not yet had time to read them. This Town has 30,000 inhabitants, and is surrounded by Walls, laid out as walks, and evidently not at present intended to be besieged, —for which reason, this morning, I merely walked on them round the Town, and did not besiege them....

"The Cathedral [of Lucca] contains some Relics; which have undoubtedly worked miracles on the imagination of the people hereabouts. The Grandfather of all Relics (as the Arabs would say) in the place is the *Volto Santo*, which is a Face of the Saviour appertaining to a wooden Crucifix. Now you must know that, after the ascension of Christ, Nicodemus was ordered by an Angel to carve an image of him; and went accordingly with a hatchet, and cut down a cedar for that purpose. He then proceeded to carve the figure; and being tired, fell asleep before he had done the face; which however, on awaking, he found completed by celestial aid. This image was brought to Lucca, from Leghorn, I think, where it had arrived in a ship, 'more than a thousand years ago, ' and has ever since been kept, in purple and fine linen and gold and diamonds, quietly working miracles. I saw the gilt Shrine of it; and also a Hatchet which refused to cut off the head of an innocent man, who had been condemned to death, and who prayed to the *Volto Santo*. I suppose it is by way of economy (they being a frugal people) that the Italians have their Book of Common Prayer and their Arabian Nights' Entertainments condensed into one. "

To the Same.

"*Pisa, December 2d*, 1838. —Pisa is very unfairly treated in all the Books I have read. It seems to me a quiet, but very agreeable place; with wide clean streets, and a look of stability and comfort; and I admire the Cathedral and its appendages more, the more I see them. The leaning of the Tower is to my eye decidedly unpleasant; but it is a beautiful building nevertheless, and the view from the top is, under a bright sky, remarkably lively and satisfactory. The Lucchese Hills form a fine mass, and the sea must in clear weather be very distinct. There was some haze over it when I was up, though the land was all clear. I could just see the Leghorn Light-house. Leghorn itself I shall not be able to visit....

"The quiet gracefulness of Italian life, and the mental maturity and vigor of Germany, have a great charm when compared with the restless whirl of England, and the chorus of mingled yells and groans sent up by our parties and sects, and by the suffering and bewildered crowds of the laboring people. Our politics make my heart ache, whenever I think of them. The base selfish frenzies of factions seem to me, at this distance, half diabolic; and I am out of the way of knowing anything that may be quietly a-doing to elevate the standard of wise and temperate manhood in the country, and to diffuse the means of physical and moral well-being among all the people.... I will write to my Father as soon as I can after reaching the capital of his friend the Pope, —who, if he had happened to be born an English gentleman, would no doubt by this time be a respectable old-gentlemanly gouty member of the Carlton. I have often amused myself by thinking what a mere accident it is that Phillpotts is not Archbishop of Tuam, and M'Hale Bishop of Exeter; and how slight a change of dress, and of a few catchwords, would even now enable them to fill those respective posts with all the propriety and discretion they display in their present positions. "

At Rome he found the Crawfords, known to him long since; and at different dates other English friends old and new; and was altogether in the liveliest humor, no end to his activities and speculations. Of all which, during the next four months, the Letters now before me give abundant record, —far too abundant for our objects here. His grand pursuit, as natural at Rome, was Art; into which metaphysical domain we shall not follow him; preferring to pick out, here and there, something of concrete and human. Of his interests, researches, speculations and descriptions on this subject of Art, there is always rather a superabundance, especially in the Italian Tour. Unfortunately, in the hard weather, poor Calvert fell ill; and Sterling, along with his Art-studies, distinguished himself as a sick-nurse till his poor comrade got afoot again. His general impressions of the scene and what it held for him may be read in the following excerpts. The Letters are all dated *Rome*, and addressed to his Father or Mother: —

"*December 21st*, 1838. —Of Rome itself, as a whole, there are infinite things to be said, well worth saying; but I shall confine myself to two remarks: first, that while the Monuments and works of Art gain in wondrousness and significance by familiarity with them, the actual life of Rome, the Papacy and its pride, lose; and though one gets accustomed to Cardinals and Friars and Swiss Guards, and ragged beggars and the finery of London and Paris, all rolling on together, and sees how it is that they subsist in a sort of spurious unity, one loses all tendency to idealize the Metropolis and System of the Hierarchy into anything higher than a piece of showy stage-declamation, at bottom, in our day, thoroughly mean and prosaic. My other remark is, that Rome, seen from the tower of the Capitol, from the Pincian or the Janiculum, is at this day one of the most beautiful spectacles which eyes ever beheld. The company of great domes rising from a mass of large and solid buildings, with a few stone-pines and scattered edifices on the outskirts; the broken bare Campagna all around; the Alban Hills not far, and the purple range of Sabine Mountains in the distance with a cope of snow; —this seen in the clear air, and the whole spiritualized by endless recollections, and a sense of the grave and lofty reality of human existence which has had this place for a main theatre, fills at once the eyes and heart more forcibly, and to me delightfully, than I can find words to say. "

"*January 22d*, 1839. —The Modern Rome, Pope and all inclusive, are a shabby attempt at something adequate to fill the place of the old Commonwealth. It is easy enough to live among them, and there is much to amuse and even interest a spectator; but the native existence of the place is now thin and hollow, and there is a stamp of littleness, and childish poverty of taste, upon all the great Christian buildings I have seen here, —not excepting St. Peter's; which is crammed with bits of colored marble and gilding, and Gog-and-Magog colossal statues of saints (looking prodigiously small), and mosaics from the worst pictures in Rome; and has altogether, with most imposing size and lavish splendor, a tang of Guildhall finery about it that contrasts oddly with the melancholy vastness and simplicity of the Ancient Monuments, though these have not the Athenian elegance. I recur perpetually to the galleries of Sculpture in the Vatican, and to the Frescos of Raffael and Michael Angelo, of inexhaustible beauty and greatness, and to the general aspect of the City and the Country round it, as the most impressive scene on earth. But the Modern City, with its churches, palaces, priests and beggars, is far from sublime. "

Of about the same date, here is another paragraph worth inserting: "Gladstone has three little agate crosses which he will give you for my little girls. Calvert bought them, as a present, for 'the bodies, ' at Martigny in Switzerland, and I have had no earlier opportunity of sending them. Will you despatch them to Hastings when you have an opportunity? I have not yet seen Gladstone's *Church and State*; but as there is a copy in Rome, I hope soon to lay hands on it. I saw yesterday in the *Times* a furious, and I am sorry to say, most absurd attack on him and it, and the new Oxonian school. "

"*February 28th, 1839*. —There is among the people plenty of squalid misery; though not nearly so much as, they say, exists in Ireland; and here there is a certain freedom and freshness of manners, a dash of Southern enjoyment in the condition of the meanest and most miserable. There is, I suppose, as little as well can be of conscience or artificial cultivation of any kind; but there is not the affectation of a virtue which they do not possess, nor any feeling of being despised for the want of it; and where life generally is so inert, except as to its passions and material wants, there is not the bitter consciousness of having been beaten by the more prosperous, in a race which the greater number have never thought of running. Among the laboring poor of Rome, a bribe will buy a crime; but if common work procures enough for a day's food or idleness, ten times the sum will not induce them to toil on, as an English workman would, for the sake of rising in the world. Sixpence any day will put any of them at the top of the only tree they care for, —that on which grows the fruit of idleness. It is striking to see the way in which, in magnificent churches, the most ragged beggars kneel on the pavement before some favorite altar in the midst of well-dressed women and of gazing foreigners. Or sometimes you will see one with a child come in from the street where she has been begging, put herself in a corner, say a prayer (probably for the success of her petitions), and then return to beg again. There is wonderfully little of any moral strength connected with this devotion; but still it is better than nothing, and more than is often found among the men of the upper classes in Rome. I believe the Clergy to be generally profligate, and the state of domestic morals as bad as it has ever been represented."—

Or, in sudden contrast, take this other glance homeward; a Letter to his eldest child; in which kind of Letters, more than in any other, Sterling seems to me to excel. Readers recollect the hurricane in St. Vincent; the hasty removal to a neighbor's house, and the birth of a son there, soon after. The boy has grown to some articulation, during these seven years; and his Father, from the new foreign scene of Priests and Dilettanti, thus addresses him: —

"To Master Edward C. Sterling, Hastings.
"ROME, 21st January, 1839.

"MY DEAR EDWARD, —I was very glad to receive your Letter, which showed me that you have learned something since I left home. If you knew how much pleasure it gave me to see your handwriting, I am sure you would take pains to be able to write well, that you might often send me letters, and tell me a great many things which I should like to know about Mamma and your Sisters as well as yourself.

"If I go to Vesuvius, I will try to carry away a bit of the lava, which you wish for. There has lately been a great eruption, as it is called, of that Mountain; which means a great breaking-out of hot ashes and fire, and of melted stones which is called lava.

"Miss Clark is very kind to take so much pains with you; and I trust you will show that you are obliged to her, by paying attention to all she tells you. When you see how much more grown people know than you, you ought to be anxious to learn all you can from those who teach you; and as there are so many wise and good things written in Books, you ought to try to read early and carefully; that you may learn something of what God has made you able to know. There are Libraries containing very many thousands of Volumes; and all that is written in these is, —accounts of some part or other of the World which God has made, or of the Thoughts which he has enabled men to have in their minds. Some Books are descriptions of the earth itself, with its rocks and ground and water, and of the air and clouds, and the stars and moon and sun, which shine so beautifully in the sky. Some tell you about the things that grow upon the ground; the many millions of plants, from little mosses and threads of grass up to great trees and forests. Some also contain accounts of living things: flies, worms, fishes, birds and four-legged beasts. And some, which are the most, are about men and their thoughts and doings. These are the most important of all; for men are the best and most wonderful creatures of God in the world; being the only ones able to know him and love him, and to try of their own accord to do his will.

"These Books about men are also the most important to us, because we ourselves are human beings, and may learn from such Books what we ought to think and to do and to try to be. Some of them describe what sort of people have lived in old times and in other countries. By reading them, we know what is the difference between ourselves in England now, and the famous nations which lived in former days. Such were the Egyptians who built the Pyramids, which are the greatest heaps of stone upon the face of the earth: and the Babylonians, who had a city with huge walls, built of bricks, having writing on them that no one in our time has been able to make out. There were also the Jews, who were the only ancient people that knew how wonderful and how good God is: and the Greeks, who were the wisest of all in thinking about men's lives and hearts, and who knew best how to make fine statues and buildings, and to write wise books. By Books also we may learn what sort of people the old Romans were, whose chief city was Rome, where I am now; and how brave and skilful they were in war; and how well they could govern and teach many nations which they had conquered. It is from Books, too, that you must learn what kind of men were our Ancestors in the Northern part of Europe, who belonged to the tribes that did the most towards pulling down the power of the Romans: and you will see in the same way how Christianity was sent among them by God, to make them wiser and more peaceful, and more noble in their minds; and how all the nations that now are in Europe, and especially the Italians and the Germans, and the French and the English, came to be what they now are. —It is well worth knowing (and it can be known only by reading) how the Germans found out the Printing of Books, and what great changes this has made in the world. And everybody in England ought to try to understand how the English came to have their Parliaments and Laws; and to have fleets that sail over all seas of the world.

"Besides learning all these things, and a great many more about different times and countries, you may learn from Books, what is the truth of God's will, and what are the best and wisest thoughts, and the most beautiful words; and how men are able to lead very right lives, and to do a great deal to better the world. I have spent a great part of my life in reading; and I hope you will come to like it as much as I do, and to learn in this way all that I know.

"But it is a still more serious matter that you should try to be obedient and gentle; and to command your temper; and to think of other people's pleasure rather than your own, and of what you *ought* to do rather than what you *like*. If you try to be better for all you read, as well as wiser, you will find Books a great help towards goodness as well as knowledge, and above all other Books, the Bible; which tells us of the will of God, and of the love of Jesus Christ towards God and men.

"I had a Letter from Mamma to-day, which left Hastings on the 10th of this month. I was very glad to find in it that you were all well and happy; but I know Mamma is not well, and is likely to be more uncomfortable every day for some time. So I hope you will all take care to give her as little trouble as possible. After sending you so much advice, I shall write a little Story to divert you. —I am, my dear Boy,

"Your affectionate Father,
"JOHN STERLING. "

The "Story" is lost, destroyed, as are many such which Sterling wrote, with great felicity, I am told, and much to the satisfaction of the young folk, when the humor took him.

Besides these plentiful communications still left, I remember long Letters, not now extant, principally addressed to his Wife, of which we and the circle at Knightsbridge had due perusal, treating with animated copiousness about all manner of picture-galleries, pictures, statues and objects of Art at Rome, and on the road to Rome and from it, wheresoever his course led him into neighborhood of such objects. That was Sterling's habit. It is expected in this Nineteenth Century that a man of culture shall understand and worship Art: among the windy gospels addressed to our poor Century there are few louder than this of Art; —and if the Century expects that every man shall do his duty, surely Sterling was not the man to balk it! Various extracts from these picture-surveys are given in Hare; the others, I suppose, Sterling himself subsequently destroyed, not valuing them much.

Certainly no stranger could address himself more eagerly to reap what artistic harvest Rome offers, which is reckoned the peculiar produce of Rome among cities under the sun; to all galleries, churches, sistine chapels, ruins, coliseums, and artistic or dilettante shrines he zealously pilgrimed; and had much to say then and afterwards, and with real technical and historical knowledge I believe, about the objects of devotion there. But it often struck me as a question, Whether all this even to himself was not, more or less, a nebulous kind of element; prescribed not by Nature and her verities, but by the Century expecting every man to do his duty? Whether not perhaps, in good part, temporary dilettante cloudland of our poor Century; —or can it be the real diviner Pisgah height, and everlasting mount of vision, for man's soul in any Century? And I think Sterling himself bent towards a negative conclusion, in the course of years. Certainly, of all subjects this was the one I cared least to hear even Sterling talk of: indeed it is a subject on which earnest men, abhorrent of hypocrisy and speech that has no meaning, are admonished to silence in this sad time, and had better, in such a Babel as we have got into for the present, "perambulate their picture-gallery with little or no speech. "

Here is another and to me much more earnest kind of "Art, " which renders Rome unique among the cities of the world; of this we will, in preference; take a glance through Sterling's eyes: —

"January 22d, 1839. —On Friday last there was a great Festival at St. Peter's; the only one I have seen. The Church was decorated with crimson hangings, and the choir fitted up with seats and galleries, and a throne for the Pope. There were perhaps a couple of hundred guards of different kinds; and three or four hundred English ladies, and not so many foreign male spectators; so that the place looked empty. The Cardinals in scarlet, and Monsignori in purple, were there; and a body of officiating Clergy. The Pope was carried in in his chair on men's shoulders, wearing the Triple Crown; which I have thus actually seen: it is something like a gigantic Egg, and of the same color, with three little bands of gold, —very large Egg-shell with three streaks of the yolk smeared round it. He was dressed in white silk robes, with gold trimmings.

"It was a fine piece of state-show; though, as there are three or four such Festivals yearly, of course there is none of the eager interest which breaks out at coronations and similar rare events; no explosion of unwonted velvets, jewels, carriages and footmen, such as London and Milan have lately enjoyed. I guessed all the people in St. Peter's, including performers and spectators, at 2,000; where 20,000 would hardly have been a crushing crowd. Mass was performed, and a stupid but short Latin sermon delivered by a lad, in honor of St. Peter, who would have been much astonished if he could have heard it. The genuflections, and train-bearings, and folding up the tails of silk petticoats while the Pontiff knelt, and the train of Cardinals going up to kiss his Ring, and so forth, —made on me the impression of something immeasurably old and sepulchral, such as might suit the Grand Lama's court, or the inside of an Egyptian Pyramid; or as if the Hieroglyphics on one of the Obelisks here should begin to pace and gesticulate, and nod their bestial heads upon the granite tablets. The careless bystanders, the London ladies with their eye-glasses and look of an Opera-box, the yawning young gentlemen of the *Guarda Nobile,* and the laugh of one of the file of vermilion Priests round the steps of the altar at the whispered good thing of his neighbor, brought one back to nothing indeed of a very lofty kind, but still to the Nineteenth Century. " —

"At the great Benediction of the City and the World on Easter Sunday by the Pope, " he writes afterwards, "there was a large crowd both native and foreign, hundreds of carriages, and thousands of the lower orders of people from the country; but even of the poor hardly one in twenty took off his hat, and a still smaller number knelt down. A few years ago, not a head was covered, nor was there a knee which did not bow. " —A very decadent "Holiness of our Lord the Pope, " it would appear! —

Sterling's view of the Pope, as seen in these his gala days, doing his big play-actorism under God's earnest sky, was much more substantial to me than his studies in the picture-galleries. To Mr. Hare also he writes: "I have seen the Pope in all his pomp at St. Peter's; and he looked to me a mere lie in livery. The Romish Controversy is doubtless a much more difficult one than the managers of the Religious-Tract Society fancy, because it is a theoretical dispute; and in dealing with notions and authorities, I can quite understand how a mere student in a library, with no eye for facts, should take either one side or other. But how any man with clear head and honest heart, and capable of seeing realities, and distinguishing them from scenic falsehoods, should, after living in a Romanist country, and especially at Rome, be inclined to side with Leo against Luther, I cannot understand. "[20]

It is fit surely to recognize with admiring joy any glimpse of the Beautiful and the Eternal that is hung out for us, in color, in form or tone, in canvas, stone, or atmospheric air, and made accessible by any sense, in this world: but it is greatly fitter still (little as we are used that way) to shudder in pity and abhorrence over the scandalous tragedy, transcendent nadir of human ugliness and contemptibility, which under the daring title of religious worship, and practical recognition of the Highest God, daily and hourly everywhere transacts itself there. And, alas, not there only, but elsewhere, everywhere more or less; whereby our sense is so blunted to it; —whence, in all provinces of human life, these tears! —

But let us take a glance at the Carnival, since we are here. The Letters, as before, are addressed to Knightsbridge; the date *Rome*: —

"*February 5th*, 1839. —The Carnival began yesterday. It is a curious example of the trifling things which will heartily amuse tens of thousands of grown people, precisely because they are trifling, and therefore a relief from serious business, cares and labors. The Corso is a street about a mile long, and about as broad as Jermyn Street; but bordered by much loftier houses, with many palaces and churches, and has two or three small squares opening into it. Carriages, mostly open, drove up and down it for two or three hours; and the contents were shot at with handfuls of comfits from the windows, —in the hope of making them as non-content as possible, —while they returned the fire to the best of their inferior ability. The populace, among whom was I, walked about; perhaps one in fifty were masked in character; but there was little in the masquerade either of splendor of costume or liveliness of mimicry. However, the whole scene was very gay; there were a good many troops about, and some of them heavy dragoons, who flourished their swords with the magnanimity of our Life-Guards, to repel the encroachments of too ambitious little boys. Most of the windows and balconies were hung with colored drapery; and there were flags, trumpets, nosegays and flirtations of all shapes and sizes. The best of all was, that there was laughter enough to have frightened Cassius out of his thin carcass, could the lean old homicide have been present, otherwise than as a fleshless ghost; —in which capacity I thought I had a glimpse of him looking over the shoulder of a particolored clown, in a carriage full of London Cockneys driving towards the Capitol. This good-humored foolery will go on for several days to come, ending always with the celebrated Horse-race, of horses without riders. The long street is cleared in the centre by troops, and half a dozen quadrupeds, ornamented like Grimaldi in a London pantomime, scamper away, with the mob closing and roaring at their heels. "

"*February* 9th, 1839. —The usual state of Rome is quiet and sober. One could almost fancy the actual generation held their breath, and stole by on tiptoe, in presence of so memorable a past. But during the Carnival all mankind, womankind and childkind think it unbecoming not to play the fool. The modern donkey pokes its head out of the lion's skin of old Rome, and brays out the absurdest of asinine roundelays. Conceive twenty thousand grown people in a long street, at the windows, on the footways, and in carriages, amused day after day for several hours in pelting and being pelted with handfuls of mock or real sugar-plums; and this no name or presence, but real downright showers of plaster comfits, from which people guard their eyes with meshes of wire. As sure as a carriage passes under a window or balcony where are acquaintances of theirs, down comes a shower of hail, ineffectually returned from below. The parties in two crossing carriages similarly assault each other; and there are long balconies hung the whole way with a deep canvas pocket full of this mortal shot. One Russian Grand Duke goes with a troop of youngsters in a wagon, all dressed in brown linen frocks and masked, and pelts among the most furious, also being pelted. The children are of course preeminently vigorous, and there is a considerable circulation of real sugar-plums, which supply consolation for all disappointments. "

The whole to conclude, as is proper, with a display, with two displays, of fireworks; in which art, as in some others, Rome is unrivalled: —

"*February 9th*, 1839. —It seems to be the ambition of all the lower classes to wear a mask and showy grotesque disguise of some kind; and I believe many of the upper ranks do the same. They even put St. Peter's into masquerade; and make it a Cathedral of Lamplight instead of a stone one. Two evenings ago this feat was performed; and I was able to see it from the rooms of a friend near this, which command an excellent view of it. I never saw so beautiful an effect of artificial light. The evening was perfectly serene and clear; the principal lines of the building, the columns, architrave and pediment of the front, the two inferior cupolas, the curves of the dome from which the dome rises, the ribs of the dome itself, the small oriel windows between them, and the lantern and ball and cross, —all were delineated in the clear vault of air by lines of pale yellow fire. The dome of another great Church, much nearer to the eye, stood up as a great black mass, —a funereal contrast to the luminous tabernacle.

"While I was looking at this latter, a red blaze burst from the summit, and at the same moment seemed to flash over the whole building, filling up the pale outline with a simultaneous burst of fire. This is a celebrated display; and is done, I believe, by the employment of a very great number of men to light, at the same instant, the torches which are fixed for the purpose all over the building. After the first glare of fire, I did not think the second aspect of the building so beautiful as the first; it wanted both softness and distinctness. The two most animated days of the Carnival are still to come. "

"*April 4th*, 1839. —We have just come to the termination of all the Easter spectacles here. On Sunday evening St. Peter's was a second time illuminated; I was in the Piazza, and admired the sight from a nearer point than when I had seen it before at the time of the Carnival.

"On Monday evening the celebrated fire-works were let off from the Castle of St. Angelo; they were said to be, in some respects more brilliant than usual. I certainly never saw any fireworks comparable to them for beauty. The Girandola is a discharge of many thousands of rockets at once, which of course fall back, like the leaves of a lily, and form for a minute a very beautiful picture. There was also in silvery light a very long Facade of a Palace, which looked a residence for Oberon and Titania, and beat Aladdin's into darkness. Afterwards a series of cascades of red fire poured down the faces of the Castle and of the scaffoldings round it, and seemed a burning Niagara. Of course there were abundance of serpents, wheels and cannon-shot; there was also a display of dazzling white light, which made a strange appearance on the houses, the river, the bridge, and the faces of the multitude. The whole ended with a second and a more splendid Girandola. "

Take finally, to people the scene a little for us, if our imagination be at all lively, these three small entries, of different dates, and so wind up: —

"*December 30th*, 1838. —I received on Christmas-day a packet from Dr. Carlyle, containing Letters from the Maurices; which were a very pleasant arrival. The Dr. wrote a few lines with them, mentioning that he was only at Civita Vecchia while the steamer baited on its way to Naples. I have written to thank him for his despatches. "

"*March 16th*, 1839. —I have seen a good deal of John Mill, whose society I like much. He enters heartily into the interest of the things which I most care for here, and I have seldom had more pleasure than in taking him to see Raffael's Loggie, where are the Frescos called his Bible, and to the Sixtine Chapel, which I admire and love more and more. He is in very weak health, but as fresh and clear in mind as possible.... English politics seem in a queer state, the Conservatives creeping on, the Whigs losing ground; like combatants on the top of a breach, while there is a social mine below which will probably blow both parties into the air. "

"*April 4th*, 1839. —I walked out on Tuesday on the Ancona Road, and about noon met a travelling carriage, which from a distance looked very suspicious, and on nearer approach was found really to contain Captain Sterling and an Albanian manservant on the front, and behind under the hood Mrs. A. Sterling and the she portion of the tail. They seemed very well; and, having turned the Albanian back to the rear of the whole machine, I sat by Anthony, and entered Rome in triumph. "—Here is indeed a conquest! Captain A. Sterling, now on his return from service in Corfu, meets his Brother in this manner; and the remaining Roman days are of a brighter complexion. As these suddenly ended, I believe he turned southward, and found at Naples the Dr. Carlyle above mentioned (an extremely intimate acquaintance of mine), who was still there. For we are a most travelling people, we of this Island in this time; and, as the Prophet threatened, see ourselves, in so many senses, made "like unto a wheel! " —

Sterling returned from Italy filled with much cheerful imagery and reminiscence, and great store of artistic, serious, dilettante and other speculation for the time; improved in health, too; but probably little enriched in real culture or spiritual strength; and indeed not permanently altered by his tour in any respect to a sensible extent, that one could notice. He returned rather in haste, and before the expected time; summoned, about the middle of April, by his Wife's domestic situation at Hastings; who, poor lady, had been brought to bed before her calculation, and had in few days lost her infant; and now saw a household round her much needing the master's presence. He hurried off to Malta, dreading the Alps at that season; and came home, by steamer, with all speed, early in May, 1839.

PART III.

CHAPTER I.
CLIFTON.

Matters once readjusted at Hastings, it was thought Sterling's health had so improved, and his activities towards Literature so developed themselves into congruity, that a permanent English place of abode might now again be selected, —on the Southwest coast somewhere, —and the family once more have the blessing of a home, and see its *lares* and *penates* and household furniture unlocked from the Pantechnicon repositories, where they had so long been lying.

Clifton, by Bristol, with its soft Southern winds and high cheerful situation, recommended too by the presence of one or more valuable acquaintances there, was found to be the eligible place; and thither in this summer of 1839, having found a tolerable lodging, with the prospect by and by of an agreeable house, he and his removed. This was the end of what I call his "third peregrinity; " —or reckoning the West Indies one, his fourth. This also is, since Bayswater, the fourth time his family has had to shift on his account. Bayswater; then to Bordeaux, to Blackheath and Knightsbridge (during the Madeira time), to Hastings (Roman time); and now to Clifton, not to stay there either: a sadly nomadic life to be prescribed to a civilized man!

At Clifton his habitation was speedily enough set up; household conveniences, methods of work, daily promenades on foot or horseback, and before long even a circle of friends, or of kindly neighborhoods ripening into intimacy, were established round him. In all this no man could be more expert or expeditious, in such cases. It was with singular facility, in a loving, hoping manner, that he threw himself open to the new interests and capabilities of the new place; snatched out of it whatsoever of human or material would suit him; and in brief, in all senses had pitched his tent-habitation, and grew to look on it as a house. It was beautiful too, as well as pathetic. This man saw himself reduced to be a dweller in tents, his house is but a stone tent; and he can so kindly accommodate himself to that arrangement; —healthy faculty and diseased necessity, nature and habit, and all manner of things primary and secondary, original and incidental, conspiring now to make it easy for him. With the evils of nomadism, he participated to the full in whatever benefits lie in it for a man.

He had friends enough, old and new, at Clifton, whose intercourse made the place human for him. Perhaps among the most valued of the former sort may be mentioned Mrs. Edward Strachey, Widow of the late Indian Judge, who now resided here; a cultivated, graceful, most devout and high-minded lady; whom he had known in old years, first probably as Charles Buller's Aunt, and whose esteem was constant for him, and always precious to him. She was some ten or twelve years older than he; she survived him some years, but is now also gone from us. Of new friends acquired here, besides a skilful and ingenious Dr. Symonds, physician as well as friend, the principal was Francis Newman, then and still an ardently inquiring soul, of fine University and other attainments, of sharp-cutting, restlessly advancing intellect, and the mildest pious enthusiasm; whose worth, since better known to all the world, Sterling highly estimated; —and indeed practically testified the same; having by will appointed him, some years hence, guardian to his eldest Son; which pious function Mr. Newman now successfully discharges.

Sterling was not long in certainty as to his abode at Clifton: alas, where could he long be so? Hardly six months were gone when his old enemy again overtook him; again admonished him how frail his hopes of permanency were. Each winter, it turned out, he had to fly; and after the second of these, he quitted the place altogether. Here, meanwhile, in a Letter to myself, and in Excerpts from others, are some glimpses of his advent and first summer there: —

To his Mother.

"*Clifton, June 11th,* 1839. —As yet I am personally very uncomfortable from the general confusion of this house, which deprives me of my room to sit and read and write in; all being more or less lumbered by boxes, and invaded by servile domesticities aproned, handled, bristled, and of nondescript varieties. We have very fine warm weather, with occasional showers; and the verdure of the woods and fields is very beautiful. Bristol seems as busy as need be; and the shops and all kinds of practical conveniences are excellent; but those of Clifton have the usual sentimental, not to say meretricious fraudulence of commercial establishments in Watering-places.

"The bag which Hannah forgot reached us safely at Bath on Friday morning; but I cannot quite unriddle the mystery of the change of padlocks, for I left the right one in care of the Head Steam-engine at

Paddington, which seemed a very decent person with a good black coat on, and a pen behind its ear. I have been meditating much on the story of Palarea's 'box of papers;' which does not appear to be in my possession, and I have a strong impression that I gave it to young Florez Calderon. I will write to say so to Madam Torrijos speedily. " Palarea, Dr. Palarea, I understand, was "an old guerilla leader whom they called *El Medico.* " Of him and of the vanished shadows, now gone to Paris, to Madrid, or out of the world, let us say nothing!

To Mr. Carlyle.

"*June 15th,* 1839. —We have a room now occupied by Robert Barton [a brother-in-law]; to which Anthony may perhaps succeed; but which after him, or in lieu of him, would expand itself to receive you. Is there no hope of your coming? I would undertake to ride with you at all possible paces, and in all existing directions.

"As yet my books are lying as ghost books, in a limbo on the banks of a certain Bristolian Styx, humanly speaking, a *Canal*; but the other apparatus of life is gathered about me, and performs its diurnal functions. The place pleases me better than I expected: a far lookout on all sides, over green country; a sufficient old City lying in the hollow near; and civilization, in no tumultuous state, rather indeed stagnant, visible in the Rows of Houses and Gardens which call themselves Clifton. I hope soon to take a lease of a house, where I may arrange myself more methodically; keep myself equably boiling in my own kitchen; and spread myself over a series of book-shelves.... I have just been interrupted by a visit from Mrs. Strachey; with whom I dined yesterday. She seems a very good and thoroughly kind-hearted woman; and it is pleasant to have her for a neighbor.... I have read Emerson's Pamphlets. I should find it more difficult than ever to write to him. "

To his Father.

"*June 30th,* 1839. —Of Books I shall have no lack, though no plethora; and the Reading-room supplies all one can want in the way of Papers and Reviews. I go there three or four times a week, and inquire how the human race goes on. I suppose this Turco-Egyptian War will throw several diplomatists into a state of great excitement, and massacre a good many thousands of Africans and Asiatics? — For the present, it appears, the English Education Question is settled. I wish the Government had said that, in their inspection and superintendence, they would look only to secular matters, and leave religious ones to the persons who set up the schools, whoever these might be. It seems to me monstrous that the State should be prevented taking any efficient measures for teaching Roman Catholic children to read, write and cipher, merely because they believe in the Pope, and the Pope is an impostor, —which I candidly confess he is! There is no question which I can so ill endure to see made a party one as that of Education. "—The following is of the same day: —

"*To Thomas Carlyle, Esq., Chelsea, London.*
"MANOR HOUSE, CLIFTON PLACE, CLIFTON,
"30th June, 1839.

"MY DEAR CARLYLE, —I have heard, this morning, from my Father, that you are to set out on Tuesday for Scotland: so I have determined to fillip away some spurt of ink in your direction, which may reach you before you move towards Thule.

"Writing to you, in fact, is considerably easier than writing about you; which has been my employment of late, at leisure moments, — that is, moments of leisure from idleness, not work. As you partly guessed, I took in hand a Review of *Teufelsdrockh*—for want of a better Heuschrecke to do the work; and when I have been well enough, and alert enough, during the last fortnight, have tried to set down some notions about Tobacco, Radicalism, Christianity, Assafoetida and so forth. But a few abortive pages are all the result as yet. If my speculations should ever see daylight, they may chance to get you into scrapes, but will certainly get me into worse.... But one must work; *sic itur ad astra*, —and the *astra* are always there to befriend one, at least as asterisks, filling up the gaps which yawn in vain for words.

"Except my unsuccessful efforts to discuss you and your offences, I have done nothing that leaves a trace behind; —unless the endeavor to teach my little boy the Latin declensions shall be found, at some time short of the Last Day, to have done so. I have—rather I think from dyspepsia than dyspneumony—been often and for days disabled from doing anything but read. In this way I have gone through a good deal of Strauss's Book; which is exceedingly clever and clearheaded; with more of insight, and less of destructive rage than I expected. It will work deep and far, in such a time as ours. When so many minds are distracted about the history, or rather genesis of the Gospel, it is a great thing for partisans on the one side to have, what the other never have wanted, a Book of which they can say, This is our Creed and Code, —or rather Anti-creed and Anti-code. And Strauss seems perfectly secure against the sort of answer to which Voltaire's critical and historical shallowness perpetually exposed him. I mean to read the Book through. It seems admitted that the orthodox theologians have failed to give any sufficient answer. —I have also looked through Michelet's *Luther*, with great delight; and have read the fourth volume of Coleridge's *Literary Remains*, in which there are things that would interest you. He has a great hankering after Cromwell, and explicitly defends the execution of Charles.

"Of Mrs. Strachey we have seen a great deal; and might have seen more, had I had time and spirits for it. She is a warm-hearted, enthusiastic creature, whom one cannot but like. She seems always excited by the wish for more excitement than her life affords. And such a person is always in danger of doing something less wise than his best knowledge and aspirations; because he must do something, and circumstances do not allow him to do what he desires. Thence, after the first glow of novelty, endless self-tormenting comes from the contrast between aims and acts. She sets out, with her daughter and two boys, for a Tour in Wales to-morrow morning. Her talk of you is always most affectionate; and few, I guess, will read *Sartor* with more interest than she.

"I am still in a very extempore condition as to house, books, &c. One which I have hired for three years will be given up to me in the middle of August; and then I may hope to have something like a house, —so far as that is possible for any one to whom Time itself is often but a worse or a better kind of cave in the desert. We have had rainy and cheerless weather almost since the day of our arrival. But the sun now shines more lovingly, and the skies seem less disdainful of man and his perplexities. The earth is green, abundant and beautiful. But human life, so far as I can learn, is mean and meagre enough in its purposes, however striking to the speculative or sentimental bystander. Pray be assured that whatever you may say of the 'landlord at Clifton, '[21] the more I know of him, the less I shall like him. Well with me if I can put up with him for the present, and make use of him, till at last I can joyfully turn him off forever!

"Love to you Wife and self. My little Charlotte desires me to tell you that she has new shoes for her Doll, which she will show you when you come.

"Yours,

"JOHN STERLING. "

The visit to Clifton never took effect; nor to any of Sterling's subsequent homes; which now is matter of regret to me. Concerning the "Review of *Teufelsdrockh*" there will be more to say anon. As to "little Charlotte and her Doll, " I remember well enough and was more than once reminded, this bright little creature, on one of my first visits to Bayswater, had earnestly applied to me to put her Doll's shoes on for her; which feat was performed. —The next fragment indicates a household settled, fallen into wholesome routine again; and may close the series here: —

To his Mother.

"*July 22d*, 1839. —A few evenings ago we went to Mr. Griffin's, and met there Dr. Prichard, the author of a well-known Book on the *Races of Mankind*, to which it stands in the same relation among English books as the Racing Calendar does to those of Horsekind. He is a very intelligent, accomplished person. We had also there the Dean; a certain Dr. —— of Corpus College, Cambridge (a booby); and a clever fellow, a Mr. Fisher, one of the Tutors of Trinity in my days. We had a very pleasant evening. " —

At London we were in the habit of expecting Sterling pretty often; his presence, in this house as in others, was looked for, once in the month or two, and came always as sunshine in the gray weather to me and mine. My daily walks with him had long since been cut short without renewal; that walk to Eltham and Edgeworth's perhaps the last of the kind he and I had: but our intimacy, deepening and widening year after year, knew no interruption or abatement of increase; an honest, frank and truly human mutual relation, valuable or even invaluable to both parties, and a lasting loss, hardly to be replaced in this world, to the survivor of the two.

His visits, which were usually of two or three days, were always full of business, rapid in movement as all his life was. To me, if possible, he would come in the evening; a whole cornucopia of talk and speculation was to be discharged. If the evening would not do, and my affairs otherwise permitted, I had to mount into cabs with him; fly far and wide, shuttling athwart the big Babel, wherever his calls and pauses had to be. This was his way to husband time! Our talk, in such straitened circumstances, was loud or low as the circumambient groaning rage of wheels and sound prescribed, —very loud it had to be in such thoroughfares as London Bridge and Cheapside; but except while he was absent, off for minutes into some banker's office, lawyer's, stationer's, haberdasher's or what office there might be, it never paused. In this way extensive strange dialogues were carried on: to me also very strange, —private friendly colloquies, on all manner of rich subjects, held thus amid the chaotic roar of things. Sterling was full of speculations, observations and bright sallies; vividly awake to what was passing in the world; glanced pertinently with victorious clearness, without spleen, though often enough with a dash of mockery, into its Puseyisms, Liberalisms, literary Lionisms, or what else the mad hour might be producing, —always prompt to recognize what grain of sanity might be in the same. He was opulent in talk, and the rapid movement and vicissitude on such occasions seemed to give him new excitement.

Once, I still remember, —it was some years before, probably in May, on his return from Madeira, —he undertook a day's riding with me; once and never again. We coursed extensively, over the Hampstead and Highgate regions, and the country beyond, sauntering or galloping through many leafy lanes and pleasant places, in ever-flowing, ever-changing talk; and returned down Regent Street at nightfall: one of the cheerfulest days I ever had; —not to be repeated, said the Fates. Sterling was charming on such occasions: at once a child and a gifted man. A serious fund of thought he always had, a serious drift you never missed in him: nor indeed had he much depth of real laughter or sense of the ludicrous, as I have elsewhere said; but what he had was genuine, free and continual: his sparkling sallies bubbled up as from aerated natural fountains; a mild dash of gayety was native to the man, and had moulded his physiognomy in a very graceful way. We got once into a cab, about Charing Cross; I know not now whence or well whitherward, nor that our haste was at all special; however, the cabman, sensible that his pace was slowish, took to whipping, with a steady, passionless, businesslike assiduity which, though the horse seemed lazy rather than weak, became afflictive; and I urged remonstrance with the savage fellow: "Let him alone, " answered Sterling; "he is kindling the enthusiasm of his horse, you perceive; that is the first thing, then we shall do very well! " —as accordingly we did.

At Clifton, though his thoughts began to turn more on poetic forms of composition, he was diligent in prose elaborations too, —doing Criticism, for one thing, as we incidentally observed. He wrote there, and sent forth in this autumn of 1839, his most important contribution to John Mill's Review, the article on *Carlyle*, which stands also in Mr. Hare's collection. [22] What its effect on the public was I knew not, and know not; but remember well, and may here be permitted to acknowledge, the deep silent joy, not of a weak or ignoble nature, which it gave to myself in my then mood and situation; as it well might. The first generous human recognition, expressed with heroic emphasis, and clear conviction visible amid its fiery exaggeration, that one's poor battle in this world is not quite a mad and futile, that it is perhaps a worthy and manful one, which will come to something yet: this fact is a memorable one in every history; and for me Sterling, often enough the stiff gainsayer in our private communings, was the doer of this. The thought burnt in me like a lamp, for several days; lighting up into a kind of heroic splendor the sad volcanic wrecks, abysses, and convulsions of said poor battle, and secretly I was very grateful to my daring friend, and am still, and ought to be. What the public might be thinking about him and his audacities, and me in consequence, or whether it thought at all, I never learned, or much heeded to learn.

Sterling's gainsaying had given way on many points; but on others it continued stiff as ever, as may be seen in that article; indeed he fought Parthian-like in such cases, holding out his last position as doggedly as the first: and to some of my notions he seemed to grow in stubbornness of opposition, with the growing inevitability, and never would surrender. Especially that doctrine of the "greatness and fruitfulness of Silence, " remained afflictive and incomprehensible: "Silence? " he would say: "Yes, truly; if they give you leave to proclaim silence by cannon-salvos! My Harpocrates-Stentor! " In like manner, "Intellect and Virtue, " how they are proportional, or are indeed one gift in us, the same great summary of gifts; and again, "Might and Right, " the identity of these two, if a man will understand this God's-Universe, and that only he who conforms to the law of it can in the long-run have any "might: " all this, at the first blush, often awakened Sterling's musketry upon me, and many volleys I have had to stand, —the thing not being decidable by that kind of weapon or strategy.

In such cases your one method was to leave our friend in peace. By small-arms practice no mortal could dislodge him: but if you were in the right, the silent hours would work continually for you; and Sterling, more certainly than any man, would and must at length swear fealty to the right, and passionately adopt it, burying all hostilities under foot. A more candid soul, once let the stormful velocities of it expend themselves, was nowhere to be met with. A son of light, if I have ever seen one; recognizing the truth, if truth there were; hurling overboard his vanities, petulances, big and small interests, in ready loyalty to truth: very beautiful; at once a loyal child, as I said, and a gifted man! —Here is a very pertinent passage from one of his Letters, which, though the name continues blank, I will insert: —

To his Father.

"*October 15th*, 1839. —As to my 'over-estimate of — —, ' your expressions rather puzzle me. I suppose there may be, at the outside, a hundred persons in England whose opinions on such a matter are worth as much as mine. If by 'the public' you and my Mother mean the other ninety-nine, I submit. I have no doubt that, on any matter not relating peculiarly to myself, the judgment of the ninety-nine most philosophical heads in the country, if unanimous, would be right, and mine, if opposed to them, wrong. But then I am at a loss to make out, How the decision of the very few really competent persons has been ascertained to be thus in contradiction to me? And on the other hand, I conceive myself, from my opportunities, knowledge and attention to the subject, to be alone quite entitled to outvote tens of thousands of gentlemen, however much my superiors as men of business, men of the world, or men of merely dry or merely frivolous literature.

"I do not remember ever before to have heard the saying, whether of Talleyrand or of any one else, That *all* the world is a wiser man than any man in the world. Had it been said even by the Devil, it would nevertheless be false. I have often indeed heard the saying, *On peut etre plus FIN qu'un autre, mais pas plus FIN que tous les autres.* But observe that '*fin*' means *cunning*, not *wise*. The difference between this assertion and the one you refer to is curious and worth examining. It is quite certain, there is always some one man in the world wiser than all the rest; as Socrates was declared by the oracle to be; and as, I suppose, Bacon was in his day, and perhaps Burke in his. There is also some one, whose opinion would be probably true, if opposed to that of all around him; and it is always indubitable that the wise men are the scores, and the unwise the millions. The millions indeed come round, in the course of a generation or two, to the opinions of the wise; but by that time a new race of wise men have again shot ahead of their contemporaries: so it has always been, and so, in the nature of things, it always must be. But with cunning, the matter is quite different. Cunning is not *dishonest wisdom*, which would be a contradiction in terms; it is *dishonest prudence*, acuteness in practice, not in thought: and though there must always be some one the most cunning in the world, as well as some one the most wise, these two superlatives will fare very differently in the world. In the case of cunning, the shrewdness of a whole people, of a whole generation, may doubtless be combined against that of the one, and so triumph over it; which was pretty much the case with Napoleon. But although a man of the greatest cunning can hardly conceal his designs and true character from millions of unfriendly eyes, it is quite impossible thus to club the eyes of the mind, and to constitute by the union of ten thousand follies an equivalent for a single wisdom. A hundred school-boys can easily unite and thrash their one master; but a hundred thousand school-boys would not be nearer than a score to knowing as much Greek among them as Bentley or Scaliger. To all which, I believe, you will assent as readily as I; —and I have written it down only because I have nothing more important to say. " —

Besides his prose labors, Sterling had by this time written, publishing chiefly in *Blackwood*, a large assortment of verses, *Sexton's Daughter*, *Hymns of a Hermit*, and I know not what other extensive stock of pieces; concerning which he was now somewhat at a loss as to his true course. He could write verses with astonishing facility, in any given form of metre; and to various readers they seemed excellent, and high judges had freely called them so, but he himself had grave misgivings on that latter essential point. In fact here once more was a parting of the ways, "Write in Poetry; write in Prose? " upon which, before all else, it much concerned him to come to a settlement.

My own advice was, as it had always been, steady against Poetry; and we had colloquies upon it, which must have tried his patience, for in him there was a strong leaning the other way. But, as I remarked and urged: Had he not already gained superior excellence in delivering, by way of *speech* or prose, what thoughts were in him, which is the grand and only intrinsic function of a writing man, call him by what title you will? Cultivate that superior excellence till it become a perfect and superlative one. Why *sing* your bits of thoughts, if you *can* contrive to speak them? By your thought, not by your mode of delivering it, you must live or die. —Besides I had to observe there was in Sterling intrinsically no depth of *tune*; which surely is the real test of a Poet or Singer, as distinguished from a Speaker? In music proper he had not the slightest ear; all music was mere impertinent noise to him, nothing in it perceptible but the mere march or time. Nor in his way of conception and utterance, in the verses he wrote, was there any contradiction, but a constant confirmation to me, of that fatal prognostic; —as indeed the whole man, in ear and heart and tongue, is one; and he whose soul does not sing, need not try to do it with his throat. Sterling's verses had a monotonous rub-a-dub, instead of tune; no trace of music deeper than that of a well-beaten drum; to which limited range of excellence the substance also corresponded; being intrinsically always a rhymed and slightly rhythmical *speech*, not a *song*.

In short, all seemed to me to say, in his case: "You can speak with supreme excellence; sing with considerable excellence you never can. And the Age itself, does it not, beyond most ages, demand and require clear speech; an Age incapable of being sung to, in any but a trivial manner, till these convulsive agonies and wild revolutionary overturnings readjust themselves? Intelligible word of command, not musical psalmody and fiddling, is possible in this fell storm of battle. Beyond all ages, our Age admonishes whatsoever thinking or writing man it has: Oh, speak to me some wise intelligible speech; your wise meaning in the shortest and clearest way; behold I am dying for want of wise meaning, and insight into the devouring fact: speak, if you have any wisdom! As to song so called, and your fiddling talent, —even if you have one, much more if you have none, —we will talk of that a couple of centuries hence, when things are calmer again. Homer shall be thrice welcome; but only when Troy is *taken*: alas, while the siege lasts, and battle's fury rages everywhere, what can I do with the Homer? I want Achilleus and Odysseus, and am enraged to see them trying to be Homers!"—

Sterling, who respected my sincerity, and always was amenable enough to counsel, was doubtless much confused by such contradictory diagnosis of his case. The question, Poetry or Prose? became more and more pressing, more and more insoluble. He decided, at last, to appeal to the public upon it; —got ready, in the late autumn, a small select Volume of his verses; and was now busy pushing it through the press. Unfortunately, in the mean while, a grave illness, of the old pulmonary sort, overtook him, which at one time threatened to be dangerous. This is a glance again into his interior household in these circumstances: —

To his Mother.

"*December 21st*, 1839. —The Tin box came quite safe, with all its miscellaneous contents. I suppose we are to thank you for the *Comic Almanac*, which, as usual, is very amusing; and for the Book on *Watt*, which disappointed me. The scientific part is no doubt very good, and particularly clear and simple; but there is nothing remarkable in the account of Watt's character; and it is an absurd piece of French impertinence in Arago to say, that England has not yet learnt to appreciate men like Watt, because he was not made a peer; which, were our peerage an institution like that of France, would have been very proper.

"I have now finished correcting the proofs of my little Volume of Poems. It has been a great plague to me, and one that I would not have incurred, had I expected to be laid up as I have been; but the matter was begun before I had any notion of being disabled by such an illness, —the severest I have suffered since I went to the West Indies. The Book will, after all, be a botched business in many respects; and I much doubt whether it will pay its expenses: but I try to consider it as out of my hands, and not to fret myself about it. I shall be very curious to see Carlyle's Tractate on *Chartism*; which" — But we need not enter upon that.

Sterling's little Book was printed at his own expense; [23] published by Moxon in the very end of this year. It carries an appropriate and pretty Epigraph: —

> "Feeling, Thought, and Fancy be
> Gentle sister Graces three:
> If these prove averse to me,
> They will punish, —pardon Ye! "

He had dedicated the little Volume to Mr. Hare; —and he submitted very patiently to the discouraging neglect with which it was received by the world; for indeed the "Ye" said nothing audible, in the way of pardon or other doom; so that whether the "sister Graces" were averse or not, remained as doubtful as ever.

CHAPTER II.
TWO WINTERS.

As we said above, it had been hoped by Sterling's friends, not very confidently by himself, that in the gentler air of Clifton his health might so far recover as to enable him to dispense with autumnal voyages, and to spend the year all round in a house of his own. These hopes, favorable while the warm season lasted, broke down when winter came. In November of this same year, while his little Volume was passing through the press, bad and worse symptoms, spitting of blood to crown the sad list, reappeared; and Sterling had to equip himself again, at this late season, for a new flight to Madeira; wherein the good Calvert, himself suffering, and ready on all grounds for such an adventure, offered to accompany him. Sterling went by land to Falmouth, meaning there to wait for Calvert, who was to come by the Madeira Packet, and there take him on board.

Calvert and the Packet did arrive, in stormy January weather; which continued wildly blowing for weeks; forbidding all egress Westward, especially for invalids. These elemental tumults, and blustering wars of sea and sky, with nothing but the misty solitude of Madeira in the distance, formed a very discouraging outlook. In the mean while Falmouth itself had offered so many resources, and seemed so tolerable in climate and otherwise, while this wintry ocean looked so inhospitable for invalids, it was resolved our voyagers should stay where they were till spring returned. Which accordingly was done; with good effect for that season, and also with results for the coming seasons. Here again, from Letters to Knightsbridge, are some glimpses of his winter-life: —

"*Falmouth, February 5th*, 1840. —I have been to-day to see a new tin-mine, two or three miles off, which is expected to turn into a copper-mine by and by, so they will have the two constituents of bronze close together. This, by the way, was the 'brass' of Homer and the Ancients generally, who do not seem to have known our brass made of copper and zinc. Achilles in his armor must have looked like a bronze statue. —I took Sheridan's advice, and did not go down the mine. "

"*February 15th*. —To some iron-works the other day; where I saw half the beam of a great steam-engine, a piece of iron forty feet long and seven broad, cast in about five minutes. It was a very striking spectacle. I hope to go to Penzance before I leave this country, and will not fail to tell you about it. " He did make trial of Penzance, among other places, next year; but only of Falmouth this.

"February 20th. —I am going on *asy* here, in spite of a great change of weather. The East-winds are come at last, bringing with them snow, which has been driving about for the last twenty-four hours; not falling heavily, nor lying long when fallen. Neither is it as yet very cold, but I suppose there will be some six weeks of unpleasant temperature. The marine climate of this part of England will, no doubt, modify and mollify the air into a happier sort of substance than that you breathe in London.

"The large vessels that had been lying here for weeks, waiting for a wind, have now sailed; two of them for the East Indies, and having three hundred soldiers on board. It is a curious thing that the long-continued westerly winds had so prevented the coasters arriving, that the Town was almost on the point of a famine as to bread. The change has brought in abundance of flour. —The people in general seem extremely comfortable; their houses are excellent, almost all of stone. Their habits are very little agricultural, but mining and fishing seem to prosper with them. There are hardly any gentry here; I have not seen more than two gentlemen's carriages in the Town; indeed I think the nearest one comes from five miles off....

"I have been obliged to try to occupy myself with Natural Science, in order to give some interest to my walks; and have begun to feel my way in Geology. I have now learnt to recognize three or four of the common kinds of stone about here, when I see them; but I find it stupid work compared with Poetry and Philosophy. In the mornings, however, for an hour or so before I get up, I generally light my candle, and try to write some verses; and since I have been here, I have put together short poems, almost enough for another small volume. In the evenings I have gone on translating some of Goethe. But six or seven hours spent on my legs, in the open air, do not leave my brain much energy for thinking. Thus my life is a dull and unprofitable one, but still better than it would have been in Madeira or on board ship. I hear from Susan every day, and write to her by return of post. "

At Falmouth Sterling had been warmly welcomed by the well-known Quaker family of the Foxes, principal people in that place, persons of cultivated opulent habits, and joining to the fine purities and pieties of their sect a reverence for human intelligence in all kinds; to whom such a visitor as Sterling was naturally a welcome windfall. The family had grave elders, bright cheery younger branches, men and women; truly amiable all, after their sort: they made a pleasant image of home for Sterling in his winter exile. "Most worthy, respectable and highly cultivated people, with a great deal of money among them, " writes Sterling in the end of February; "who make the place pleasant to me. They are connected with all the large Quaker circle, the Gurneys, Frys, &c., and also with Buxton the Abolitionist. It is droll to hear them talking of all the common topics of science, literature, and life, and in the midst of it: 'Does thou know Wordsworth? ' or, 'Did thou see the Coronation? ' or 'Will thou take some refreshment? ' They are very kind and pleasant people to know. "

"Calvert, " continues our Diarist, "is better than he lately was, though he has not been at all laid up. He shoots little birds, and dissects and stuffs them; while I carry a hammer, and break flints and slates, to look for diamonds and rubies inside; and admire my success in the evening, when I empty my great-coat pocket of its specimens. On the whole, I doubt whether my physical proceedings will set the Thames on fire. Give my love to Anthony's Charlotte; also remember me affectionately to the Carlyles. " —

At this time, too, John Mill, probably encouraged by Sterling, arrived in Falmouth, seeking refuge of climate for a sickly younger Brother, to whom also, while he continued there, and to his poor patient, the doors and hearts of this kind family were thrown wide open. Falmouth, during these winter weeks, especially while Mill continued, was an unexpectedly engaging place to Sterling; and he left it in spring, for Clifton, with a very kindly image of it in his thoughts. So ended, better than it might have done, his first year's flight from the Clifton winter.

In April, 1840, he was at his own hearth again; cheerily pursuing his old labors, —struggling to redeem, as he did with a gallant constancy, the available months and days, out of the wreck of so many that were unavailable, for the business allotted him in this world. His swift, decisive energy of character; the valiant rally he made again and ever again, starting up fresh from amid the wounded, and cheerily storming in anew, was admirable, and showed a noble fund of natural health amid such an element of disease. Somehow one could never rightly fancy that he was diseased; that those fatal ever-recurring downbreaks were not almost rather the penalties paid for exuberance of health, and of faculty for living and working; criminal forfeitures, incurred by excess of self-exertion and such irrepressible over-rapidity of movement: and the vague hope was habitual with us, that increase of years, as it deadened this over-energy, would first make the man secure of life, and a sober prosperous worker among his fellows. It was always as if with a kind of blame that one heard of his being ill again! Poor Sterling; —no man knows another's burden: these things were not, and were not to be, in the way we had fancied them!

Summer went along in its usual quiet tenor at Clifton; health good, as usual while the warm weather lasted, and activity abundant; the scene as still as the busiest could wish. "You metropolitan signors," writes Sterling to his Father, "cannot conceive the dulness and scantiness of our provincial chronicle." Here is a little excursion to the seaside; the lady of the family being again, —for good reasons, — in a weakly state: —

"To Edward Sterling, Esq., Knightsbridge, London.
"PORTSHEAD, BRISTOL, 1st Sept., 1840.

"MY DEAR FATHER, —This place is a southern headland at the mouth of the Avon. Susan, and the Children too, were all suffering from languor; and as she is quite unfit to travel in a carriage, we were obliged to move, if at all, to some place accessible by water; and this is the nearest where we could get the fresher air of the Bristol Channel. We sent to take a house, for a week; and came down here in a steamer yesterday morning. It seems likely to do every one good. We have a comfortable house, with eight rather small bedrooms, for which we pay four guineas and a half for the week. We have brought three of our own maids, and leave one to take care of the house at Clifton.

"A week ago my horse fell with me, but did not hurt seriously either himself or me: it was, however, rather hard that, as there were six legs to be damaged, the one that did scratch itself should belong to the part of the machine possessing only two, instead of the quadrupedal portion. I grazed about the size of a halfpenny on my left knee; and for a couple of days walked about as if nothing had happened. I found, however, that the skin was not returning correctly; and so sent for a doctor: he treated the thing as quite insignificant, but said I must keep my leg quiet for a few days. It is still not quite healed; and I lie all day on a sofa, much to my discomposure; but the thing is now rapidly disappearing; and I hope, in a day or two more, I shall be free again. I find I can do no work, while thus crippled in my leg. The man in Horace who made verses *stans pede in uno* had the advantage of me.

"The Great Western came in last night about eleven, and has just been making a flourish past our windows; looking very grand, with four streamers of bunting, and one of smoke. Of course I do not yet know whether I have Letters by her, as if so they will have gone to Clifton first. This place is quiet, green and pleasant; and will suit us very well, if we have good weather, of which there seems every appearance.

"Milnes spent last Sunday with me at Clifton; and was very amusing and cordial. It is impossible for those who know him well not to like him. —I send this to Knightsbridge, not knowing where else to hit you. Love to my Mother.

"Your affectionate,
"JOHN STERLING. "

The expected "Letters by the Great Western" are from Anthony, now in Canada, doing military duties there. The "Milnes" is our excellent Richard, whom all men know, and truly whom none can know well without even doing as Sterling says. —In a week the family had returned to Clifton; and Sterling was at his poetizings and equitations again. His grand business was now Poetry; all effort, outlook and aim exclusively directed thither, this good while.

Of the published Volume Moxon gave the worst tidings; no man had hailed it with welcome; unsold it lay, under the leaden seal of general neglect; the public when asked what it thought, had answered hitherto by a lazy stare. It shall answer otherwise, thought Sterling; by no means taking that as the final response. It was in this same September that he announced to me and other friends, under seal of secrecy as usual, the completion, or complete first-draught, of "a new Poem reaching to two thousand verses. " By working "three hours every morning" he had brought it so far. This Piece, entitled *The Election*, of which in due time we obtained perusal, and had to give some judgment, proved to be in a new vein, —what might be called the mock-heroic, or sentimental Hudibrastic, reminding one a little, too, of Wieland's *Oberon*; —it had touches of true drollery combined not ill with grave clear insight; showed spirit everywhere, and a plainly improved power of execution. Our stingy verdict was to the effect, "Better, but still not good enough: —why follow that sad 'metrical' course, climbing the loose sandhills, when you have a firm path along the plain? " To Sterling himself it remained dubious whether so slight a strain, new though it were, would suffice to awaken the sleeping public; and the Piece was thrown away and taken up again, at intervals; and the question, Publish or not publish? lay many months undecided.

Meanwhile his own feeling was now set more and more towards Poetry; and in spite of symptoms and dissuasions, and perverse prognostics of outward wind and weather, he was rallying all his force for a downright struggle with it; resolute to see which *was* the stronger. It must be owned, he takes his failures in the kindliest manner; and goes along, bating no jot of heart or hope. Perhaps I should have more admired this than I did! My dissuasions, in that case, might have been fainter. But then my sincerity, which was all the use of my poor counsel in assent or dissent, would have been less. He was now furthermore busy with a *Tragedy of Strafford*, the theme of many failures in Tragedy; planning it industriously in his head; eagerly reading in *Whitlocke, Rushworth* and the Puritan Books, to attain a vesture and local habitation for it. Faithful assiduous studies I do believe; —of which, knowing my stubborn realism, and savage humor towards singing by the Thespian or other methods, he told me little, during his visits that summer.

The advance of the dark weather sent him adrift again; to Torquay, for this winter: there, in his old Falmouth climate, he hoped to do well; —and did, so far as well-doing was readily possible, in that sad wandering way of life. However, be where he may, he tries to work "two or three hours in the morning, " were it even "with a lamp, " in bed, before the fires are lit; and so makes something of it. From abundant Letters of his now before me, I glean these two or three small glimpses; sufficient for our purpose at present. The general date is "Tor, near Torquay: " —

To Mrs. Charles Fox, Falmouth.

Tor, November 30th, 1840. —I reached this place on Thursday; having, after much hesitation, resolved to come here, at least for the next three weeks, —with some obscure purpose of embarking, at the New

Year, from Falmouth for Malta, and so reaching Naples, which I have not seen. There was also a doubt whether I should not, after Christmas, bring my family here for the first four months of the year. All this, however, is still doubtful. But for certain inhabitants of Falmouth and its neighborhood, this place would be far more attractive than it. But I have here also friends, whose kindness, like much that I met with last winter, perpetually makes me wonder at the stock of benignity in human nature. A brother of my friend Julius Hare, Marcus by name, a Naval man, and though not a man of letters, full of sense and knowledge, lives here in a beautiful place, with a most agreeable and excellent wife, a daughter of Lord Stanley of Alderley. I had hardly seen them before; but they are fraternizing with me, in a much better than the Jacobin fashion; and one only feels ashamed at the enormity of some people's good-nature. I am in a little rural sort of lodging; and as comfortable as a solitary oyster can expect to be. " —

To C. Barton.

"*December 5th.* — This place is extremely small, much more so than Falmouth even; but pretty, cheerful, and very mild in climate. There are a great many villas in and about the little Town, having three or four reception-rooms, eight or ten bedrooms; and costing about fifteen hundred or two thousand pounds each, and occupied by persons spending a thousand or more pounds a year. If the Country would acknowledge my merits by the gift of one of these, I could prevail on myself to come and live here; which would be the best move for my health I could make in England; but, in the absence of any such expression of public feeling, it would come rather dear. " —

To Mrs. Fox again.

"*December 22d.* — By the way, did you ever read a Novel? If you ever mean to do so hereafter, let it be Miss Martineau's *Deerbrook.* It is really very striking; and parts of it are very true and very beautiful. It is not so true, or so thoroughly clear and harmonious, among delineations of English middle-class gentility, as Miss Austen's books, especially as *Pride and Prejudice,* which I think exquisite; but it is worth reading. *The hour and the Man* is eloquent, but an absurd exaggeration. — I hold out so valorously against this Scandinavian weather, that I deserve to be ranked with Odin and Thor; and fancy I may go to live at Clifton or Drontheim. Have you had the same icy desolation as prevails here? "

To W. Coningham, Esq.

"*December 28th.* —Looking back to him [a deceased Uncle, father of his correspondent], as I now very often do, I feel strongly, what the loss of other friends has also impressed on me, how much Death deepens our affection; and sharpens our regret for whatever has been even slightly amiss in our conduct towards those who are gone. What trifles then swell into painful importance; how we believe that, could the past be recalled, life would present no worthier, happier task, than that of so bearing ourselves towards those we love, that we might ever after find nothing but melodious tranquillity breathing about their graves! Yet, too often, I feel the difficulty of always practicing such mild wisdom towards those who are still left me. —You will wonder less at my rambling off in this way, when I tell you that my little lodging is close to a picturesque old Church and Churchyard, where, every day, I brush past a tombstone, recording that an Italian, of Manferrato, has buried there a girl of sixteen, his only daughter: '*L' unica speranza di mia vita.* '—No doubt, as you say, our Mechanical Age is necessary as a passage to something better; but, at least, do not let us go back. " —

At the New-year time, feeling unusually well, he returns to Clifton. His plans, of course, were ever fluctuating; his movements were swift and uncertain. Alas, his whole life, especially his winter-life, had to be built as if on wavering drift-sand; nothing certain in it, except if possible the "two or three hours of work" snatched from the general whirlpool of the dubious four-and-twenty!

To Dr. Carlyle.

"*Clifton, January 10th*, 1841. —I stood the sharp frost at Torquay with such entire impunity, that at last I took courage, and resolved to return home. I have been here a week, in extreme cold; and have suffered not at all; so that I hope, with care I may prosper in spite of medical prognostics, —if you permit such profane language. I am even able to work a good deal; and write for some hours every morning, by dint of getting up early, which an Arnott stove in my study enables me to do. "—But at Clifton he cannot continue. Again, before long, the rude weather has driven him Southward; the spring finds him in his former haunts; doubtful as ever what to decide upon for the future; but tending evidently towards a new change of residence for household and self: —

To W. Coningham, Esq.

"*Penzance, April 19th*, 1841. —My little Boy and I have been wandering about between Torquay and this place; and latterly have had my Father for a few days with us, —he left us yesterday. In all probability I shall endeavor to settle either at Torquay, at Falmouth, or here; as it is pretty clear that I cannot stand the sharp air of Clifton, and still less the London east-winds. Penzance is, on the whole, a pleasant-looking, cheerful place; with a delightful mildness of air, and a great appearance of comfort among the people: the view of Mount's Bay is certainly a very noble one. Torquay would suit the health of my Wife and Children better; or else I should be glad to live here always, London and its neighborhood being impracticable. "— Such was his second wandering winter; enough to render the prospect of a third at Clifton very uninviting.

With the Falmouth friends, young and old, his intercourse had meanwhile continued cordial and frequent. The omens were pointing towards that region at his next place of abode. Accordingly, in few weeks hence, in the June of this Summer, 1841, his dubitations and inquirings are again ended for a time; he has fixed upon a house in Falmouth, and removed thither; bidding Clifton, and the regretful Clifton friends, a kind farewell. This was the *fifth* change of place for his family since Bayswater; the fifth, and to one chief member of it the last. Mrs. Sterling had brought him a new child in October last; and went hopefully to Falmouth, dreading *other* than what befell there.

CHAPTER III.
FALMOUTH: POEMS.

At Falmouth, as usual, he was soon at home in his new environment; resumed his labors; had his new small circle of acquaintance, the ready and constant centre of which was the Fox family, with whom he lived on an altogether intimate, honored and beloved footing; realizing his best anticipations in that respect, which doubtless were among his first inducements to settle in this new place. Open cheery heights, rather bare of wood: fresh southwestern breezes; a brisk laughing sea, swept by industrious sails, and the nets of a most stalwart, wholesome, frank and interesting population: the clean little fishing, trading and packet Town; hanging on its slope towards the Eastern sun, close on the waters of its basin and intricate bay, — with the miniature Pendennis Castle seaward on the right, the miniature St. Mawes landward to left, and the mining world and the farming world open boundlessly to the rear: —all this made a pleasant outlook and environment. And in all this, as in the other new elements of his position, Sterling, open beyond most men to the worth of things about him, took his frank share. From the first, he had liked the general aspect of the population, and their healthy, lively ways; not to speak of the special friendships he had formed there, which shed a charm over them all. "Men of strong character, clear heads and genuine goodness, " writes he, "are by no means wanting. " And long after: "The common people here dress better than in most parts of England; and on Sundays, if the weather be at all fine, their appearance is very pleasant. One sees them all round the Town, especially towards Pendennis Castle, streaming in a succession of little groups, and seeming for the most part really and quietly happy. " On the whole he reckoned himself lucky; and, so far as locality went, found this a handsome shelter for the next two years of his life. Two years, and not without an interruption; that was all. Here we have no continuing city; he less than any of us! One other flight for shelter; and then it is ended, and he has found an inexpugnable refuge. Let us trace his remote footsteps, as we have opportunity: —

To Dr. Symonds, Clifton.

"*Falmouth, June 28th,* 1841. —Newman writes to me that he is gone to the Rhine. I wish I were! And yet the only 'wish' at the bottom of my heart, is to be able to work vigorously in my own way anywhere, were it in some Circle of Dante's Inferno. This, however, is the secret of my soul, which I disclose only to a few. "

To his Mother.

"*Falmouth, July 6th,* 1841. —I have at last my own study made comfortable; the carpet being now laid down, and most of my appurtenances in tolerable order. By and by I shall, unless stopped by illness, get myself together, and begin living an orderly life and doing my daily task. I have swung a cot in my dressing-room; partly as a convenience for myself, partly as a sort of memorial of my poor Uncle, in whose cot in his dressing-room at Lisworney I remember to have slept when a child. I have put a good large bookcase in my drawing-room, and all the rest of my books fit very well into the study. "

To Mr. Carlyle.

"*July 6th.* —No books have come in my way but Emerson's, which I value full as much as you, though as yet I have read only some corners of it. We have had an Election here, of the usual stamp; to me a droll 'realized Ideal, ' after my late metrical adventures in that line. But the oddest sign of the Times I know, is a cheap Translation of Strauss's *Leben Jesu*, now publishing in numbers, and said to be circulating far and wide. What does—or rather, what does not—this portend? " —

With the Poem called *The Election*, here alluded to, which had been more than once revised and reconsidered, he was still under some hesitations; but at last had well-nigh resolved, as from the first it was clear he would do, on publishing it. This occupied some occasional portion of his thoughts. But his grand private affair, I believe, was now *Strafford*; to which, or to its adjuncts, all working hours were devoted. Sterling's notions of Tragedy are high enough. This is what he writes once, in reference to his own task in these weeks: "Few, I fancy, know how much harder it is to write a Tragedy than to realize or be one. Every man has in his heart and lot, if he pleases, and too many whether they please or no, all the woes of OEdipus and Antigone. But it takes the One, the Sophocles of a thousand years, to utter these in the full depth and harmony of creative song. Curious, by the way, how that Dramatic Form of the old Greek, with only some superficial changes, remains a law not only for the stage, but for the thoughts of all Poets; and what a charm it has even for the reader who never saw a theatre. The Greek Plays and Shakspeare have interested a hundred as books, for one who has seen their writings acted. How lightly does the mere clown, the idle school-girl, build a private theatre in the fancy, and laugh or weep with Falstaff and Macbeth: with how entire an oblivion of the artificial nature of the whole contrivance, which thus compels them to be their own architects, machinists, scene-painters, and actors! In fact, the artifice succeeds, —becomes grounded in the substance of the soul: and every one loves to feel how he is thus brought face to face with the brave, the fair, the woful and the great of all past ages; looks into their eyes, and feels the beatings of their hearts; and reads, over the shoulder, the secret written tablets of the busiest and the largest brains; while the Juggler, by whose cunning the whole strange beautiful absurdity is set in motion, keeps himself hidden; sings loud with a mouth unmoving as that of a statue, and makes the human race cheat itself unanimously and delightfully by the illusion that he preordains; while as an obscure Fate, he sits invisible, and hardly lets his being be divined by those who cannot flee him. The Lyric Art is childish, and the Epic barbarous, compared to this. But of the true and perfect Drama it may be said, as of even higher mysteries, Who is sufficient for these things? "—On this *Tragedy of Strafford*, writing it and again writing it, studying for it, and bending himself with his whole strength to do his best on it, he expended many strenuous months, —"above a year of his life, " he computes, in all.

For the rest, what Falmouth has to give him he is willing to take, and mingles freely in it. In Hare's Collection there is given a *Lecture* which he read in Autumn, 1841 (Mr. Hare says "1842, " by mistake), to a certain Public Institution in the place, —of which more anon; —a piece interesting in this, if not much in any other respect. Doubtless his friends the Foxes were at the heart of that lecturing enterprise, and had urged and solicited him. Something like proficiency in certain branches of science, as I have understood, characterized one or more of this estimable family; love of knowledge, taste for art, wish to consort with wisdom and wise men, were the tendencies of all; to opulent means superadd the Quaker beneficence, Quaker purity and reverence, there is a circle in which wise men also may love to be. Sterling made acquaintance here with whatever of notable in worthy persons or things might be afoot in those parts; and was led thereby, now and then, into pleasant reunions, in new circles of activity, which might otherwise have continued foreign to him. The good Calvert, too, was now here; and intended to remain; —which he mostly did henceforth, lodging in Sterling's neighborhood, so long as lodging in this world was permitted him. Still good and clear and cheerful; still a lively comrade, within doors or without, —a diligent rider always, —though now wearing visibly weaker, and less able to exert himself.

Among those accidental Falmouth reunions, perhaps the notablest for Sterling occurred in this his first season. There is in Falmouth an Association called the *Cornwall Polytechnic Society*, established about twenty years ago, and supported by the wealthy people of the Town and neighborhood, for the encouragement of the arts in that region; it has its Library, its Museum, some kind of Annual Exhibition withal; gives prizes, publishes reports: the main patrons, I believe, are Sir Charles Lemon, a well-known country gentleman of those parts, and the Messrs. Fox. To this, so far as he liked to go in it, Sterling was sure to be introduced and solicited. The Polytechnic meeting of 1841 was unusually distinguished; and Sterling's part in it formed one of the pleasant occurrences for him in Falmouth. It was here that, among other profitable as well as pleasant things, he made acquaintance with Professor Owen (an event of which I too had my benefit in due time, and still have): the bigger assemblage called *British Association*, which met at Plymouth this year, having now just finished its affairs there, Owen and other distinguished persons had taken Falmouth in their route from it. Sterling's account of this Polytechnic gala still remains, —in three Letters to his Father, which, omitting the extraneous portions, I will give in one, —as a piece worth reading among those still-life pictures: —

"*To Edward Sterling, Esq., Knightsbridge, London.*
"FALMOUTH, 10th August, 1841.

"MY DEAR FATHER, —I was not well for a day or two after you went; and since, I have been busy about an annual show of the Polytechnic Society here, in which my friends take much interest, and for which I have been acting as one of the judges in the department of the Fine Arts, and have written a little Report for them. As I have not said that Falmouth is as eminent as Athens or Florence, perhaps the Committee will not adopt my statement. But if they do, it will be of some use; for I have hinted, as delicately as possible, that people should not paint historical pictures before they have the power of drawing a decent outline of a pig or a cabbage. I saw Sir Charles Lemon yesterday, who was kind as well as civil in his manner; and promises to be a pleasant neighbor. There are

several of the British Association heroes here; but not Whewell, or
any one whom I know. "

"*August 17th.* —At the Polytechnic Meeting here we had several very
eminent men; among others, Professor Owen, said to be the first of
comparative anatomists, and Conybeare the geologist. Both of these
gave evening Lectures; and after Conybeare's, at which I happened
to be present, I said I would, if they chose, make some remarks on
the Busts which happened to be standing there, intended for prizes
in the department of the Fine Arts. They agreed gladly. The heads
were Homer, Pericles, Augustus, Dante and Michael Angelo. I got
into the box-like platform, with these on a shelf before me; and
began a talk which must have lasted some three quarters of an hour;
describing partly the characters and circumstances of the men,
illustrated by anecdotes and compared with their physiognomies,
and partly the several styles of sculpture exhibited in the Casts,
referring these to what I considered the true principles of the Art.
The subject was one that interests me, and I got on in famous style;
and had both pit and galleries all applauding, in a way that had had
no precedent during any other part of the meeting. Conybeare paid
me high compliments; Owen looked much pleased, —an honor well
purchased by a year's hard work; —and everybody, in short, seemed
delighted. Susan was not there, and I had nothing to make me
nervous; so that I worked away freely, and got vigorously over the
ground. After so many years' disuse of rhetoric, it was a pleasant
surprise to myself to find that I could still handle the old weapons
without awkwardness. More by good luck than good guidance, it
has done my health no harm. I have been at Sir Charles Lemon's,
though only to pay a morning visit, having declined to stay there or
dine, the hours not suiting me. They were very civil. The person I
saw most of was his sister, Lady Dunstanville; a pleasant, well-
informed and well-bred woman. He seems a most amiable, kindly
man, of fair good sense and cultivated tastes. —I had a letter to-day
from my Mother [in Scotland]; who says she sent you one which you
were to forward me; which I hope soon to have. "

"*August 29th.* —I returned yesterday from Carclew, Sir C. Lemon's
fine place about five miles off; where I had been staying a couple of
days, with apparently the heartiest welcome. Susan was asked; but
wanting a Governess, could not leave home.

"Sir Charles is a widower (his Wife was sister to Lord Ilchester)
without children; but had a niece staying with him, and his sister

Lady Dunstanville, a pleasant and very civil woman. There were also Mr. Bunbury, eldest son of Sir Henry Bunbury, a man of much cultivation and strong talents; Mr. Fox Talbot, son, I think, of another Ilchester lady, and brother of *the* Talbot of Wales, but himself a man of large fortune, and known for photogenic and other scientific plans of extracting sunbeams from cucumbers. He also is a man of known ability, but chiefly employed in that peculiar department. *Item* Professors Lloyd and Owen: the former, of Dublin, son of the late Provost, I had seen before and knew; a great mathematician and optician, and a discoverer in those matters; with a clever little Wife, who has a great deal of knowledge, quite free from pretension. Owen is a first-rate comparative anatomist, they say the greatest since Cuvier; lives in London, and lectures there. On the whole, he interested me more than any of them, —by an apparent force and downrightness of mind, combined with much simplicity and frankness.

"Nothing could be pleasanter and easier than the habits of life, with what to me was a very unusual degree of luxury, though probably nothing but what is common among people of large fortune. The library and pictures are nothing extraordinary. The general tone of good nature, good sense and quiet freedom, was what struck me most; and I think besides this there was a disposition to be cordially courteous towards me....

"I took Edward a ride of two hours yesterday on Calvert's pony, and he is improving fast in horsemanship. The school appears to answer very well. We shall have the Governess in a day or two, which will be a great satisfaction. Will you send my Mother this scribble with my love; and believe me,

"Your affectionate son,
"JOHN STERLING. "

One other little event dwells with me, out of those Falmouth times, exact date now forgotten; a pleasant little matter, in which Sterling, and principally the Misses Fox, bright cheery young creatures, were concerned; which, for the sake of its human interest, is worth mention. In a certain Cornish mine, said the Newspapers duly specifying it, two miners deep down in the shaft were engaged putting in a shot for blasting: they had completed their affair, and were about to give the signal for being hoisted up, —one at a time was all their coadjutor at the top could manage, and the second was to kindle the match, and then mount with all speed. Now it chanced while they were both still below, one of them thought the match too long; tried to break it shorter, took a couple of stones, a flat and a sharp, to cut it shorter; did cut it of the due length, but, horrible to relate, kindled it at the same time, and both were still below! Both shouted vehemently to the coadjutor at the windlass, both sprang at the basket; the windlass man could not move it with them both. Here was a moment for poor miner Jack and miner Will! Instant horrible death hangs over both, —when Will generously resigns himself: "Go aloft, Jack, " and sits down; "away; in one minute I shall be in Heaven! " Jack bounds aloft, the explosion instantly follows, bruises his face as he looks over; he is safe above ground: and poor Will? Descending eagerly they find Will too, as if by miracle, buried under rocks which had arched themselves over him, and little injured: he too is brought up safe, and all ends joyfully, say the Newspapers.

Such a piece of manful promptitude, and salutary human heroism, was worth investigating. It was investigated; found to be accurate to the letter, —with this addition and explanation, that Will, an honest, ignorant good man, entirely given up to Methodism, had been perfect in the "faith of assurance, " certain that *he* should get to Heaven if he died, certain that Jack would not, which had been the ground of his decision in that great moment; —for the rest, that he much wished to learn reading and writing, and find some way of life above ground instead of below. By aid of the Misses Fox and the rest of that family, a subscription (modest *Anti*-Hudson testimonial) was raised to this Methodist hero: he emerged into daylight with fifty pounds in his pocket; did strenuously try, for certain months, to learn reading and writing; found he could not learn those arts or either of them; took his money and bought cows with it, wedding at the same time some religious likely milkmaid; and is, last time I heard of him, a prosperous modest dairyman, thankful for the upper light and safety from the wrath to come. Sterling had some hand in this affair: but, as I said, it was the two young ladies of the family that mainly did it.

In the end of 1841, after many hesitations and revisals, *The Election* came out; a tiny Duodecimo without name attached; [24] again inquiring of the public what its suffrage was; again to little purpose. My vote had never been loud for this step, but neither was it quite adverse; and now, in reading the poor little Poem over again, after ten years' space, I find it, with a touching mixture of pleasure and repentance, considerably better than it then seemed to me. My encouragement, if not to print this poem, yet to proceed with Poetry, since there was such a resolution for it, might have been a little more decided!

This is a small Piece, but aims at containing great things; a *multum in parvo* after its sort; and is executed here and there with undeniable success. The style is free and flowing, the rhyme dances along with a certain joyful triumph; everything of due brevity withal. That mixture of mockery on the surface, which finely relieves the real earnestness within, and flavors even what is not very earnest and might even be insipid otherwise, is not ill managed: an amalgam difficult to effect well in writing; nay, impossible in writing, —unless it stand already done and effected, as a general fact, in the writer's mind and character; which will betoken a certain ripeness there.

As I said, great things are intended in this little Piece; the motto itself foreshadowing them: —

> "*Fluellen.*   Ancient Pistol, I do partly understand your
>   meaning.
> *Pistol.*   Why, then, rejoice therefor. "

A stupid commonplace English Borough has lost its Member suddenly, by apoplexy or otherwise; resolves, in the usual explosive temper of mind, to replace him by one of two others; whereupon strange stirring-up of rival-attorney and other human interests and catastrophes. "Frank Vane" (Sterling himself), and "Peter Mogg, " the pattern English blockhead of elections: these are the candidates. There are, of course, fierce rival attorneys; electors of all creeds and complexions to be canvassed: a poor stupid Borough thrown all into red or white heat; into blazing paroxysms of activity and enthusiasm, which render the inner life of it (and of England and the world through it) luminously transparent, so to speak; —of which opportunity our friend and his "Muse" take dexterous advantage, to delineate the same. His pictures are uncommonly good; brief, joyous, sometimes conclusively true: in rigorously compressed shape; all is merry freshness and exuberance: we have leafy summer embowering red bricks and small human interests, presented as in glowing miniature; a mock-heroic action fitly interwoven; —and many a clear glance is carelessly given into the deepest things by the way. Very happy also is the little love-episode; and the absorption of all the interest into that, on the part of Frank Vane and of us, when once this gallant Frank, —having fairly from his barrel-head stated his own (and John Sterling's) views on the aspects of the world, and of course having quite broken down with his attorney and his public, —handsomely, by stratagem, gallops off with the fair Anne; and leaves free field to Mogg, free field to the Hippopotamus if it like. This portrait of Mogg may be considered to have merit: —

"Though short of days, how large the mind of man;
A godlike force enclosed within a span!
To climb the skies we spurn our nature's clog,
And toil as Titans to elect a Mogg.

"And who was Mogg? O Muse! the man declare,
How excellent his worth, his parts how rare.
A younger son, he learnt in Oxford's halls
The spheral harmonies of billiard-balls,
Drank, hunted, drove, and hid from Virtue's frown
His venial follies in Decorum's gown.
Too wise to doubt on insufficient cause,
He signed old Cranmer's lore without a pause;
And knew that logic's cunning rules are taught
To guard our creed, and not invigorate thought, —
As those bronze steeds at Venice, kept for pride,
Adorn a Town where not one man can ride.

"From Isis sent with all her loud acclaims,
The Laws he studied on the banks of Thames.
Park, race and play, in his capacious plan,
Combined with Coke to form the finished man,
Until the wig's ambrosial influence shed
Its last full glories on the lawyer's head.

"But vain are mortal schemes. The eldest son
At Harrier Hall had scarce his stud begun,
When Death's pale courser took the Squire away
To lands where never dawns a hunting day:
And so, while Thomas vanished 'mid the fog,
Bright rose the morning-star of Peter Mogg. "[25]

And this little picture, in a quite opposite way: —

"Now, in her chamber all alone, the maid
Her polished limbs and shoulders disarrayed;
One little taper gave the only light,

172

One little mirror caught so dear a sight;
'Mid hangings dusk and shadows wide she stood,
Like some pale Nymph in dark-leafed solitude
Of rocks and gloomy waters all alone,
Where sunshine scarcely breaks on stump or stone
To scare the dreamy vision. Thus did she,
A star in deepest night, intent but free,
Gleam through the eyeless darkness, heeding not
Her beauty's praise, but musing o'er her lot.

"Her garments one by one she laid aside,
And then her knotted hair's long locks untied
With careless hand, and down her cheeks they fell,
And o'er her maiden bosom's blue-veined swell.
The right-hand fingers played amidst her hair,
And with her reverie wandered here and there:
The other hand sustained the only dress
That now but half concealed her loveliness;
And pausing, aimlessly she stood and thought,
In virgin beauty by no fear distraught. "

Manifold, and beautiful of their sort, are Anne's musings, in this interesting attitude, in the summer midnight, in the crisis of her destiny now near; —at last: —

"But Anne, at last her mute devotions o'er,
Perceived the feet she had forgot before
Of her too shocking nudity; and shame
Flushed from her heart o'er all the snowy frame:
And, struck from top to toe with burning dread,
She blew the light out, and escaped to bed. "[26]

—which also is a very pretty movement.

It must be owned withal, the Piece is crude in parts, and far enough from perfect. Our good painter has yet several things to learn, and to unlearn. His brush is not always of the finest; and dashes about, sometimes, in a recognizably sprawling way: but it hits many a feature with decisive accuracy and felicity; and on the palette, as usual, lie the richest colors. A grand merit, too, is the brevity of everything; by no means a spontaneous, or quite common merit with Sterling.

This new poetic Duodecimo, as the last had done and as the next also did, met with little or no recognition from the world: which was not very inexcusable on the world's part; though many a poem with far less proof of merit than this offers, has run, when the accidents favored it, through its tens of editions, and raised the writer to the demigods for a year or two, if not longer. Such as it is, we may take it as marking, in its small way, in a noticed or unnoticed manner, a new height arrived at by Sterling in his Poetic course; and almost as vindicating the determination he had formed to keep climbing by that method. Poor Poem, or rather Promise of a Poem! In Sterling's brave struggle, this little *Election* is the highest point he fairly lived to see attained, and openly demonstrated in print. His next public adventure in this kind was of inferior worth; and a third, which had perhaps intrinsically gone much higher than any of its antecessors, was cut off as a fragment, and has not hitherto been published. Steady courage is needed on the Poetic course, as on all courses! —

Shortly after this Publication, in the beginning of 1842, poor Calvert, long a hopeless sufferer, was delivered by death: Sterling's faithful fellow-pilgrim could no more attend him in his wayfarings through this world. The weary and heavy-laden man had borne his burden well. Sterling says of him to Hare: "Since I wrote last, I have lost Calvert; the man with whom, of all others, I have been during late years the most intimate. Simplicity, benevolence, practical good sense and moral earnestness were his great unfailing characteristics; and no man, I believe, ever possessed them more entirely. His illness had latterly so prostrated him, both in mind and body, that those who most loved him were most anxious for his departure. " There was something touching in this exit; in the quenching of so kind and bright a little life under the dark billows of death. To me he left a curious old Print of James Nayler the Quaker, which I still affectionately preserve.

Sterling, from this greater distance, came perhaps rather seldomer to London; but we saw him still at moderate intervals; and, through his family here and other direct and indirect channels, were kept in lively communication with him. Literature was still his constant pursuit; and, with encouragement or without, Poetic composition his chosen department therein. On the ill success of *The Election*, or any ill success with the world, nobody ever heard him utter the least murmur; condolence upon that or any such subject might have been a questionable operation, by no means called for! Nay, my own approval, higher than this of the world, had been languid, by no means enthusiastic. But our valiant friend took all quietly; and was not to be repulsed from his Poetics either by the world's coldness or by mine; he labored at his *Strafford*; —determined to labor, in all ways, till he felt the end of his tether in this direction.

He sometimes spoke, with a certain zeal, of my starting a Periodical: Why not lift up some kind of war-flag against the obese platitudes, and sickly superstitious aperies and impostures of the time? But I had to answer, "Who will join it, my friend? " He seemed to say, "I, for one; " and there was occasionally a transient temptation in the thought, but transient only. No fighting regiment, with the smallest attempt towards drill, co-operation, commissariat, or the like unspeakable advantages, could be raised in Sterling's time or mine; which truly, to honest fighters, is a rather grievous want. A grievous, but not quite a fatal one. For, failing this, failing all things and all men, there remains the solitary battle (and were it by the poorest weapon, the tongue only, or were it even by wise abstinence and silence and without any weapon), such as each man for himself can wage while he has life: an indubitable and infinitely comfortable fact for every man! Said battle shaped itself for Sterling, as we have long since seen, chiefly in the poetic form, in the singing or hymning rather than the speaking form; and in that he was cheerfully assiduous according to his light. The unfortunate *Strafford* is far on towards completion; a *Coeur-de-Lion*, of which we shall hear farther, "*Coeur-de-Lion*, greatly the best of all his Poems, " unluckily not completed, and still unpublished, already hangs in the wind.

His Letters to friends continue copious; and he has, as always, a loyally interested eye on whatsoever of notable is passing in the world. Especially on whatsoever indicates to him the spiritual condition of the world. Of "Strauss, " in English or in German, we now hear nothing more; of Church matters, and that only to special correspondents, less and less. Strauss, whom he used to mention, had interested him only as a sign of the times; in which sense alone do we find, for a year or two back, any notice of the Church, or its affairs by Sterling; and at last even this as good as ceases: "Adieu, O Church; thy road is that way, mine is this: in God's name, adieu! " "What we are going *to*, " says he once, "is abundantly obscure; but what all men are going *from*, is very plain. "—Sifted out of many pages, not of sufficient interest, here are one or two miscellaneous sentences, about the date we are now arrived at: —

To Dr. Symonds.

"*Falmouth, 3d November,* 1841. —Yesterday was my Wedding-day: eleven years of marriage; and on the whole my verdict is clear for matrimony. I solemnized the day by reading *John Gilpin* to the children, who with their Mother are all pretty well.... There is a trick of sham Elizabethan writing now prevalent, that looks plausible, but in most cases means nothing at all. Darley has real (lyrical) genius; Taylor, wonderful sense, clearness and weight of purpose; Tennyson, a rich and exquisite fancy. All the other men of our tiny generation that I know of are, in Poetry, either feeble or fraudulent. I know nothing of the Reviewer you ask about. "

To his Mother

"*December 11th.* —I have seen no new books; but am reading your last. I got hold of the two first Numbers of the *Hoggarty Diamond*; and read them with extreme delight. What is there better in Fielding or Goldsmith? The man is a true genius; and, with quiet and comfort, might produce masterpieces that would last as long as any we have, and delight millions of unborn readers. There is more truth and nature in one of these papers than in all — —'s Novels together. " —Thackeray, always a close friend of the Sterling house, will observe that this is dated 1841, not 1851, and have his own reflections on the matter!

To the Same.

"*December 17th.* —I am not much surprised at Lady — —'s views of Coleridge's little Book on *Inspiration.* —Great part of the obscurity of the Letters arises from his anxiety to avoid the difficulties and absurdities of the common views, and his panic terror of saying anything that bishops and good people would disapprove. He paid a heavy price, viz. all his own candor and simplicity, in hope of gaining the favor of persons like Lady — —; and you see what his reward is! A good lesson for us all. "

To the Same.

"*February 1st,* 1842. —English Toryism has, even in my eyes, about as much to say for itself as any other form of doctrine; but Irish Toryism is the downright proclamation of brutal injustice, and all in the name of God and the Bible! It is almost enough to make one turn Mahometan, but for the fear of the four wives. "

To his Father.

"*March 12th,* 1842. —... Important to me as these matters are, it almost seems as if there were something unfeeling in writing of them, under the pressure of such news as ours from India. If the Cabool Troops have perished, England has not received such a blow from an enemy, nor anything approaching it, since Buckingham's Expedition to the Isle of Rhe. Walcheren destroyed us by climate; and Corunna, with all its losses, had much of glory. But here we are dismally injured by mere Barbarians, in a War on our part shamefully unjust as well as foolish: a combination of disgrace and calamity that would have shocked Augustus even more than the defeat of Varus. One of the four officers with Macnaghten was George Lawrence, a brother-in-law of Nat Barton; a distinguished man, and the father of five totally unprovided children. He is a prisoner, if not since murdered. Macnaghten I do not pity; he was the prime author of the whole mad War. But Burnes; and the women; and our regiments! India, however, I feel sure, is safe. "

So roll the months at Falmouth; such is the ticking of the great World-Horologe as heard there by a good ear. "I willingly add, " so ends he, once, "that I lately found somewhere this fragment of an Arab's love-song: 'O Ghalia! If my father were a jackass, I would sell him to purchase Ghalia! ' A beautiful parallel to the French *'Avec cette sauce on mangerait son pere. '"*

CHAPTER IV.
NAPLES: POEMS.

In the bleak weather of this spring, 1842, he was again abroad for a little while; partly from necessity, or at least utility; and partly, as I guess, because these circumstances favored, and he could with a good countenance indulge a little wish he had long had. In the Italian Tour, which ended suddenly by Mrs. Sterling's illness recalling him, he had missed Naples; a loss which he always thought to be considerable; and which, from time to time, he had formed little projects, failures hitherto, for supplying. The rigors of spring were always dangerous to him in England, and it was always of advantage to get out of them: and then the sight of Naples, too; this, always a thing to be done some day, was now possible. Enough, with the real or imaginary hope of bettering himself in health, and the certain one of seeing Naples, and catching a glance of Italy again, he now made a run thither. It was not long after Calvert's death. The Tragedy of *Strafford* lay finished in his desk. Several things, sad and bright, were finished. A little intermezzo of ramble was not unadvisable.

His tour by water and by land was brief and rapid enough; hardly above two months in all. Of which the following Letters will, with some abridgment, give us what details are needful: —

> "*To Charles Barton, Esq., Leamington.*
> "FALMOUTH, 25th March, 1842.

"MY DEAR CHARLES, —My attempts to shoot you flying with my paper pellets turned out very ill. I hope young ladies succeed better when they happen to make appointments with you. Even now, I hardly know whether you have received a Letter I wrote on Sunday last, and addressed to The Cavendish. I sent it thither by Susan's advice.

"In this missive, —happily for us both, it did not contain a hundred-pound note or any trifle of that kind, —I informed you that I was compelled to plan an expedition towards the South Pole; stopping, however, in the Mediterranean; and that I designed leaving this on Monday next for Cadiz or Gibraltar, and then going on to Malta, whence Italy and Sicily would be accessible. Of course your company would be a great pleasure, if it were possible for you to join me. The delay in hearing from you, through no fault of yours, has naturally put me out a little; but, on the whole, my plan still holds, and I shall leave this on Monday for Gibraltar, where the *Great Liverpool* will catch me, and carry me to Malta. The *Great Liverpool* leaves Southampton on the 1st of April, and Falmouth on the 2d; and will reach Gibraltar in from four to five days.

"Now, if you *should* be able and disposed to join me, you have only to embark in that sumptuous tea-kettle, and pick me up under the guns of the Rock. We could then cruise on to Malta, Sicily, Naples, Rome, &c., *a discretion*. It is just *possible*, though extremely improbable, that my steamer of Monday (most likely the *Montrose*) may not reach Gibraltar so soon as the *Liverpool*. If so, and if you should actually be on board, you must stop at Gibraltar. But there are ninety-nine chances to one against this. Write at all events to Susan, to let her know what you propose.

"I do not wait till the *Great Liverpool* goes, because the object for me is to get into a warm climate as soon as possible. I am decidedly better.

"Your affectionate Brother,

"JOHN STERLING. "

Barton did not go with him, none went; but he arrives safe, and not *hurt* in health, which is something.

"*To Mrs. Sterling, Knightsbridge, London.*

"MALTA, 14th April, 1842.

"DEAREST MOTHER, —I am writing to Susan through France, by to-morrow's mail; and will also send you a line, instead of waiting for the longer English conveyance.

"We reached this the day before yesterday, in the evening; having had a strong breeze against us for a day or two before; which made me extremely uncomfortable, —and indeed my headache is hardly gone yet. From about the 4th to the 9th of the month, we had beautiful weather, and I was happy enough. You will see by the map that the straightest line from Gibraltar to this place goes close along the African coast; which accordingly we saw with the utmost clearness; and found it generally a line of mountains, the higher peaks and ridges covered with snow. We went close in to Algiers; which looks strong, but entirely from art. The town lies on the slope

179

of a straight coast; and is not at all embayed, though there is some little shelter for shipping within the mole. It is a square patch of white buildings huddled together; fringed with batteries; and commanded by large forts on the ridge above: a most uncomfortable-looking place; though, no doubt, there are *cafes* and billiard-rooms and a theatre within, —for the French like to have their Houris, &c., on *this* side of Paradise, if possible.

"Our party of fifty people (we had taken some on board at Gibraltar) broke up, on reaching this; never, of course, to meet again. The greater part do not proceed to Alexandria. Considering that there was a bundle of midshipmen, ensigns, &c., we had as much reason among us as could perhaps be looked for; and from several I gained bits of information and traits of character, though nothing very remarkable....

"I have established myself in an inn, rather than go to Lady Louis's; [27] I not feeling quite equal to company, except in moderate doses. I have, however, seen her a good deal; and dine there to-day, very privately, for Sir John is not quite well, and they will have no guests. The place, however, is full of official banqueting, for various unimportant reasons. When here before, I was in much distress and anxiety, on my way from Rome; and I suppose this it was that prevented its making the same impression on me as now, when it seems really the stateliest town I have ever seen. The architecture is generally of a corrupt Roman kind; with something of the varied and picturesque look, though much more massive, of our Elizabethan buildings. We have the finest English summer and a pellucid sky.... Your affectionate

"JOHN STERLING. "

At Naples next, for three weeks, was due admiration of the sceneries and antiquities, Bay and Mountain, by no means forgetting Art and the Museum: "to Pozzuoli, to Baiae, round the Promontory of Sorrento; "—above all, "twice to Pompeii, " where the elegance and classic simplicity of Ancient Housekeeping strikes us much; and again to Paestum, where "the Temple of Neptune is far the noblest building I have ever seen; and makes both Greek and Revived Roman seem quite barbaric.... Lord Ponsonby lodges in the same house with me; —but, of course, I do not countenance an adherent of a beaten Party! "[28]—Or let us take this more compendious account, which has much more of human in it, from an onward stage, ten days later: —

"To Thomas Carlyle, Esq., Chelsea, London.
"ROME, 13th May, 1842,

"MY DEAR CARLYLE, —I hope I wrote to you before leaving England, to tell you of the necessity for my doing so. Though coming to Italy, there was little comfort in the prospect of being divided from my family, and pursuits which grew on me every day. However, I tried to make the best of it, and have gained both health and pleasure.

"In spite of scanty communications from England (owing to the uncertainty of my position), a word or two concerning you and your dear Wife have reached me. Lately it has often occurred to me, that the sight of the Bay of Naples, of the beautiful coast from that to this place, and of Rome itself, all bathed in summer sunshine, and green with spring foliage, would be some consolation to her. [29] Pray give her my love.

"I have been two days here; and almost the first thing I did was to visit the Protestant burial-ground, and the graves of those I knew when here before. But much as being now alone here, I feel the difference, there is no scene where Death seems so little dreadful and miserable as in the lonelier neighborhoods of this old place. All one's impressions, however, as to that and everything else, appear to me, on reflection, more affected than I had for a long time any notion of, by one's own isolation. All the feelings and activities which family, friends and occupation commonly engage, are turned, here in one's solitude, with strange force into the channels of mere observation and contemplation; and the objects one is conversant with seem to gain a tenfold significance from the abundance of spare interest one now has to bestow on them. This explains to me a good deal of the peculiar effect that Italy has always had on me: and something of that artistic enthusiasm which I remember you used to think so singular in Goethe's *Travels*. Darley, who is as much a brooding hermit in England as here, felt nothing but disappointment from a country which fills me with childish wonder and delight.

"Of you I have received some slight notice from Mrs. Strachey; who is on her way hither; and will (she writes) be at Florence on the 15th, and here before the end of the month. She notices having received a

Letter of yours which had pleased her much. She now proposes spending the summer at Sorrento, or thereabouts; and if mere delight of landscape and climate were enough, Adam and Eve, had their courier taken them to that region, might have done well enough without Paradise, —and not been tempted, either, by any Tree of Knowledge; a kind that does not flourish in the Two Sicilies.

"The ignorance of the Neapolitans, from the highest to the lowest, is very eminent; and excites the admiration of all the rest of Italy. In the great building containing all the Works of Art, and a Library of 150,000 volumes, I asked for the best existing Book (a German one published ten years ago) on the Statues in that very Collection; and, after a rabble of clerks and custodes, got up to a dirty priest, who bowing to the ground regretted 'they did not possess it, ' but at last remembered that 'they *had* entered into negotiations on the subject, which as yet had been unsuccessful. '—The favorite device on the walls at Naples is a vermilion Picture of a Male and Female Soul respectively up to the waist (the waist of a *soul*) in fire, and an Angel above each, watering the sufferers from a watering-pot. This is intended to gain alms for Masses. The same populace sit for hours on the Mole, listening to rhapsodists who recite Ariosto. I have seen I think five of them all within a hundred yards of each other, and some sets of fiddlers to boot. Yet there are few parts of the world where I have seen less laughter than there. The Miracle of Januarius's Blood is, on the whole, my most curious experience. The furious entreaties, shrieks and sobs, of a set of old women, yelling till the Miracle was successfully performed, are things never to be forgotten.

"I spent three weeks in this most glittering of countries, and saw most of the usual wonders, —the Paestan Temples being to me much the most valuable. But Pompeii and all that it has yielded, especially the Fresco Paintings, have also an infinite interest. When one considers that this prodigious series of beautiful designs supplied the place of our common room-papers, —the wealth of poetic imagery among the Ancients, and the corresponding traditional variety and elegance of pictorial treatment, seem equally remarkable. The Greek and Latin Books do not give one quite so fully this sort of impression; because they afford no direct measure of the extent of their own diffusion. But these are ornaments from the smaller class of decent houses in a little Country Town; and the greater number of them, by the slightness of the execution, show very clearly that they were adapted to ordinary taste, and done by mere artisans. In general clearness, symmetry and simplicity of feeling, I cannot say that, on the whole, the works of Raffaelle equal them; though of course he has endless beauties such as we could not find unless in the great original works from which these sketches at Pompeii were taken. Yet with all my much increased reverence for the Greeks, it seems more plain than ever that they had hardly anything of the peculiar devotional feeling of Christianity.

"Rome, which I loved before above all the earth, now delights me more than ever; —though at this moment there is rain falling that would not discredit Oxford Street. The depth, sincerity and splendor that there once was in the semi-paganism of the old Catholics comes out in St. Peter's and its dependencies, almost as grandly as does Greek and Roman Art in the Forum and the Vatican Galleries. I wish you were here: but, at all events, hope to see you and your Wife once more during this summer.

"Yours,
"JOHN STERLING. "

At Paris, where he stopped a day and night, and generally through his whole journey from Marseilles to Havre, one thing attended him: the prevailing epidemic of the place and year; now gone, and nigh forgotten, as other influenzas are. He writes to his Father: "I have not yet met a single Frenchman, who could give me any rational explanation *why* they were all in such a confounded rage against us. Definite causes of quarrel a statesman may know how to deal with, inasmuch as the removal of them may help to settle the dispute. But it must be a puzzling task to negotiate about instincts; to which class, as it seems to me, we must have recourse for an understanding of the present abhorrence which everybody on the other side of the Channel not only feels, but makes a point to boast of, against the name of Britain. France is slowly arming, especially with Steam, *en attendant* a more than possible contest, in which they reckon confidently on the eager co-operation of the Yankees; as, *vice versa*, an American told me that his countrymen do on that of France. One person at Paris (M. — — whom you know) provoked me to tell him that 'England did not want another battle of Trafalgar; but if France did, she might compel England to gratify her. '"—After a couple of pleasant and profitable months, he was safe home again in the first days of June; and saw Falmouth not under gray iron skies, and whirls of March dust, but bright with summer opulence and the roses coming out.

It was what I call his "*fifth* peregrinity; " his fifth and last. He soon afterwards came up to London; spent a couple of weeks, with all his old vivacity, among us here. The AEsculapian oracles, it would appear, gave altogether cheerful prophecy; the highest medical authority "expresses the most decided opinion that I have gradually mended for some years; and in truth I have not, for six or seven, been so free from serious symptoms of illness as at present. " So uncertain are all oracles, AEsculapian and other!

During this visit, he made one new acquaintance which he much valued; drawn thither, as I guess, by the wish to take counsel about *Strafford*. He writes to his Clifton friend, under date, 1st July 1842: "Lockhart, of the *Quarterly Review*, I made my first oral acquaintance with; and found him as neat, clear and cutting a brain as you would expect; but with an amount of knowledge, good nature and liberal anti-bigotry, that would much surprise many. The tone of his children towards him seemed to me decisive of his real kindness. He quite agreed with me as to the threatening seriousness of our present social perplexities, and the necessity and difficulty of doing something effectual for so satisfying the manual multitude as not to overthrow all legal security...."

"Of other persons whom I saw in London, " continues he, "there are several that would much interest you, —though I missed Tennyson, by a mere chance.... John Mill has completely finished, and sent to the bookseller, his great work on Logic; the labor of many years of a singularly subtle, patient and comprehensive mind. It will be our chief speculative monument of this age. Mill and I could not meet above two or three times; but it was with the openness and freshness of school-boy friends, though our friendship only dates from the manhood of both. "

He himself was busier than ever; occupied continually with all manner of Poetic interests. *Coeur-de-Lion*, a new and more elaborate attempt in the mock-heroic or comico-didactic vein, had been on hand for some time, the scope of it greatly deepening and expanding itself since it first took hold of him; and now, soon after the Naples journey, it rose into shape on the wider plan; shaken up probably by this new excitement, and indebted to Calabria, Palermo and the Mediterranean scenes for much of the vesture it had. With this, which opened higher hopes for him than any of his previous efforts, he was now employing all his time and strength; —and continued to do so, this being the last effort granted him among us.

Already, for some months, *Strafford* lay complete: but how to get it from the stocks; in what method to launch it? The step was questionable. Before going to Italy he had sent me the Manuscript; still loyal and friendly; and willing to hear the worst that could be said of his poetic enterprise. I had to afflict him again, the good brave soul, with the deliberate report that I could *not* accept this Drama as his Picture of the Life of Strafford, or as any *Picture* of that strange Fact. To which he answered, with an honest manfulness, in a tone which is now pathetic enough to me, that he was much grieved yet much obliged, and uncertain how to decide. On the other hand, Mr. Hare wrote, warmly eulogizing. Lockhart too spoke kindly, though taking some exceptions. It was a questionable case. On the whole, *Strafford* remained, for the present, unlaunched; and *Coeur de-Lion* was getting its first timbers diligently laid down. So passed, in peaceable seclusion, in wholesome employment and endeavor, the autumn and winter of 1842-43. On Christmas-day, he reports to his Mother: —

"I wished to write to you yesterday; but was prevented by the important business of preparing a Tree, in the German fashion, for the children. This project answered perfectly, as it did last year; and gave them the greatest pleasure. I wish you and my Father could have been here to see their merry faces. Johnny was in the thick of the fun, and much happier than Lord Anson on capturing the galleon. We are all going on well and quietly, but with nothing very new among us.... The last book I have lighted on is Moffat's *Missionary Labors in South Africa*; which is worth reading. There is the best collection of lion stories in it that I have ever seen. But the man is, also, really a very good fellow; and fit for something much better than most lions are. He is very ignorant, and mistaken in some things; but has strong sense and heart; and his Narrative adds another to the many proofs of the enormous power of Christianity on rude minds. Nothing can be more chaotic, that is human at all, than the notions of these poor Blacks, even after what is called their conversion; but the effect is produced. They do adopt pantaloons, and abandon polygamy; and I suppose will soon have newspapers and literary soirees. "

CHAPTER V.
DISASTER ON DISASTER.

DURING all these years of struggle and wayfaring, his Father's household at Knightsbridge had stood healthful, happy, increasing in wealth, free diligence, solidity and honest prosperity: a fixed sunny islet, towards which, in all his voyagings and overclouded roamings, he could look with satisfaction, as to an ever-open port of refuge.

The elder Sterling, after many battles, had reached his field of conquest in these years; and was to be regarded as a victorious man. Wealth sufficient, increasing not diminishing, had rewarded his labors in the *Times*, which were now in their full flower; he had influence of a sort; went busily among busy public men; and enjoyed, in the questionable form attached to journalism and anonymity, a social consideration and position which were abundantly gratifying to him. A singular figure of the epoch; and when you came to know him, which it was easy to fail of doing if you had not eyes and candid insight, a gallant, truly gifted, and manful figure, of his kind. We saw much of him in this house; much of all his family; and had grown to love them all right well, —him too, though that was the difficult part of the feat. For in his Irish way he played the conjurer very much, —"three hundred and sixty-five opinions in the year upon every subject, " as a wag once said. In fact his talk, ever ingenious, emphatic and spirited in detail, was much defective in earnestness, at least in clear earnestness, of purport and outcome; but went tumbling as if in mere welters of explosive unreason; a volcano heaving under vague deluges of scoriae, ashes and imponderous pumice-stones, you could not say in what direction, nor well whether in any. Not till after good study did you see the deep molten lava-flood, which simmered steadily enough, and showed very well by and by whither it was bound. For I must say of Edward Sterling, after all his daily explosive sophistries, and fallacies of talk, he had a stubborn instinctive sense of what was manful, strong and worthy; recognized, with quick feeling, the charlatan under his solemnest wig; knew as clearly as any man a pusillanimous tailor in buckram, an ass under the lion's skin, and did with his whole heart despise the same.

The sudden changes of doctrine in the *Times*, which failed not to excite loud censure and indignant amazement in those days, were first intelligible to you when you came to interpret them as his changes. These sudden whirls from east to west on his part, and total changes of party and articulate opinion at a day's warning, lay in the nature of the man, and could not be helped; products of his fiery impatience, of the combined impetuosity and limitation of an intellect, which did nevertheless continually gravitate towards what was loyal, true and right on all manner of subjects. These, as I define them, were the mere scoriae and pumice wreck of a steady central lava-flood, which truly was volcanic and explosive to a strange degree, but did rest as few others on the grand fire-depths of the world. Thus, if he stormed along, ten thousand strong, in the time of the Reform Bill, indignantly denouncing Toryism and its obsolete insane pretensions; and then if, after some experience of Whig management, he discerned that Wellington and Peel, by whatever name entitled, were the men to be depended on by England, —there lay in all this, visible enough, a deeper consistency far more important than the superficial one, so much clamored after by the vulgar. Which is the lion's-skin; which is the real lion? Let a man, if he is prudent, ascertain that before speaking; —but above and beyond all things, *let* him ascertain it, and stand valiantly to it when ascertained! In the latter essential part of the operation Edward Sterling was honorably successful to a really marked degree; in the former, or prudential part, very much the reverse, as his history in the Journalistic department at least, was continually teaching him.

An amazingly impetuous, hasty, explosive man, this "Captain Whirlwind, " as I used to call him! Great sensibility lay in him, too; a real sympathy, and affectionate pity and softness, which he had an over-tendency to express even by tears, —a singular sight in so leonine a man. Enemies called them maudlin and hypocritical, these tears; but that was nowise the complete account of them. On the whole, there did conspicuously lie a dash of ostentation, a self-consciousness apt to become loud and braggart, over all he said and did and felt: this was the alloy of the man, and you had to be thankful for the abundant gold along with it.

Quizzing enough he got among us for all this, and for the singular *chiaroscuro* manner of procedure, like that of an Archimagus Cagliostro, or Kaiser Joseph Incognito, which his anonymous known-unknown thunderings in the *Times* necessitated in him; and much we laughed, —not without explosive counter-banterings on his part; —but, in fine, one could not do without him; one knew him at heart for a right brave man. "By Jove, sir! " thus he would swear to you, with radiant face; sometimes, not often, by a deeper oath. With persons of dignity, especially with women, to whom he was always very gallant, he had courtly delicate manners, verging towards the wire-drawn and elaborate; on common occasions, he bloomed out at once into jolly familiarity of the gracefully boisterous kind, reminding you of mess-rooms and old Dublin days. His off-hand mode of speech was always precise, emphatic, ingenious: his laugh, which was frequent rather than otherwise, had a sincerity of banter, but no real depth of sense for the ludicrous; and soon ended, if it grew too loud, in a mere dissonant scream. He was broad, well-built, stout of stature; had a long lowish head, sharp gray eyes, with large strong aquiline face to match; and walked, or sat, in an erect decisive manner. A remarkable man; and playing, especially in those years 1830-40, a remarkable part in the world.

For it may be said, the emphatic, big-voiced, always influential and often strongly unreasonable *Times* Newspaper was the express emblem of Edward Sterling; he, more than any other man or circumstance, *was* the *Times* Newspaper, and thundered through it to the shaking of the spheres. And let us assert withal that his and its influence, in those days, was not ill grounded but rather well; that the loud manifold unreason, often enough vituperated and groaned over, was of the surface mostly; that his conclusions, unreasonable, partial, hasty as they might at first be, gravitated irresistibly towards the right: in virtue of which grand quality indeed, the root of all good insight in man, his *Times* oratory found acceptance and influential audience, amid the loud whirl of an England itself logically very stupid, and wise chiefly by instinct.

England listened to this voice, as all might observe; and to one who knew England and it, the result was not quite a strange one, and was honorable rather than otherwise to both parties. A good judge of men's talents has been heard to say of Edward Sterling: "There is not a *faculty of improvising* equal to this in all my circle. Sterling rushes out into the clubs, into London society, rolls about all day, copiously talking modish nonsense or sense, and listening to the like, with the multifarious miscellany of men; comes home at night; redacts it into a *Times* Leader, —and is found to have hit the essential purport of the world's immeasurable babblement that day, with an accuracy beyond all other men. This is what the multifarious Babel sound did mean to say in clear words; this, more nearly than anything else. Let the most gifted intellect, capable of writing epics, try to write such a Leader for the Morning Newspapers! No intellect but Edward

Sterling's can do it. An improvising faculty without parallel in my experience. "—In this "improvising faculty, " much more nobly developed, as well as in other faculties and qualities with unexpectedly new and improved figure, John Sterling, to the accurate observer, showed himself very much the son of Edward.

Connected with this matter, a remarkable Note has come into my hands; honorable to the man I am writing of, and in some sort to another higher man; which, as it may now (unhappily for us all) be published without scruple, I will not withhold here. The support, by Edward Sterling and the *Times*, of Sir Robert Peel's first Ministry, and generally of Peel's statesmanship, was a conspicuous fact in its day; but the return it met with from the person chiefly interested may be considered well worth recording. The following Letter, after meandering through I know not what intricate conduits, and consultations of the Mysterious Entity whose address it bore, came to Edward Sterling as the real flesh-and-blood proprietor, and has been found among his papers. It is marked *Private*: —

"(Private) *To the Editor of the Times*.
"WHITEHALL, 18th April, 1835.

"SIR, —Having this day delivered into the hands of the King the Seals of Office, I can, without any imputation of an interested motive, or any impediment from scrupulous feelings of delicacy, express my deep sense of the powerful support which that Government over which I had the honor to preside received from the *Times* Newspaper.

"If I do not offer the expressions of personal gratitude, it is because I feel that such expressions would do injustice to the character of a support which was given exclusively on the highest and most independent grounds of public principle. I can say this with perfect truth, as I am addressing one whose person even is unknown to me, and who during my tenure of power studiously avoided every species of intercourse which could throw a suspicion upon the motives by which he was actuated. I should, however, be doing injustice to my own feelings, if I were to retire from Office without one word of acknowledgment; without at least assuring you of the admiration with which I witnessed, during the arduous contest in which I was engaged, the daily exhibition of that extraordinary ability to which I was indebted for a support, the more valuable because it was an impartial and discriminating support. —I have the honor to be, Sir,

"Ever your most obedient and faithful servant,
"ROBERT PEEL. "

To which, with due loftiness and diplomatic gravity and brevity, there is Answer, Draught of Answer in Edward Sterling's hand, from the Mysterious Entity so honored, in the following terms: —

"To the Right Hon. Sir Robert Peel, Bart., &c. &c. &c.

"SIR, —It gives me sincere satisfaction to learn from the Letter with which you have honored me, bearing yesterday's date, that you estimate so highly the efforts which have been made during the last five months by the *Times* Newspaper to support the cause of rational and wholesome Government which his Majesty had intrusted to your guidance; and that you appreciate fairly the disinterested motive, of regard to the public welfare, and to that alone, through which this Journal has been prompted to pursue a policy in accordance with that of your Administration. It is, permit me to say, by such motives only, that the *Times,* ever since I have known it, has been influenced, whether in defence of the Government of the day, or in constitutional resistance to it: and indeed there exist no other motives of action for a Journalist, compatible either with the safety of the press, or with the political morality of the great bulk of its readers. —With much respect, I have the honor to be, Sir, &c. &c. &c.

"THE EDITOR OF THE 'TIMES. '"

Of this Note I do not think there was the least whisper during Edward Sterling's lifetime; which fact also one likes to remember of him, so ostentatious and little-reticent a man. For the rest, his loyal admiration of Sir Robert Peel, —sanctioned, and as it were almost consecrated to his mind, by the great example of the Duke of Wellington, whom he reverenced always with true hero-worship, — was not a journalistic one, but a most intimate authentic feeling, sufficiently apparent in the very heart of his mind. Among the many opinions "liable to three hundred and sixty-five changes in the course of the year, " this in reference to Peel and Wellington was one which ever changed, but was the same all days and hours. To which, equally genuine, and coming still oftener to light in those times, there might one other be added, one and hardly more: fixed contempt, not unmingled with detestation, for Daniel O'Connell. This latter feeling, we used often laughingly to say, was his grand political principle, the one firm centre where all else went revolving. But internally the other also was deep and constant; and indeed these were properly his *two* centres, —poles of the same axis, negative and positive, the one presupposing the other.

O'Connell he had known in young Dublin days; —and surely no man could well venerate another less! It was his deliberate, unalterable opinion of the then Great O, that good would never come of him; that only mischief, and this in huge measure, would come. That however showy, and adroit in rhetoric and management, he was a man of incurably commonplace intellect, and of no character but a hollow, blustery, pusillanimous and unsound one; great only in maudlin patriotisms, in speciosities, astucities, —in the miserable gifts for becoming Chief *Demagogos*, Leader of a deep-sunk Populace towards *its* Lands of Promise; which trade, in any age or country, and especially in the Ireland of this age, our indignant friend regarded (and with reason) as an extremely ugly one for a man. He had himself zealously advocated Catholic Emancipation, and was not without his Irish patriotism, very different from the Orange sort; but the "Liberator" was not admirable to him, and grew daily less so to an extreme degree. Truly, his scorn of the said Liberator, now riding in supreme dominion on the wings of *blarney*, devil-ward of a surety, with the Liberated all following and huzzaing; his fierce gusts of wrath and abhorrence over him, —rose occasionally almost to the sublime. We laughed often at these vehemences: —and they were not wholly laughable; there was something very serious, and very true, in them! This creed of Edward Sterling's would not now, in either pole of its axis, look so strange as it then did in many quarters.

During those ten years which might be defined as the culminating period of Edward Sterling's life, his house at South Place, Knights bridge, had worn a gay and solid aspect, as if built at last on the high table-land of sunshine and success, the region of storms and dark weather now all victoriously traversed and lying safe below. Health, work, wages, whatever is needful to a man, he had, in rich measure; and a frank stout heart to guide the same: he lived in such style as pleased him; drove his own chariot up and down (himself often acting as Jehu, and reminding you a little of *Times* thunder even in driving); consorted, after a fashion, with the powerful of the world; saw in due vicissitude a miscellany of social faces round him, —

pleasant parties, which he liked well enough to garnish by a lord; "Irish lord, if no better might be, " as the banter went. For the rest, he loved men of worth and intellect, and recognized them well, whatever their title: this was his own patent of worth which Nature had given him; a central light in the man, which illuminated into a kind of beauty, serious or humorous, all the artificialities he had accumulated on the surface of him. So rolled his days, not quietly, yet prosperously, in manifold commerce with men. At one in the morning, when all had vanished into sleep, his lamp was kindled in his library; and there, twice or thrice a week, for a three-hours' space, he launched his bolts, which next morning were to shake the high places of the world.

John's relation to his Father, when one saw John here, was altogether frank, joyful and amiable: he ignored the *Times* thunder for most part, coldly taking the Anonymous for non-extant; spoke of it floutingly, if he spoke at all: indeed a pleasant half-bantering dialect was the common one between Father and Son; and they, especially with the gentle, simple-hearted, just-minded Mother for treble-voice between them, made a very pretty glee-harmony together.

So had it lasted, ever since poor John's voyagings began; his Father's house standing always as a fixed sunny islet with safe harbor for him. So it could not always last. This sunny islet was now also to break and go down: so many firm islets, fixed pillars in his fluctuating world, pillar after pillar, were to break and go down; till swiftly all, so to speak, were sunk in the dark waters, and he with them! Our little History is now hastening to a close.

In the beginning of 1843 news reached us that Sterling had, in his too reckless way, encountered a dangerous accident: maids, in the room where he was, were lifting a heavy table; he, seeing them in difficulty, had snatched at the burden; heaved it away, —but had broken a blood-vessel by the business; and was now, after extensive hemorrhage, lying dangerously ill. The doctors hoped the worst was over; but the case was evidently serious. In the same days, too, his Mother had been seized here by some painful disease, which from its continuance grew alarming. Sad omens for Edward Sterling, who by this time had as good as ceased writing or working in the *Times*, having comfortably winded up his affairs there; and was looking forward to a freer idle life befitting his advanced years henceforth. Fatal eclipse had fallen over that household of his; never to be lifted off again till all darkened into night.

By dint of watchful nursing, John Sterling got on foot once more: but his Mother did not recover, quite the contrary. Her case too grew very questionable. Disease of the heart, said the medical men at last; not immediately, not perhaps for a length of years, dangerous to life, said they; but without hope of cure. The poor lady suffered much; and, though affecting hope always, grew weaker and weaker. John ran up to Town in March; I saw him, on the morrow or next day after, in his own room at Knightsbridge: he had caught fresh cold overnight, the servant having left his window up, but I was charged to say nothing of it, not to flutter the already troubled house: he was going home again that very day, and nothing ill would come of it. We understood the family at Falmouth, his Wife being now near her confinement again, could at any rate comport with no long absence. He was cheerful, even rudely merry; himself pale and ill, his poor Mother's cough audible occasionally through the wall. Very kind, too, and gracefully affectionate; but I observed a certain grimness in his mood of mind, and under his light laughter lay something unusual, something stern, as if already dimmed in the coming shadows of Fate. "Yes, yes, you are a good man: but I understand they mean to appoint you to Rhadamanthus's post, which has been vacant for some time; and you will see how you like that! " This was one of the things he said; a strange effulgence of wild drollery flashing through the ice of earnest pain and sorrow. He looked paler than usual: almost for the first time, I had myself a twinge of misgiving as to his own health; for hitherto I had been used to blame as much as pity his fits of dangerous illness, and would often angrily remonstrate with him that he might have excellent health, would he but take reasonable care of himself, and learn the art of sitting still. Alas, as if he *could* learn it; as if Nature had not laid her ban on him even there, and said in smiles and frowns manifoldly, "No, that thou shalt not learn! "

He went that day; he never saw his good true Mother more. Very shortly afterwards, in spite of doctors' prophecies, and affectionate illusions, she grew alarmingly and soon hopelessly worse. Here are his last two Letters to her: —

"To Mrs. Sterling, Knightsbridge, London.
"FALMOUTH 8th April, 1843.

"DEAREST MOTHER, —I could do you no good, but it would be the greatest comfort to me if I could be near you. Nothing would detain me but Susan's condition. I feel that until her confinement is over, I ought to remain here, —unless you wished me to go to you; in which case she would be the first to send me off. Happily she is doing as well as possible, and seems even to gain strength every day. She sends her love to you.

"The children are all doing well. I rode with Edward to-day through some of the pleasant lanes in the neighborhood; and was delighted, as I have often been at the same season, to see the primroses under every hedge. It is pleasant to think that the Maker of them can make other flowers for the gardens of his other mansions. We have here a softness in the air, a smoothness of the clouds, and a mild sunshine, that combine in lovely peace with the first green of spring and the mellow whiteness of the sails upon the quiet sea. The whole aspect of the world is full of a quiet harmony, that influences even one's bodily frame, and seems to make one's very limbs aware of something living, good and immortal in all around us. Knowing how you suffer, and how weak you are, anything is a blessing to me that helps me to rise out of confusion and grief into the sense of God and joy. I could not indeed but feel how much happier I should have been, this morning, had you been with me, and delighting as you would have done in all the little as well as the large beauty of the world. But it was still a satisfaction to feel how much I owe to you of the power of perceiving meaning, reality and sweetness in all healthful life. And thus I could fancy that you were still near me; and that I could see you, as I have so often seen you, looking with earnest eyes at wayside flowers.

"I would rather not have written what must recall your thoughts to your present sufferings: but, dear Mother, I wrote only what I felt; and perhaps you would rather have it so, than that I should try to find other topics. I still hope to be with you before long. Meanwhile and always, God bless you, is the prayer of

"Your affectionate son,
"JOHN STERLING. "

To the same.
"FALMOUTH, 12th April, 1843.

"DEAREST MOTHER, —I have just received my Father's Letter; which gives me at least the comfort of believing that you do not suffer very much pain. That your mind has remained so clear and strong, is an infinite blessing.

"I do not know anything in the world that would make up to me at all for wanting the recollection of the days I spent with you lately, when I was amazed at the freshness and life of all your thoughts. It brought back far-distant years, in the strangest, most peaceful way. I felt myself walking with you in Greenwich Park, and on the seashore at Sandgate; almost even I seemed a baby, with you bending over me. Dear Mother, there is surely something uniting us that cannot perish. I seem so sure of a love which shall last and reunite us, that even the remembrance, painful as that is, of all my own follies and ill tempers, cannot shake this faith. When I think of you, and know how you feel towards me, and have felt for every moment of almost forty years, it would be too dark to believe that we shall never meet again. It was from you that I first learnt to think, to feel, to imagine, to believe; and these powers, which cannot be extinguished, will one day enter anew into communion with you. I have bought it very dear by the prospect of losing you in this world, —but since you have been so ill, everything has seemed to me holier, loftier and more lasting, more full of hope and final joy.

"It would be a very great happiness to see you once more even here; but I do not know if that will be granted to me. But for Susan's state, I should not hesitate an instant; as it is, my duty seems to be to remain, and I have no right to repine. There is no sacrifice that she would not make for me, and it would be too cruel to endanger her by mere anxiety on my account. Nothing can exceed her sympathy with my sorrow. But she cannot know, no one can, the recollections of all you have been and done for me; which now are the most sacred and deepest, as well as most beautiful, thoughts that abide with me. May God bless you, dearest Mother. It is much to believe that He feels for you all that you have ever felt for your children.

"JOHN STERLING. "

A day or two after this, "on Good Friday, 1843, " his Wife got happily through her confinement, bringing him, he writes, "a stout little girl, who and the Mother are doing as well as possible. " The little girl still lives and does well; but for the Mother there was another lot. Till the Monday following she too did altogether well, he affectionately watching her; but in the course of that day, some change for the worse was noticed, though nothing to alarm either the doctors or him; he watched by her bedside all night, still without alarm; but sent again in the morning, Tuesday morning, for the doctors, —Who did not seem able to make much of the symptoms.

She appeared weak and low, but made no particular complaint. The London post meanwhile was announced; Sterling went into another room to learn what tidings of his Mother it brought him. Returning speedily with a face which in vain strove to be calm, his Wife asked, How at Knightsbridge? "My Mother is dead, " answered Sterling; "died on Sunday: She is gone. " "Poor old man! " murmured the other, thinking of old Edward Sterling now left alone in the world; and these were her own last words: in two hours more she too was dead. In two hours Mother and Wife were suddenly both snatched away from him.

"It came with awful suddenness! " writes he to his Clifton friend. "Still for a short time I had my Susan: but I soon saw that the medical men were in terror; and almost within half an hour of that fatal Knightsbridge news, I began to suspect our own pressing danger. I received her last breath upon my lips. Her mind was much sunk, and her perceptions slow; but a few minutes before the last, she must have caught the idea of dissolution; and signed that I should kiss her. She faltered painfully, 'Yes! yes! '—returned with fervency the pressure of my lips; and in a few moments her eyes began to fix, her pulse to cease. She too is gone from me! " It was Tuesday morning, April 18th, 1843. His Mother had died on the Sunday before.

He had loved his excellent kind Mother, as he ought and well might: in that good heart, in all the wanderings of his own, there had ever been a shrine of warm pity, of mother's love and blessed soft affections for him; and now it was closed in the Eternities forevermore. His poor Life-partner too, his other self, who had faithfully attended him so long in all his pilgrimings, cheerily footing the heavy tortuous ways along with him, can follow him no farther; sinks now at his side: "The rest of your pilgrimings alone, O Friend, —adieu, adieu! " She too is forever hidden from his eyes; and he stands, on the sudden, very solitary amid the tumult of fallen and falling things. "My little baby girl is doing well; poor little wreck cast upon the sea-beach of life. My children require me tenfold now. What I shall do, is all confusion and darkness. "

The younger Mrs. Sterling was a true good woman; loyal-hearted, willing to do well, and struggling wonderfully to do it amid her languors and infirmities; rescuing, in many ways, with beautiful female heroism and adroitness, what of fertility their uncertain, wandering, unfertile way of life still left possible, and cheerily making the most of it. A genial, pious and harmonious fund of character was in her; and withal an indolent, half-unconscious force of intellect, and justness and delicacy of perception, which the casual acquaintance scarcely gave her credit for. Sterling much respected her decision in matters literary; often altering and modifying where her feeling clearly went against him; and in verses especially trusting to her ear, which was excellent, while he knew his own to be worth little. I remember her melodious rich plaintive tone of voice; and an exceedingly bright smile which she sometimes had, effulgent with sunny gayety and true humor, among other fine qualities.

Sterling has lost much in these two hours; how much that has long been can never again be for him! Twice in one morning, so to speak, has a mighty wind smitten the corners of his house; and much lies in dismal ruins round him.

CHAPTER VI.
VENTNOR: DEATH.

In this sudden avalanche of sorrows Sterling, weak and worn as we have seen, bore up manfully, and with pious valor fronted what had come upon him. He was not a man to yield to vain wailings, or make repinings at the unalterable: here was enough to be long mourned over; but here, for the moment, was very much imperatively requiring to be done. That evening, he called his children round him; spoke words of religious admonition and affection to them; said, "He must now be a Mother as well as Father to them. " On the evening of the funeral, writes Mr. Hare, he bade them good-night, adding these words, "If I am taken from you, God will take care of you. " He had six children left to his charge, two of them infants; and a dark outlook ahead of them and him. The good Mrs. Maurice, the children's young Aunt, present at this time and often afterwards till all ended, was a great consolation.

Falmouth, it may be supposed, had grown a sorrowful place to him, peopled with haggard memories in his weak state; and now again, as had been usual with him, change of place suggested itself as a desirable alleviation; —and indeed, in some sort, as a necessity. He has "friends here, " he admits to himself, "whose kindness is beyond all price, all description; " but his little children, if anything befell him, have no relative within two hundred miles. He is now sole watcher over them; and his very life is so precarious; nay, at any rate, it would appear, he has to leave Falmouth every spring, or run the hazard of worse. Once more, what is to be done? Once more, —and now, as it turned out, for the last time.

A still gentler climate, greater proximity to London, where his Brother Anthony now was and most of his friends and interests were: these considerations recommended Ventnor, in the beautiful Southeastern corner of the Isle of Wight; where on inquiry an eligible house was found for sale. The house and its surrounding piece of ground, improvable both, were purchased; he removed thither in June of this year 1843; and set about improvements and adjustments on a frank scale. By the decease of his Mother, he had become rich in money; his share of the West-India properties having now fallen to him, which, added to his former incomings, made a revenue he could consider ample and abundant. Falmouth friends looked lovingly towards him, promising occasional visits; old

Herstmonceux, which he often spoke of revisiting but never did, was not far off; and London, with all its resources and remembrances, was now again accessible. He resumed his work; and had hopes of again achieving something.

The Poem of *Coeur-de-Lion* has been already mentioned, and the wider form and aim it had got since he first took it in hand. It was above a year before the date of these tragedies and changes, that he had sent me a Canto, or couple of Cantos, of *Coeur-de-Lion*; loyally again demanding my opinion, harsh as it had often been on that side. This time I felt right glad to answer in another tone: "That here was real felicity and ingenuity, on the prescribed conditions; a decisively rhythmic quality in this composition; thought and phraseology actually *dancing*, after a sort. What the plan and scope of the Work might be, he had not said, and I could not judge; but here was a light opulence of airy fancy, picturesque conception, vigorous delineation, all marching on as with cheerful drum and fife, if without more rich and complicated forms of melody: if a man *would* write in metre, this sure enough was the way to try doing it. " For such encouragement from that stinted quarter, Sterling, I doubt not, was very thankful; and of course it might co-operate with the inspirations from his Naples Tour to further him a little in this his now chief task in the way of Poetry; a thought which, among my many almost pathetic remembrances of contradictions to his Poetic tendency, is pleasant for me.

But, on the whole, it was no matter. With or without encouragement, he was resolute to persevere in Poetry, and did persevere. When I think now of his modest, quiet steadfastness in this business of Poetry; how, in spite of friend and foe, he silently persisted, without wavering, in the form of utterance he had chosen for himself; and to what length he carried it, and vindicated himself against us all; —his character comes out in a new light to me, with more of a certain central inflexibility and noble silent resolution than I had elsewhere noticed in it. This summer, moved by natural feelings, which were sanctioned, too, and in a sort sanctified to him, by the remembered counsel of his late Wife, he printed the *Tragedy of Strafford*. But there was in the public no contradiction to the hard vote I had given about it: the little Book fell dead-born; and Sterling had again to take his disappointment; —which it must be owned he cheerfully did; and, resolute to try it again and ever again, went along with his *Coeur-de-Lion*, as if the public had been all with him. An honorable capacity to stand single against the whole world; such as all men need, from time to time! After all, who knows whether, in his overclouded, broken, flighty way of life, incapable of long hard drudgery, and so shut out from the solid forms of Prose, this Poetic Form, which he could well learn as he could all forms, was not the suitablest for him?

This work of *Coeur-de-Lion* he prosecuted steadfastly in his new home; and indeed employed on it henceforth all the available days that were left him in this world. As was already said, he did not live to complete it; but some eight Cantos, three or four of which I know to possess high worth, were finished, before Death intervened, and there he had to leave it. Perhaps it will yet be given to the public; and in that case be better received than the others were, by men of judgment; and serve to put Sterling's Poetic pretensions on a much truer footing. I can say, that to readers who do prefer a poetic diet, this ought to be welcome: if you can contrive to love the thing which is still called "poetry" in these days, here is a decidedly superior article in that kind, —richer than one of a hundred that you smilingly consume.

In this same month of June, 1843, while the house at Ventnor was getting ready, Sterling was again in London for a few days. Of course at Knightsbridge, now fallen under such sad change, many private matters needed to be settled by his Father and Brother and him. Captain Anthony, now minded to remove with his family to London and quit the military way of life, had agreed to purchase the big family house, which he still occupies; the old man, now rid of that encumbrance, retired to a smaller establishment of his own; came ultimately to be Anthony's guest, and spent his last days so. He was much lamed and broken, the half of his old life suddenly torn away; —and other losses, which he yet knew not of, lay close ahead of him. In a year or two, the rugged old man, borne down by these pressures, quite gave way; sank into paralytic and other infirmities; and was released from life's sorrows, under his son Anthony's roof, in the fall of 1847. —The house in Knightsbridge was, at the time we now speak of, empty except of servants; Anthony having returned to Dublin, I suppose to conclude his affairs there, prior to removal. John lodged in a Hotel.

We had our fair share of his company in this visit, as in all the past ones; but the intercourse, I recollect, was dim and broken, a disastrous shadow hanging over it, not to be cleared away by effort. Two American gentlemen, acquaintances also of mine, had been recommended to him, by Emerson most likely: one morning Sterling appeared here with a strenuous proposal that we should come to Knightsbridge, and dine with him and them. Objections, general dissuasions were not wanting: The empty dark house, such needless trouble, and the like; —but he answered in his quizzing way, "Nature herself prompts you, when a stranger comes, to give him a dinner. There are servants yonder; it is all easy; come; both of you are bound to come. " And accordingly we went. I remember it as one of the saddest dinners; though Sterling talked copiously, and our friends, Theodore Parker one of them, were pleasant and distinguished men. All was so haggard in one's memory, and half consciously in one's anticipations; sad, as if one had been dining in a will, in the crypt of a mausoleum. Our conversation was waste and logical, I forget quite on what, not joyful and harmoniously effusive: Sterling's silent sadness was painfully apparent through the bright mask he had bound himself to wear. Withal one could notice now, as on his last visit, a certain sternness of mood, unknown in better days; as if strange gorgon-faces of earnest Destiny were more and more rising round him, and the time for sport were past. He looked always hurried, abrupt, even beyond wont; and indeed was, I suppose, overwhelmed in details of business.

One evening, I remember, he came down hither, designing to have a freer talk with us. We were all sad enough; and strove rather to avoid speaking of what might make us sadder. Before any true talk had been got into, an interruption occurred, some unwelcome arrival; Sterling abruptly rose; gave me the signal to rise; and we unpolitely walked away, adjourning to his Hotel, which I recollect was in the Strand, near Hungerford Market; some ancient comfortable quaint-looking place, off the street; where, in a good warm queer old room, the remainder of our colloquy was duly finished. We spoke of Cromwell, among other things which I have now forgotten; on which subject Sterling was trenchant, positive, and in some essential points wrong, —as I said I would convince him some day. "Well, well! " answered he, with a shake of the head. — We parted before long; bedtime for invalids being come: he escorted me down certain carpeted backstairs, and would not be forbidden: we took leave under the dim skies; —and alas, little as I then dreamt of it, this, so far as I can calculate, must have been the last time I ever saw him in the world. Softly as a common evening, the last of the evenings had passed away, and no other would come for me forevermore.

Through the summer he was occupied with fitting up his new residence, selecting governesses, servants; earnestly endeavoring to set his house in order, on the new footing it had now assumed. Extensive improvements in his garden and grounds, in which he took due interest to the last, were also going on. His Brother, and Mr. Maurice his brother-in-law, —especially Mrs. Maurice the kind sister, faithfully endeavoring to be as a mother to her poor little nieces, —were occasionally with him. All hours available for labor on his literary tasks, he employed, almost exclusively I believe, on *Coeur-de-Lion*; with what energy, the progress he had made in that Work, and in the art of Poetic composition generally, amid so many sore impediments, best testifies. I perceive, his life in general lay heavier on him than it had done before; his mood of mind is grown more sombre; —indeed the very solitude of this Ventnor as a place, not to speak of other solitudes, must have been new and depressing. But he admits no hypochondria, now or ever; occasionally, though rarely, even flashes of a kind of wild gayety break through. He works steadily at his task, with all the strength left him; endures the past as he may, and makes gallant front against the world. "I am going on quietly here, rather than happily, " writes he to his friend Newman; "sometimes quite helpless, not from distinct illness, but from sad thoughts and a ghastly dreaminess. The heart is gone out of my life. My children, however, are doing well; and the place is cheerful and mild. "

From Letters of this period I might select some melancholy enough; but will prefer to give the following one (nearly the last I can give), as indicative of a less usual temper: —

"*To Thomas Carlyle, Esq., Chelsea, London.*
"VENTNOR, 7th December, 1843.

"MY DEAR CARLYLE, —My Irish Newspaper was *not* meant as a hint that I wanted a Letter. It contained an absurd long Advertisement, —some project for regenerating human knowledge, &c. &c. ; to which I prefixed my private mark (a blot), thinking that you might be pleased to know of a fellow-laborer somewhere in Tipperary.

"Your Letter, like the Scriptural oil, —(they had no patent lamps then, and used the best oil, 7s. per gallon), —has made my face to shine. There is but one person in the world, I shall not tell you who, from whom a Letter would give me so much pleasure. It would be nearly as good at Pekin, in the centre of the most enlightened Mandarins; but here at Ventnor, where there are few Mandarins and no enlightenment, —fountains in the wilderness, even were they miraculous, are nothing compared with your handwriting. Yet it is sad that you should be so melancholy. I often think that though Mercury was the pleasanter fellow, and probably the happier, Saturn was the greater god; —rather cannibal or so, but one excuses it in him, as in some other heroes one knows of.

"It is, as you say, your destiny to write about Cromwell: and you will make a book of him, at which the ears of our grandchildren will tingle; —and as one may hope that the ears of human nature will be growing longer and longer, the tingling will be proportionately greater than we are accustomed to. Do what you can, I fear there will be little gain from the Royalists. There is something very small about the biggest of them that I have ever fallen in with, unless you count old Hobbes a Royalist.

"Curious to see that you have them exactly preserved in the Country Gentlemen of our day; while of the Puritans not a trace remains except in History. Squirism had already, in that day, become the *caput mortuum* that it is now; and has therefore, like other mummies, been able to last. What was opposed to it was the Life of Puritanism, —then on the point of disappearing; and it too has left its mummy at Exeter Hall on the platform and elsewhere. One must go back to the Middle Ages to see Squirism as rampant and vivacious as Biblicism was in the Seventeenth Century: and I suppose our modern Country Gentlemen are about as near to what the old Knights and Barons were who fought the Crusades, as our modern Evangelicals to the fellows who sought the Lord by the light of their own pistol-shots.

"Those same Crusades are now pleasant matter for me. You remember, or perhaps you do not, a thing I once sent you about Coeur-de-Lion. Long since, I settled to make the Cantos you saw part of a larger Book; and worked at it, last autumn and winter, till I had a bad illness. I am now at work on it again; and go full sail, like *my* hero. There are six Cantos done, roughly, besides what you saw. I have struck out most of the absurdest couplets, and given the whole a higher though still sportive tone. It is becoming a kind of *Odyssey*, with a laughing and Christian Achilles for hero. One may manage to wrap, in that chivalrous brocade, many things belonging to our Time, and capable of interesting it. The thing is not bad; but will require great labor. Only it is labor that I thoroughly like; and which keeps the maggots out of one's brain, until their time.

"I have never spoken to you, never been able to speak to you, of the change in my life, —almost as great, one fancies, as one's own death. Even now, although it seems as if I had so much to say, I cannot. If one could imagine—... But it is no use; I cannot write wisely on this matter. I suppose no human being was ever devoted to another more entirely than she; and that makes the change not less but more bearable. It seems as if she could not be gone quite; and that indeed is my faith.

"Mr. James, your New-England friend, was here only for a few days; I saw him several times, and liked him. They went, on the 24th of last month, back to London, —or so purposed, —because there is no pavement here for him to walk on. I want to know where he is, and thought I should be able to learn from you. I gave him a Note for Mill, who perhaps may have seen him. I think this is all at present from,

"Yours,

"JOHN STERLING. "

Of his health, all this while, we had heard little definite; and understood that he was very quiet and careful; in virtue of which grand improvement we vaguely considered all others would follow. Once let him learn well to be *slow* as the common run of men are, would not all be safe and well? Nor through the winter, or the cold spring months, did bad news reach us; perhaps less news of any kind than had been usual, which seemed to indicate a still and wholesome way of life and work. Not till "April 4th, 1844, " did the new alarm occur: again on some slight accident, the breaking of a blood-vessel; again prostration under dangerous sickness, from which this time he never rose.

There had been so many sudden failings and happy risings again in our poor Sterling's late course of health, we had grown so accustomed to mingle blame of his impetuosity with pity for his sad overthrows, we did not for many weeks quite realize to ourselves the stern fact that here at length had the peculiar fall come upon us, — the last of all these falls! This brittle life, which had so often held together and victoriously rallied under pressures and collisions, could not rally always, and must one time be shivered. It was not till the summer came and no improvement; and not even then without lingering glimmers of hope against hope, that I fairly had to own what had now come, what was now day by day sternly advancing with the steadiness of Time.

From the first, the doctors spoke despondently; and Sterling himself felt well that there was no longer any chance of life. He had often said so, in his former illnesses, and thought so, yet always till now with some tacit grain of counter-hope; he had never clearly felt so as now: Here *is* the end; the great change is now here! —Seeing how it was, then, he earnestly gathered all his strength to do this last act of his tragedy, as he had striven to do the others, in a pious and manful manner. As I believe we can say he did; few men in any time *more* piously or manfully. For about six months he sat looking steadfastly, at all moments, into the eyes of Death; he too who had eyes to *see* Death and the Terrors and Eternities; and surely it was with perfect courage and piety, and valiant simplicity of heart, that he bore himself, and did and thought and suffered, in this trying predicament, more terrible than the usual death of men. All strength left to him he still employed in working: day by day the end came nearer, but day by day also some new portion of his adjustments was completed, by some small stage his task was nearer done. His domestic and other affairs, of all sorts, he settled to the last item. Of his own Papers he saved a few, giving brief pertinent directions about them; great quantities, among which a certain Autobiography begun some years ago at Clifton, he ruthlessly burnt, judging that the best. To his friends he left messages, memorials of books: I have a *Gough's Camden*, and other relics, which came to me in that way, and are among my sacred possessions. The very Letters of his friends he sorted and returned; had each friend's Letters made into a packet, sealed with black, and duly addressed for delivery when the time should come.

At an early period of his illness, all visitors had of course been excluded, except his most intimate ones: before long, so soon as the end became apparent, he took leave even of his Father, to avoid excitements and intolerable emotions; and except his Brother and the Maurices, who were generally about him coming and going, none were admitted. This latter form of life, I think, continued for above three months. Men were still working about his grounds, of whom he took some charge; needful works, great and small, let them not pause on account of him. He still rose from bed; had still some portion of his day which he could spend in his Library. Besides

Life of John Sterling

business there, he read a good deal, —earnest books; the Bible, most earnest of books, his chief favorite. He still even wrote a good deal. To his eldest Boy, now Mr. Newman's ward, who had been removed to the Maurices' since the beginning of this illness, he addressed, every day or two, sometimes daily, for eight or nine weeks, a Letter, of general paternal advice and exhortation; interspersing sparingly, now and then, such notices of his own feelings and condition as could be addressed to a boy. These Letters, I have lately read: they give, beyond any he has written, a noble image of the intrinsic Sterling; —the same face we had long known; but painted now as on the azure of Eternity, serene, victorious, divinely sad; the dusts and extraneous disfigurements imprinted on it by the world, now washed away. One little Excerpt, not the best, but the fittest for its neighborhood here, will be welcome to the reader: —

"To Master Edward C. Sterling, London.
"HILLSIDE, VENTNOR, 29th June, 1844.

"MY DEAR BOY, —We have been going on here as quietly as possible, with no event that I know of. There is nothing except books to occupy me. But you may suppose that my thoughts often move towards you, and that I fancy what you may be doing in the great City, —the greatest on the Earth, —where I spent so many years of my life. I first saw London when I was between eight and nine years old, and then lived in or near it for the whole of the next ten, and more there than anywhere else for seven years longer. Since then I have hardly ever been a year without seeing the place, and have often lived in it for a considerable time. There I grew from childhood to be a man. My little Brothers and Sisters, and since, my Mother, died and are buried there. There I first saw your Mamma, and was there married. It seems as if, in some strange way, London were a part of Me or I of London. I think of it often, not as full of noise and dust and confusion, but as something silent, grand and everlasting.

"When I fancy how you are walking in the same streets, and moving along the same river, that I used to watch so intently, as if in a dream, when younger than you are, —I could gladly burst into tears, not of grief, but with a feeling that there is no name for. Everything is so wonderful, great and holy, so sad and yet not bitter, so full of Death and so bordering on Heaven. Can you understand anything of this? If you can, you will begin to know what a serious matter our Life is; how unworthy and stupid it is to trifle it away without heed; what a wretched, insignificant, worthless creature any one comes to be, who does not as soon as possible bend his whole strength, as in stringing a stiff bow, to doing whatever task lies first before him....

"We have a mist here to-day from the sea. It reminds me of that which I used to see from my house in St, Vincent, rolling over the great volcano and the mountains round it. I used to look at it from our windows with your Mamma, and you a little baby in her arms.

"This Letter is not so well written as I could wish, but I hope you will be able to read it.

"Your affectionate Papa,
"JOHN STERLING. "

These Letters go from June 9th to August 2d, at which latter date vacation-time arrived, and the Boy returned to him. The Letters are preserved; and surely well worth preserving.

In this manner he wore the slow doomed months away. Day after day his little period of Library went on waning, shrinking into less and less; but I think it never altogether ended till the general end came. —For courage, for active audacity we had all known Sterling; but such a fund of mild stoicism, of devout patience and heroic composure, we did not hitherto know in him. His sufferings, his sorrows, all his unutterabilities in this slow agony, he held right manfully down; marched loyally, as at the bidding of the Eternal, into the dread Kingdoms, and no voice of weakness was heard from him. Poor noble Sterling, he had struggled so high and gained so little here! But this also he did gain, to be a brave man; and it was much.

Summer passed into Autumn: Sterling's earthly businesses, to the last detail of them, were now all as good as done: his strength too was wearing to its end, his daily turn in the Library shrunk now to a span. He had to hold himself as if in readiness for the great voyage at any moment. One other Letter I must give; not quite the last message I had from Sterling, but the last that can be inserted here: a brief Letter, fit to be forever memorable to the receiver of it: —

"To Thomas Carlyle, Esq., Chelsea, London.
"HILLSIDE, VENTNOR, 10th August, 1844.

MY DEAR CARLYLE, —For the first time for many months it seems possible to send you a few words; merely, however, for Remembrance and Farewell. On higher matters there is nothing to say. I tread the common road into the great darkness, without any thought of fear, and with very much of hope. Certainty indeed I have none. With regard to You and Me I cannot begin to write; having nothing for it but to keep shut the lid of those secrets with all the iron weights that are in my power. Towards me it is still more true than towards England that no man has been and done like you. Heaven bless you! If I can lend a hand when THERE, that will not be wanting. It is all very strange, but not one hundredth part so sad as it seems to the standers-by.

"Your Wife knows my mind towards her, and will believe it without asseverations.

"Yours to the last,
"JOHN STERLING. "

It was a bright Sunday morning when this letter came to me: if in the great Cathedral of Immensity I did no worship that day, the fault surely was my own. Sterling affectionately refused to see me; which also was kind and wise. And four days before his death, there are some stanzas of verse for me, written as if in star-fire and immortal tears; which are among my sacred possessions, to be kept for myself alone.

His business with the world was done; the one business now to await silently what may lie in other grander worlds. "God is great, " he was wont to say: "God is great. " The Maurices were now constantly near him; Mrs. Maurice assiduously watching over him. On the evening of Wednesday the 18th of September, his Brother, as he did every two or three days, came down; found him in the old temper, weak in strength but not very sensibly weaker; they talked calmly together for an hour; then Anthony left his bedside, and retired for the night, not expecting any change. But suddenly, about eleven o'clock, there came a summons and alarm: hurrying to his Brother's room, he found his Brother dying; and in a short while more the faint last struggle was ended, and all those struggles and strenuous often-foiled endeavors of eight-and-thirty years lay hushed in death.

CHAPTER VII.
CONCLUSION.

Sterling was of rather slim but well-boned wiry figure, perhaps an inch or two from six feet in height; of blonde complexion, without color, yet not pale or sickly; dark-blonde hair, copious enough, which he usually wore short. The general aspect of him indicated freedom, perfect spontaneity, with a certain careless natural grace. In his apparel, you could notice, he affected dim colors, easy shapes; cleanly always, yet even in this not fastidious or conspicuous: he sat or stood, oftenest, in loose sloping postures; walked with long strides, body carelessly bent, head flung eagerly forward, right hand perhaps grasping a cane, and rather by the middle to swing it, than by the end to use it otherwise. An attitude of frank, cheerful impetuosity, of hopeful speed and alacrity; which indeed his physiognomy, on all sides of it, offered as the chief expression. Alacrity, velocity, joyous ardor, dwelt in the eyes too, which were of brownish gray, full of bright kindly life, rapid and frank rather than deep or strong. A smile, half of kindly impatience, half of real mirth, often sat on his face. The head was long; high over the vertex; in the brow, of fair breadth, but not high for such a man.

In the voice, which was of good tenor sort, rapid and strikingly distinct, powerful too, and except in some of the higher notes harmonious, there was a clear-ringing *metallic* tone, —which I often thought was wonderfully physiognomic. A certain splendor, beautiful, but not the deepest or the softest, which I could call a splendor as of burnished metal, —fiery valor of heart, swift decisive insight and utterance, then a turn for brilliant elegance, also for ostentation, rashness, &c. &c., —in short, a flash as of clear-glancing sharp-cutting steel, lay in the whole nature of the man, in his heart and in his intellect, marking alike the excellence and the limits of them both. His laugh, which on light occasions was ready and frequent, had in it no great depth of gayety, or sense for the ludicrous in men or things; you might call it rather a good smile become vocal than a deep real laugh: with his whole man I never saw him laugh. A clear sense of the humorous he had, as of most other things; but in himself little or no true humor; —nor did he attempt that side of things. To call him deficient in sympathy would seem strange, him whose radiances and resonances went thrilling over all the world, and kept him in brotherly contact with all: but I may say his sympathies dwelt rather with the high and sublime than with the low or ludicrous; and were, in any field, rather light, wide and lively, than deep, abiding or great.

There is no Portrait of him which tolerably resembles. The miniature Medallion, of which Mr. Hare has given an Engraving, offers us, with no great truth in physical details, one, and not the best, superficial expression of his face, as if that with vacuity had been what the face contained; and even that Mr. Hare's engraver has disfigured into the nearly or the utterly irrecognizable. Two Pencil-sketches, which no artist could approve of, hasty sketches done in some social hour, one by his friend Spedding, one by Banim the Novelist, whom he slightly knew and had been kind to, tell a much truer story so far as they go: of these his Brother has engravings; but these also I must suppress as inadequate for strangers.

Nor in the way of Spiritual Portraiture does there, after so much writing and excerpting, anything of importance remain for me to say. John Sterling and his Life in this world were—such as has been already said. In purity of character, in the so-called moralities, in all manner of proprieties of conduct, so as tea-tables and other human tribunals rule them, he might be defined as perfect, according to the world's pattern: in these outward tangible respects the world's criticism of him must have been praise and that only. An honorable man, and good citizen; discharging, with unblamable correctness, all functions and duties laid on him by the customs (*mores*) of the society he lived in, —with correctness and something more. In all these particulars, a man perfectly *moral*, or of approved virtue according to the rules.

Nay in the far more essential tacit virtues, which are not marked on stone tables, or so apt to be insisted on by human creatures over tea or elsewhere, —in clear and perfect fidelity to Truth wherever found, in childlike and soldier-like, pious and valiant loyalty to the Highest, and what of good and evil that might send him, —he excelled among good men. The joys and the sorrows of his lot he took with true simplicity and acquiescence. Like a true son, not like a miserable mutinous rebel, he comported himself in this Universe. Extremity of distress—and surely his fervid temper had enough of contradiction in this world—could not tempt him into impatience at any time. By no chance did you ever hear from him a whisper of those mean repinings, miserable arraignings and questionings of the Eternal Power, such as weak souls even well disposed will sometimes give way to in the pressure of their despair; to the like of this he never yielded, or showed the least tendency to yield; —which surely was well on his part. For the Eternal Power, I still remark, will not answer the like of this, but silently and terribly accounts it impious, blasphemous and damnable, and now as heretofore will visit it as such. Not a rebel but a son, I said; willing to suffer when Heaven said, Thou shalt; —and withal, what is perhaps rarer in such a combination, willing to rejoice also, and right cheerily taking the good that was sent, whensoever or in whatever form it came.

A pious soul we may justly call him; devoutly submissive to the will of the Supreme in all things: the highest and sole essential form which Religion can assume in man, and without which all forms of religion are a mockery and a delusion in man. Doubtless, in so clear and filial a heart there must have dwelt the perennial feeling of silent worship; which silent feeling, as we have seen, he was eager enough to express by all good ways of utterance; zealously adopting such appointed forms and creeds as the dignitaries of the World had fixed upon and solemnly named recommendable; prostrating his heart in such Church, by such accredited rituals and seemingly fit or half-fit methods, as his poor time and country had to offer him, —not rejecting the said methods till they stood convicted of palpable unfitness and then doing it right gently withal, rather letting them drop as pitiably dead for him, than angrily hurling them out of doors as needing to be killed. By few Englishmen of his epoch had the thing called Church of England been more loyally appealed to as a spiritual mother.

And yet, as I said before, it may be questioned whether piety, what we call devotion or worship, was the principle deepest in him. In spite of his Coleridge discipleship, and his once headlong operations following thereon, I used to judge that his piety was prompt and pure rather than great or intense; that, on the whole, religious devotion was not the deepest element of him. His reverence was ardent and just, ever ready for the thing or man that deserved revering, or seemed to deserve it: but he was of too joyful, light and hoping a nature to go to the depths of that feeling, much more to dwell perennially in it. He had no fear in his composition; terror and awe did not blend with his respect of anything. In no scene or epoch could he have been a Church Saint, a fanatic enthusiast, or have worn out his life in passive martyrdom, sitting patient in his grim coal-mine, looking at the "three ells" of Heaven high overhead there. In sorrow he would not dwell; all sorrow he swiftly subdued, and shook away from him. How could you have made an Indian Fakir of the Greek Apollo, "whose bright eye lends brightness, and never yet saw a shadow"? —I should say, not religious reverence, rather artistic admiration was the essential character of him: a fact connected with all other facts in the physiognomy of his life and self, and giving a tragic enough character to much of the history he had among us.

Poor Sterling, he was by nature appointed for a Poet, then, —a Poet after his sort, or recognizer and delineator of the Beautiful; and not for a Priest at all? Striving towards the sunny heights, out of such a level and through such an element as ours in these days is, he had strange aberrations appointed him, and painful wanderings amid the miserable gaslights, bog-fires, dancing meteors and putrid phosphorescences which form the guidance of a young human soul at present! Not till after trying all manner of sublimely illuminated places, and finding that the basis of them was putridity, artificial gas and quaking bog, did he, when his strength was all done, discover his true sacred hill, and passionately climb thither while life was fast ebbing! —A tragic history, as all histories are; yet a gallant, brave and noble one, as not many are. It is what, to a radiant son of the Muses, and bright messenger of the harmonious Wisdoms, this poor world—if he himself have not strength enough, and *inertia* enough, and amid his harmonious eloquences silence enough—has provided at present. Many a high-striving, too hasty soul, seeking guidance towards eternal excellence from the official Black-artists, and successful Professors of political, ecclesiastical, philosophical, commercial, general and particular Legerdemain, will recognize his own history in this image of a fellow-pilgrim's.

Over-haste was Sterling's continual fault; over-haste, and want of the due strength, —alas, mere want of the due *inertia* chiefly; which is so common a gift for most part; and proves so inexorably needful withal! But he was good and generous and true; joyful where there was joy, patient and silent where endurance was required of him; shook innumerable sorrows, and thick-crowding forms of pain, gallantly away from him; fared frankly forward, and with scrupulous care to tread on no one's toes. True, above all, one may call him; a man of perfect veracity in thought, word and deed. Integrity towards all men, —nay integrity had ripened with him into chivalrous generosity; there was no guile or baseness anywhere found in him. Transparent as crystal; he could not hide anything sinister, if such there had been to hide. A more perfectly transparent soul I have never known. It was beautiful, to read all those interior movements; the little shades of affectations, ostentations; transient spurts of anger, which never grew to the length of settled spleen: all so naive, so childlike, the very faults grew beautiful to you.

And so he played his part among us, and has now ended it: in this first half of the Nineteenth Century, such was the shape of human destinies the world and he made out between them. He sleeps now, in the little burying-ground of Bonchurch; bright, ever-young in the memory of others that must grow old; and was honorably released from his toils before the hottest of the day.

All that remains, in palpable shape, of John Sterling's activities in this world are those Two poor Volumes; scattered fragments gathered from the general waste of forgotten ephemera by the piety of a friend: an inconsiderable memorial; not pretending to have achieved greatness; only disclosing, mournfully, to the more observant, that a promise of greatness was there. Like other such lives, like all lives, this is a tragedy; high hopes, noble efforts; under thickening difficulties and impediments, ever-new nobleness of valiant effort; —and the result death, with conquests by no means corresponding. A life which cannot challenge the world's attention; yet which does modestly solicit it, and perhaps on clear study will be found to reward it.

On good evidence let the world understand that here was a remarkable soul born into it; who, more than others, sensible to its influences, took intensely into him such tint and shape of feature as the world had to offer there and then; fashioning himself eagerly by whatsoever of noble presented itself; participating ardently in the world's battle, and suffering deeply in its bewilderments; —whose Life-pilgrimage accordingly is an emblem, unusually significant, of the world's own during those years of his. A man of infinite susceptivity; who caught everywhere, more than others, the color of the element he lived in, the infection of all that was or appeared honorable, beautiful and manful in the tendencies of his Time; — whose history therefore is, beyond others, emblematic of that of his Time.

In Sterling's Writings and Actions, were they capable of being well read, we consider that there is for all true hearts, and especially for young noble seekers, and strivers towards what is highest, a mirror in which some shadow of themselves and of their immeasurably complex arena will profitably present itself. Here also is one encompassed and struggling even as they now are. This man also had said to himself, not in mere Catechism-words, but with all his instincts, and the question thrilled in every nerve of him, and pulsed in every drop of his blood: "What is the chief end of man? Behold, I too would live and work as beseems a denizen of this Universe, a child of the Highest God. By what means is a noble life still possible for me here? Ye Heavens and thou Earth, oh, how? "—The history of this long-continued prayer and endeavor, lasting in various figures for near forty years, may now and for some time coming have something to say to men!

Nay, what of men or of the world? Here, visible to myself, for some while, was a brilliant human presence, distinguishable, honorable and lovable amid the dim common populations; among the million little beautiful, once more a beautiful human soul: whom I, among others, recognized and lovingly walked with, while the years and the hours were. Sitting now by his tomb in thoughtful mood, the new times bring a new duty for me. "Why write the Life of Sterling? " I imagine I had a commission higher than the world's, the dictate of Nature herself, to do what is now done. *Sic prosit.*

NOTES:

[1] *John Sterling's Essays and Tales, with Life* by Archdeacon Hare. Parker; London, 1848.

[2] *Commons Journals*, iv. 15 (l0th January, 1644-5); and again v. 307 &c., 498 (18th September, 1647-15th March, 1647-8).

[3] *Literary Chronicle*, New Series; London, Saturday, 21 June, 1828, Art. II.

[4] "The Letters of Vetus from March 10th to May 10th, 1812" (second edition, London, 1812): Ditto, "Part III., with a Preface and Notes" (ibid. 1814).

[5] Here, in a Note, is the tragic little Register, with what indications for us may lie in it: —

> (l.) Robert Sterling died, 4th June, 1815, at Queen Square, in his fourth year (John being now nine). (
>
> 2.) Elizabeth died, 12th March, 1818, at Blackfriars Road, in her second year.
>
> (3.) Edward, 30th March, 1818 (same place, same month and year), in his ninth.
>
> (4.) Hester, 21st July, 1818 (three months later), at Blackheath, in her eleventh.
>
> (5.) Catherine Hester Elizabeth, 16th January, 1821, in Seymour Street.

[6] *History of the English Universities*. (Translated from the German.)

[7] Mrs. Anthony Sterling, very lately Miss Charlotte Baird.

[8] *Biography*, by Hare, pp. xvi-xxvi.

[9] *Biography*, by Mr. Hare, p. xli.

[10] Hare, pp. xliii-xlvi.

[11] Hare, xlviii, liv, lv.

[12] Hare, p. lvi.

[13] P. lxxviii.

[14] Given in Hare (ii. 188-193).

[15] Came out, as will soon appear, in *Blackwood* (February, 1838).

[16] "*Hotel de l'Europe, Berlin,* " added in Mrs. Sterling's hand.

[17] Hare, ii. 96-167.

[18] Ib. i. 129, 188.

[19] Here in a Note they are, if they can be important to anybody. The marks of interrogation, attached to some Names as not yet consulted or otherwise questionable, are in the Secretary's hand: —

J. D. Acland, Esq.	H. Malden, Esq.
Hon. W. B. Baring.	J. S. Mill, Esq.
Rev. J. W. Blakesley.	R. M. Milnes, Esq.

W. Boxall, Esq.
T. Carlyle, Esq.
Hon. R. Cavendish (?)
H. N. Coleridge, Esq. (?)
J. W. Colville, Esq.
Allan Cunningham, Esq. (?)
Rev. H. Donn.
F. H. Doyle, Esq.
C. L. Eastlake, Esq.
Alex. Ellice, Esq.
J. F. Elliott, Esq.
Copley Fielding, Esq.
Rev. J. C. Hare.
Sir Edmund Head (?)
D. D. Heath, Esq.
G. C. Lewis, Esq.
H. L. Lushington, Esq.
The Lord Lyttleton.
C. Macarthy, Esq.

R. Monteith, Esq.
S. A. O'Brien, Esq.
Sir F. Palgrave (?)
W. F. Pollok, Esq.
Philip Pusey, Esq.
A. Rio, Esq.
C. Romilly, Esq.
James Spedding, Esq.
Rev. John Sterling.
Alfred Tennyson, Esq.
Rev. Connop Thirlwall.
Rev. W. Hepworth Thompson.
Edward Twisleton, Esq.
G. S. Venables, Esq.
Samuel Wood, Esq.
Rev. T. Worsley.

James Spedding, *Secretary*.
8th August, 1838.

[20] Hare, p. cxviii.
[21] Of Sterling himself, I suppose.
[22] Hare, ii. p. 252.
[23] *Poems by John Sterling*. London (Moxon), 1839.
[24] *The Election: a Poem, in Seven Books*. London, Murray, 1841.
[25] Pp. 7, 8.
[26] Pp. 89-93.
[27] Sister of Mrs. Strachey and Mrs. Buller: Sir John Louis was now in a high Naval post at Malta.
[28] Long Letter to his Father: Naples, 3d May, 1842.
[29] Death of her Mother, four mouths before. (*Note of* 1870.]

Lightning Source UK Ltd.
Milton Keynes UK
17 August 2009

142758UK00003BA/23/A